EASTER FAITH

and

HISTORY

EASTER FAITH

and

HISTORY

by

DANIEL P. FULLER

Dean of Faculty
and Associate Professor of Hermeneutics
Fuller Theological Seminary

WILLIAM B. EERDMANS PUBLISHING COMPANY
GRAND RAPIDS, MICHIGAN

To my father

in whose life i first saw the power of christ's resurrection

Foreword

At first sight, this book by Dr. Fuller may seem to have a heterogeneous structure. Its main part investigates the approach of liberal idealism, dialectical theology, and modern hermeneutics to the problem of Christ's resurrection. The two last chapters are concerned with Luke's solution of the same problem. However, by following the interesting exposition one will discover that scholarly attempts to explain Easter faith made since Lessing have developed in such a way that now we must be prepared to listen to the New Testament from within. In the end, a very pertinent illustration of the New Testament's testimony is given by references to Luke, especially concerning his attitude to faith and facts.

Dr. Fuller is the grandson and son of well-known men connected with Fuller Theological Seminary of California, and presently its Dean. Yet he works and lives without any dynastic conceitedness. He has qualities of his own, and in his scholarly activity permits himself to be dominated only by the biblical historical problems as such.

BO REICKE

Basel

Preface

This book is essentially the dissertation accepted by the theological Faculty of the University of Basel in the fall of 1962 in fulfillment of the requirement for the Doctor of Theology (D.Theol.) degree. As one whose field is hermeneutics, I felt increasingly and, finally, irresistibly drawn to Europe as the place to pursue this study. Until recently the term hermeneutics had all but dropped from the vocabulary of American theologians; however, since World War II, European theologians, realizing its cruciality for the whole theological discipline, have been discussing it avidly.

I am indeed grateful to Dr. Bo Reicke, professor of New Testament at Basel, for his insistence from the first that a worthwhile study in the field of hermeneutics must be centered in some concrete portion or aspect of the Biblical text, rather than be lost in the labyrinth of philosophical discussion that so often characterizes the contemporary hermeneutical debate. It became apparent that the question of the historicity of the resurrection of Jesus is a basic theme of Scripture and yet central to the hermeneutical discussion, because according to the New Testament, Christian faith must be essentially resurrection faith.

I am also grateful to Professor Oscar Cullmann, my coreferent at Basel, for helping me to see how basic is the theme of redemptive history for the message of the Bible. Likewise I am indebted to all the theological Faculty at Basel for the various ways they enriched my understanding of hermeneutics.

Drs. George E. Ladd, Edward J. Carnell, Geoffrey W. Bromiley, and Calvin Schoonhoven, colleagues at Fuller Seminary, read all or parts of the manuscript at various stages of its development, and I do appreciate their constructive criticism and stimulating interaction. Professor Wolfhart Pan-

9

nenberg of the University of Mainz was also most generous in his assistance on the section in which his approach to faith and history is considered.

And special thanks are due to my wife, who has so faithfully labored alongside of me in repeated rewritings, retypings, and proof-readings—to say nothing of encouragement rendered, especially during some of the more difficult times I encountered while preparing this work.

—DANIEL P. FULLER

Pasadena, California

Contents

Note: To reduce the number of footnotes in the book, the page
numbers of books cited have frequently been given in the
body of the text immediately following the passage quoted.
Such page numbers are always those of the book last cited
in the footnotes. Full bibliographical data for each book
cited are given in the Bibliography.

CHAPTER ONE

Posing the Question

CHRISTIANITY DISTINGUISHES ITSELF FROM MANY OTHER religions and from all speculative philosophy in that its message concerns a God who has acted in history. The God of the Bible is the creator of the world and of man, and is thus the initiator of history. He exercises his providential rule over the events of history to such an extent that even a bird's falling to the ground is a part of this rule (Matt. 10:29). But in addition to initiating and supervising history, this God enters into it from time to time to bring about a sequence of events that will climax in the redemption of the people of God in the new heavens and earth. These redemptive events are considered as completely historical, but they distinguish themselves from the rest of history in that their occurrence cannot be explained by a prior cause within history but only by the immediate intervention of God. Thus, for example, the speaking in tongues at Pentecost could not be explained by drunkenness, it being only nine o'clock in the morning; rather, these tongues occurred only because the risen Jesus had poured forth the Holy Spirit (Acts 2:15, 33).

Creation, the flood, the covenant with Abraham, the exodus, the giving of the law at Sinai, the conquest of the promised land, the establishment of the monarchy, the exile, the restoration, the coming of Jesus Christ (his ministry, death, resurrection, and ascension), Pentecost, the inauguration of the mission to the Gentiles, the preaching of the Gospel to the

13

world, the return of Jesus, the resurrection of the dead, the judgment, and the establishment of the new heavens and earth —this is the sequence of the more important divine interventions that the Bible declares to be necessary for the completion of redemption. By basing its message upon these events, Christianity thus distinguishes itself from religious philosophy, in which one seeks knowledge of God by inference from all the phenomena within experience, and from mysticism, in which one seeks such knowledge immediately through intuition. Christianity considers both philosophy and mysticism to have their place but declares that all claim to religious knowledge gained in these ways should be controlled by the Biblical report and interpretation of redemptive events.

Orthodox Judaism and Islam also claim to be historical religions based upon God's redemptive events within history. In fact, those events near the beginning and end of the sequence comprising Christianity are essential to these religions. Both Judaism and Islam find great significance in the call of Abraham and in the future judgment. But the heart of Christianity lies in the person of Jesus Christ, with his appearance at the center of redemptive history. Judaism and Islam, of course, would not agree to this. In particular the New Testament makes clear that central to Jesus' life is his resurrection from the dead, and that upon this all God's redemptive acts are based. Paul said, "If Christ has not been raised, then our preaching is in vain and your faith is in vain" (I Cor. 15:14).

I. The Centrality of the Resurrection

Paul was echoing the feeling of the whole primitive church when he asserted that the resurrection of Jesus was central to the Christian faith. Oscar Cullmann has shown that one of the best ways to get back to the very earliest stratum of Christian thinking is to examine those statements in the New Testament that appear originally to have been set formulas for confessing the faith. Such an examination reveals that the most

central idea is that Jesus is Lord because of his resurrection.[1]
A prime example of such a confession is Romans 10:9: "If
you confess with your lips that Jesus is Lord and believe in
your heart that God raised him from the dead, you will be
saved." When the early Christians called Jesus Lord, they
ascribed to him the highest of all titles. The Septuagint trans-
lators had used the Greek word *kyrios*, which had the general
meaning of "master," to translate *Yahweh* or *Adonai*, the usual
Hebrew words for God. The early Christians took over the
Old Testament meaning of the word *kyrios* when they assigned
this title to Jesus. Thus they equated Jesus with God,[2] and
their reason for so doing was his resurrection and exaltation.
Paul said, "For to this end Christ died and lived again, that
he might be Lord both of the dead and of the living" (Rom.
14:9).

Likewise the resurrection is the basis for also calling Jesus
the Messiah, or the Christ. According to the Old Testament,
the Christ was the one who would come to save Israel and
enable her to fulfill her God-given destiny in the world. Thus
in the first Christian sermon (Acts 2:22-36) Peter declared
that the promise in Psalms 16:11 that God would not suffer
his Holy One to see corruption predicted the resurrection of
the Christ, and since Jesus had risen, he was therefore the
Christ. The sermon concluded by asserting that because of the
resurrection of Jesus the house of Israel should assuredly
know that Jesus is both Lord and Christ (Acts 2:36).

According to the New Testament, the resurrection of Jesus
also verifies that he is the Son of God. Jesus was "designated
Son of God in power according to the Spirit of holiness by his
resurrection from the dead" (Rom. 1:4). When Jesus is called
"Son of God" in the New Testament, more is meant than that
he exemplified the filial relation with God that every man has
by virtue of creation. Jesus never declared that his relationship
to God and that of his disciples were identical. Rather, he

[1] O. Cullmann, *The Earliest Christian Confessions*, pp. 58f.
[2] V. Taylor, *The Names of Jesus*, pp. 50f.; E. Stauffer, *The Theology of the New Testament*, pp. 114f.

differentiated his relationship from theirs, for he spoke of his
Father and their Father, never of "our Father."[3] Thus when
the New Testament calls Jesus the Son, it asserts that Jesus'
relationship to God was unique, that he was the Messiah who
himself was God. In Psalms 45:6 the Messianic King is spoken
of as God who is himself anointed by God, and Hebrews 1:8
applies this verse to Jesus. Speaking of him as the Son, it says,
"Thy throne, O God, is for ever and ever, the righteous scepter
is the scepter of thy kingdom."

It is generally acknowledged that Matthew 11:25-27 is the
classical passage for discerning the basic meaning of Jesus
as the Son. Here Jesus declares that no man knows him, the
Son, except the Father, and no one knows the Father except
the Son and he to whom the Son reveals him. While the doctrine of Jesus' equality with the Father is not spelled out
theologically in these words, there can be no doubt, as Vincent
Taylor has put it,[4] that these words imply a knowledge of God
by which Jesus conceives of himself as a distinction within the
unity of the Godhead. Because he is the Son of God, in the
sense of being God's Messiah who is himself God, therefore he
alone has the power to reveal God to men. While it is through
his resurrection that Jesus became openly designated as the
Son (Rom. 1:4), yet because he was deity and therefore
eternal, he is termed as the "Son" before the resurrection. In
addition to Matthew 11:25-27 and Mark 12:6, where Jesus
called himself the Son, there are the incidents of his baptism
and transfiguration (Mark 1:11; 9:7), where God calls him
the Son. The demons likewise called him the Son (Mark 5:7).

Consequently, the New Testament sees Jesus as Lord,
Christ, and Son because of his resurrection. Because these
titles denoted deity to the early Christians, it is not surprising
that the New Testament should view all previous redemptive
events in the light of Jesus and see all subsequent redemptive

---

[3] Cf. John 20:17. The "our Father" of the Lord's prayer is what the
disciples were to say as they prayed. The "our" included the disciples
but not Christ. F. Foakes-Jackson and Kirsopp Lake, *The Beginnings of
Christianity*, I, 402. A. McNeile, *The Gospel according to Matthew*, p. 77.
[4] *Op. cit.*, p. 61.

events as based on Jesus and his resurrection. The early church regarded Jesus as the mediator of creation. The fourth Gospel declares that "all things were made through him." In I Corinthians 8:6 Paul echoes one of the early confessions of faith when he says, "There is one Lord Jesus, by whom are all things and we through him." If the resurrection shows forth Jesus as God, then he must always have been God, and therefore he must have participated in the work of creation.[5]

Following the same reasoning, the New Testament understands Jesus as participating in the redemptive events of the Old Testament. Jesus was already existing at the time of Abraham (John 8:58). For Moses to leave Pharaoh's palace and to side with the Israelites in their bondage was to participate in the sufferings of Christ (Heb. 11:26). Christ was the one who provided the Israelites with food and drink during their wilderness wanderings (I Cor. 10:4). David understood that one of his posterity would be the Messiah, who would enjoy life free from the threat of death (Acts 2:25-31). The prophets spoke under the influence of the Spirit of Christ (I Pet. 1:11), and thus Isaiah saw the glory of Christ (John 12:38-41).

The New Testament also sees Jesus as promised in the Old Testament. The sufferings and glory of the servant of God depicted in Isaiah are realized in Jesus, for in the second Christian sermon Peter declared, "The God of Abraham and of Isaac and of Jacob, the God of our fathers, glorified his servant Jesus, whom you delivered up and denied in the presence of Pilate" (Acts 3:13). In this sermon Jesus is the prophet who was predicted in Deuteronomy 18:15. The early Christians regarded the Old Testament as their Bible, for they believed that Moses, the prophets, and the Psalms found their fulfillment in Christ (Luke 24:44). Their ability to see the Old Testament in this light came through the resurrection of Christ, for it was the risen Christ who opened the eyes of the Emmaus disciples to understand the Old Testament Scriptures as centering in Jesus (Luke 24:45).

[5] O. Cullmann, *The Christology of the New Testament,* p. 169.

17

The resurrection also functions as the basis for the redemptive events set forth in the New Testament. The cross of Jesus Christ has redemptive meaning because it was so closely related to the resurrection. Paul declared that Jesus "was put to death for our trespasses and raised for our justification" (Rom. 4:25). Consequently, "If Christ has not been raised . . . you are still in your sins" (I Cor. 15:17).

The outpouring of the Holy Spirit at Pentecost, too, is based on the resurrection: "This Jesus God raised up . . . . Being therefore exalted at the right hand of God, and having received from the Father the promise of the Holy Spirit, he has poured out this which you see and hear" (Acts 2:31-32). It is the risen Jesus who commissions the disciples to carry out the Great Commission (Matt. 28:18-20). By virtue of the absolute authority and power that he has, he will remain with his followers and thus enable the Gospel to be preached to all the nations (Matt. 24:14). It is the risen Jesus who appears to Paul and commissions him to launch the mission to the Gentiles (Acts 26:16-18), and it is through the Spirit of Jesus that Paul is led step by step on this mission (Acts 16:7).

Between the first and second comings of Jesus, the powers of sin and death still hold sway. To be sure, the followers of Jesus make progress in overcoming sin by the Spirit of the risen Jesus (Rom. 8:9-13), but they are still subject to physical death as are other men. However, since Jesus rose from the dead, believers will be resurrected at his second coming and death will be conquered:

> Christ has been raised from the dead, the first fruits of those who have fallen asleep . . . . But each in his own order: Christ the first fruits, then at his coming those who belong to Christ. Then cometh the end, when he delivers the kingdom to God the Father after destroying every rule and every authority and power. For he must reign until he has put all enemies under his feet. The last enemy to be destroyed is death (I Cor. 15:20, 23-26).

At this time the redeemed will be made perfect by virtue of Jesus' resurrection (Phil. 3:10-14, 20-21). Likewise, according to Acts 17:30-31, the resurrection of Jesus is the certification to all men that there will be a future judgment in which God will hold all men accountable for their deeds. The reasoning is that since Jesus' resurrection insures the final triumph over death and evil, God will not always allow evil to triumph but will bring men to answer for their sins.

Hence the resurrection of the dead and the final judgment will mark the ultimate triumph over evil and the inauguration of the new heavens and earth. According to Hebrews 2:5-10, man was originally made to be crowned with glory and honor and to have all the created world in subjection to him. But because man sinned he was dethroned from his position of authority and glory and now spends his short lifetime in bondage to the fear of death and to Satan, who has the power of death. However, while death still exercises its power, the Christian beholds Jesus now crowned with glory and honor. Because of his resurrection, Jesus therefore enjoys the glory man was originally destined to have. Through Jesus many sons are to be brought to their original destiny of glory (v. 11), and consequently, they will inherit the world to come (v. 5). Hence the resurrection and exaltation of Jesus certify that the people of God will reign in the new heavens and earth. As Cullmann has put it, "Christians are now looking forward with certainty to the V-E day, because the decisive battle, which insures the ultimate victory, has already been won."[6]

Thus it becomes apparent how the New Testament conceives of the resurrection of Jesus as the basis for all of the events of redemptive history. For this reason Walter Künneth concludes his book on the resurrection by saying, "Thus the Resurrection becomes the fulcrum of theology."[7] Likewise B. F. Westcott: "When once we grasp clearly the momentous interests which are involved in the belief in the resurrection, we shall be prepared to understand how it formed the central point of the apostolic teachings; and yet more than this, how the event itself is the central point of history, primarily of religious history . . . ."[8]

[6] O. Cullmann, *Christ and Time*, p. 141.
[7] W. Künneth, *Theologie der Auferstehung*, p. 256.
[8] B. Westcott, *The Gospel of the Resurrection*, p. 6.

19

Thus the New Testament insists that redemption from sin and death will come to pass because God entered decisively and supernaturally into history in the resurrection of Jesus Christ. There can be no question that the New Testament regards the resurrection as an historical event. It happened at a certain place: "He has risen, he is not here; see the place where they laid him" (Mark 16:6). It also happened at a certain time: ". . . he was raised on the third day . . ." (I Cor. 15:4). Consequently, if Christianity's claim to be the truth is to stand, some attention must be given to the question of history to see if it is possible to know or even conceive of God so acting within history. The problem that history poses for the possibility of faith in the resurrection becomes most evident through a consideration of the historical method, the commonly accepted procedure for coming to know what has occurred in the past.

II. The Historical Method

What is the historical method? This method is used more often than it is explained, since historians are understandably more interested in proceeding with the actual business of writing and interpreting history than they are in theorizing about the method they use. A certain historian named Marc Bloch, however, has contributed a small work on the subject of the historical method. Bloch was professor of economic history at the University of Paris until 1940, when the war and his involvement in the French underground removed him from his notes and barred him from access to libraries. Being thus unable to proceed with his trade of exploring the past, he sought release from the tensions of war and satisfaction for his intellectual craving by writing down his reflections on the procedure to be followed in carrying out the historical method. In 1944 he was captured and shot, but his reflections regarding the historical method have survived in a small booklet entitled *The Historian's Craft*.[9]

[9] The subsequent page numbers appearing in the text are taken from this book.

Bloch begins his outline of historical methodology with a definition of the science of history as "the attempt to provide knowledge about the activities of men who lived in the past" (47). The only means for gaining this knowledge are the tracks that men leave behind. These tracks are of two kinds: the intentional and the unintentional. Intentional tracks are left whenever a man sits down to write a record of things that happened in a certain span of history, such as Caesar's *Gallic Wars* or Winston Churchill's *The Second World War*. Such accounts are essential in that they provide a chronological framework without which an understanding of history is impossible. Their disadvantage lies in the fact that the reader sees the subject matter in the way the historian wanted it to be seen. Unintentional tracks range all the way from the artifacts left by a cave dweller to correspondence that men have exchanged. They include anything that indicates how men lived in the past. The advantage of this kind of evidence is that since the tracks were left unintentionally and hence were not distorted by an intermediate historian, they give insights into what the situation actually was in the past. The disadvantages of these unintentional tracks is that their almost limitless variety corresponds to nothing less than the complexity of the human species itself. The proper evaluation of each variety requires such expert skill that Bloch remarks:

> Very few scholars can boast that they are equally well equipped to read critically a medieval charter, to explain correctly the etymology of place names, to date unerringly the ruins of dwellings of the prehistoric, Celtic, or Gallo-Roman periods, and to analyze the plant life proper to a pasture, field, or a moor. Without all these, however, how could one pretend to describe the history of land use? Few sciences, I believe, are forced to use so many dissimilar tools at the same time (68).

Thus Bloch asserts repeatedly that "historical investigation is the most difficult of all the sciences." Furthermore, unlike the scientist in his laboratory, the historian can only investigate his subject matter, man, through the medium of these tracks. Because of the indirectness of his inquiry and its great difficulties, "the knowledge of the past is something progressive which is constantly transforming and perfecting itself" (58). Hence historical investigation can never fully grasp the past but must ever seek for closer and closer approximations of that fixed datum.

The acquisition of this knowledge begins with determining the authenticity and reliability of the evidences. A document recording a supposed sequence of happenings must be cross-examined to determine whether its purported author and date are valid. Only by knowing the author and date can the historian determine whether the writer was in a position to know what he was talking about. The writing must also be cross-examined to learn whether its contents are an accurate representation of the facts. Such an examination must proceed on "an instinctive metaphysics of the similar and the dissimilar, of the one and the many" (116). Basic to the whole historical inquiry is the estimation that "the universe and society possess sufficient uniformity to exclude the possibility of overly pronounced deviations" (115).

Bloch illustrates this principle by showing the way the historical method works in evaluating the report of one of Napoleon's officers, Marbot, who in his *Memoirs* claimed that on the night of May 7, 1809, he crossed the raging torrents of the Danube in order to free some prisoners on the other side. The validity of this report is determined by comparing it with other documents providing knowledge of Napoleon's army in that particular historical context. But according to the orders, records of march, and reports of the opposing armies, the Austrian army was on the side of the Danube opposite from that on which Marbot claimed to have freed his prisoners. Furthermore, from Napoleon's letters it is learned that even on May 8 the flood waters had not begun. Finally, there is the record of Marbot's request for promotion, drawn up six weeks later, in which he makes no allusion to his heroic act. Which is right, Marbot's *Memoirs* or the three sources which indicate otherwise?

Both cannot be true because "the principle of contradiction pitilessly denies that an event can be and not be at the same time" (112). The decision is made on the basis of that hypothesis which accords best with a concept of a universe in which the particularities are not of such a diverse character as to deny the essential unity in society and nature. It is possible (though the probability is infinitesimally small) that both armies were completely confused about their location on the night of May 7. It is also possible that records as to the army's whereabouts on that night were falsified, although no reason for doing this can be advanced. It is also possible that Marbot, though noted for his braggadocio, was suddenly overcome with an urge to be modest. If each of these improbabilities did in fact occur, then Marbot's report of his activities on the night of May 7 is true. But this hypothesis is to be rejected because it can stand only on the assumption of a universe in which such overly pronounced deviations can occur that many different men in two armies can be independently mistaken about their location at one and the same time, and that an inveterate liar and braggart can suddenly become humble. The hypothesis that Marbot was lying in his *Memoirs* is to be accepted because one's knowledge of the uniformity of human nature assigns it such a high degree of probability as to exclude all reasonable doubt.

The objection may be raised at this point that historians are guilty of introducing an a priori by proceeding on the basis of a universe and society which exclude "the possibility of overly pronounced deviations." But it should be noted that to deny this premise would seem to mean that no knowledge of the past is possible. Historians reason that if overly pronounced deviations do occur in the universe, then there would be no way of knowing whether Marbot crossed the river or not.

But on the other hand, the unity of the universe and human behavior must not be considered so uniform that the unexpected and the surprising cannot happen. Human nature is not so uniform as to exclude the peculiarities of individuals. Thus if two soldiers use very similar wording or phraseology in reporting a battle, the historian decides that one availed himself of the other's report. The interests of truth cease to be served when such consistency is demanded between two individuals reporting the same event that one must be judged right and the other wrong when omissions and discrepancies appear in their accounts. "Thus criticism oscillates between two extremes," says Bloch, "the similarity which vindicates and that which discredits" (115).

Nature (e.g., storms, pestilences, hereditary characteristics) does affect the course of history, but human behavior in reaction to its environment is the mainspring of history. Hence most historical explanations become attempts to account for human behavior. But having rendered an explanation, the historian should avoid pronouncing a judgment, for the very thought of doing such a thing, declares Bloch, "leads to a loss of taste for explanations" (140). If an historian has an a priori standard from which to judge human behavior in advance, he will not take the needed time to understand the deep causes for it. "How much easier it is to write for or against Luther than to fathom his soul" (141). Therefore the historian must always seek to understand why, and attaining this, he has done all.

It should be noted that almost all of the crucial points in this exposition of the historical method signify difficulties for the Christian faith. It has been shown that the basis for Christianity's structure of thought lies in the resurrection conceived of as an historical event. But if the knowledge of such events comes through a method called "the most difficult of all the sciences," then the acceptance of Christianity's claim to truth would be the possibility for only the scholarly minority. The majority of those who would be Christians would either have to accept the word of the scholars or accept Christianity's claim to truth by a method that was nonhistorical.

Then there is the difficulty that as the historical method works with the tracks left by human activity in the past, it gains a body of knowledge which is progressively increasing and being perfected. One never gains more than an approximate knowledge of the past, and it was Kierkegaard who said, "An approximation is essentially incommensurable with an infinite personal interest in an eternal happiness."[10]

Again, the historical method can be carried out only on the assumption of an orderly universe in which such overly pronounced deviations as miracles cannot occur. "The assumption of a divine intervention would be unscientific," declares Bloch (32), and it has been shown why he felt that such an assumption would destroy the possibility of historical knowledge. But Christianity asserts that God not only intervened to bring about the overly pronounced deviation of a dead man returning to life, but that the whole present order of creation will be replaced by a new creation.

Therefore it becomes apparent that there is a tension between faith and the historical method. But actually the problems of the historical method are simply the problems of history itself. In view of this tension the question that needs to be posed is, Can the resurrection of Jesus stand by itself as an historical fact known through the historical method and thus provide a basis for faith, or in order to have Easter faith must one somehow receive the will to believe the resurrection as set forth in the New Testament without needing support from historical reason? But even if the resurrection is not known by dependence on historical reason, it nevertheless clashes with this reason in its assertion that an "overly-pronounced deviation" occurred in history, which for most historians would make all historical knowledge impossible.

Then, too, there is the problem of how God, who *is,* can participate in the *becomingness* of history. This problem has come into focus ever since the Hebrew-Christian tradition began to interact with Greek thought.[11] The first real heresy

---

[10] S. Kierkegaard, *Concluding Unscientific Postscript,* p. 26.

[11] The problem was felt even before the rise of Christianity, when Judaism's teachings spread to the Greek world. Thus Philo the Jew, being enamored of Greek philosophy, sought to remove from the Old Testament the idea of a God entering into history. He did this by allegorizing the redemptive events recorded in the Old Testament so that they were merely illustrations of the timeless truths of God.

to arise within the early Christian church was Gnosticism, which declared that the center of divine revelation was not to be found in certain events in history but rather in an immediate knowledge of God gained through mystical or liturgical procedures. In the third century even Origen, the church's first great theologian, made immediate knowledge of God central and Biblical history nothing more than parables or charades that were illustrative of the timeless truths of God. This concept led to Origen's famous allegorical interpretation of Scripture, which was not fully disowned by the church in any far-reaching way until the Reformation, when Luther asserted:

> Origen altogether is not worth one word of Christ. Now I have shaken off all these follies, and my best art is to deliver the Scripture in the simple sense: therein is life, strength and doctrine; all other methods are nothing but foolishness.[12]

During the post-Reformation era of the seventeenth century, however, theologians again lost sight of the historical nature of the Bible by making the chief function of Biblical interpretation that of providing disconnected proof texts, quite unrelated to their immediate or historical context, as supports for the various dogmas.

At the end of the seventeenth century, with the dawning of the Enlightenment, the intellectual mood of humanity underwent one of its most profound changes. This new mood intensified the clash between Easter faith and history and touched off a debate that has continued until the present time. The next five chapters will trace the history of this debate so that the solution proposed in the last two chapters might profit from all that can be learned from this debate and be relevant to the present phase of the discussion.

[12] Luther, *The Table Talk of Martin Luther,* p. 399.

CHAPTER TWO

The Enlightenment
and Lessing's "Ugly Ditch"

IT IS CONVENIENT TO DATE THE ENLIGHTENMENT, OR THE AGE of Reason as it is sometimes called, from the publication of Isaac Newton's *Mathematical Principles of Natural Philosophy* in 1687 to the Lisbon earthquake of 1755. The essential characteristic of this period was man's confidence in his ability to understand and order his environment so that he might achieve fulfillment. Immanuel Kant has provided a classic definition of its mood:

> The Enlightenment represents man's emergence from a self-inflicted state of minority. A minor is one who is incapable of making use of his understanding without guidance from someone else. This minority is self-inflicted whenever its cause lies not in a lack of understanding, but in a lack of determination and courage to make use of it without the guidance of another. *Sapere aude!* Have the courage to make use of your own understanding, is therefore the watchword of the Enlightenment.[1]

The confidence of this era arose in part from the discoveries of Copernicus and Galileo that the earth and the other planets revolved around the sun. Prior to this time man had followed the Ptolemaic tradition that the earth was the center around

[1] I. Kant, *Die Religion innerhalb der Grenzen der blossen Vernunft* (1794), p. 197, quoted by Karl Barth, *From Rousseau to Ritschl*, p. 152.

which the sun and stars revolved, and when Copernicus and Galileo advanced this new theory, tradition was so strongly entrenched against it that Copernicus' book was placed on the *Index,* and Galileo had to deny the theory in order to avoid being burned at the stake. However, the facts upon which these men based their systems inevitably prevailed, and the new cosmology gradually became accepted.

Copernicus and Galileo had come to this revolutionary discovery simply through their powers of observation and abstract reasoning, and a century later Isaac Newton, limiting himself to these same powers, showed how the earth revolved around the sun according to the law of gravitation. The words of Alexander Pope indicate how momentous was Newton's discovery: "Nature and Nature's laws lay hid in night:/God said, Let Newton be! and all was light."

The work of Copernicus, Galileo, and Newton gave men the courage to make use of their understanding without feeling dependent upon an authority outside of themselves. This confidence expressed itself in new theories of government and education, in music, and even in the geometrical designs by which wild nature was transformed into lovely parks. The philosopher Baron d'Holbach (1723-1789) summed up the whole mood of this era as an attempt to

> inspire man with a respect for his own reason so that he may no longer be duped by an imagination that has been led astray by authority, by the prejudices of his childhood, and thus may learn to base his morals on his own nature, on his own wants, on the real advantage of society, so that he may become a virtuous and rational being, who cannot fail to become happy.[2]

Such a mood also made its impact felt in the realm of philosophy and religion. Newton had shown how the workings of nature could be reduced to mathematical formulas, and consequently a theology called Deism came into vogue in which nature was understood as a perfectly functioning clock that God had started and that had subsequently continued in

---

[2] W. Wallbank and A. Taylor, *Civilization Past and Present,* II, 39.

and of itself. Since God by definition must be perfect, the world that he set in motion must be as perfect as is possible for limited, finite matter. Thus the German philosopher Leibnitz said, "All is for the best in this best of all possible worlds," or as Pope expressed it, "Whatever is, is right." Since man had discovered the functionings of this clock by his own reasoning, it was inferred that he was transcendent to this clock. Man was therefore regarded as enjoying an essentially harmonious relationship to God, for since man was capable of understanding the workings of this clock, then he must be in harmony with the God who initially set the clock in motion. In short, just as the world works on the basis of a reason imparted to it by God, so man's reason is divine because it is able to discern what God has done.

The interpretation of the Bible underwent a radical change when it was carried out by men whose minds were impregnated with the spirit of the Enlightenment. The Bible's moral teachings were stressed and it was implied that man could fulfill these commands by his unaided efforts. The Biblical teaching that man is a slave of sin and in need of a supernatural redemptive work was largely ignored. The death of Jesus, instead of being the work whereby God's wrath toward sinful men was propitiated, was now set forth as an example of dying for the right, an example that all men should imitate. The immortality of the soul was emphasized rather than the resurrection of the body. Only that in the Bible was acceptable that was deemed reasonable in the sense that it tended to compliment man by implying that he was in essential harmony with God.

Deistic thinking became increasingly popular until an earthquake and tidal wave killed some 15,000 people in Lisbon on November 1, 1755. Up to this time it had seemed that Deism was able to give an adequate account of evil by declaring that this was the best of all *possible* worlds. Matter, by its very nature, was finite, so that it did not always function perfectly. But if men would only understand the limitations of matter and adjust their lives accordingly, they could avoid suffering. Then, too, there was suffering in the world as the result of not acting reasonably and transgressing moral law. But the catastrophe at Lisbon implied that matter was not simply lacking in the power always to effect the greatest good but that it was capable of producing radical evil that involved men in suffering with no regard to their moral worth.

In 1759 Voltaire published *Candide*, his famous satire of Deism. Candide and his teacher, the Deistic philosopher Pangloss, are in Lisbon at the time of the earthquake. To Candide's rising doubts about the essential goodness of the world, Pangloss gives the desperate and impractical answer that all would have been well had the inhabitants of Lisbon only discerned that somewhere offshore, at the bottom of the ocean, there was a volcano which would always threaten the city of Lisbon with an earthquake and tidal wave. Later Candide becomes involved in a war in which, as Voltaire put it, "The musket bullets swept away, out of the best of all possible worlds, nine or ten thousand scoundrels that infested its surface!"

Thus experience itself belied Deism's confidence in the rationality of the world. Not only was there a radical malevolence in nature, but whole segments of mankind were capable of acting with such folly as to make it extremely doubtful that man was in harmony with God. Hence, in the second half of the eighteenth century, two ways of modifying Deism became discernible. There was Rousseau who taught that for man again to achieve fulfillment he must seek to reorient his life to the primitive state of nature. Gotthold Lessing, on the other hand, taught that man must allow his reason to develop further. When it had achieved its goal, all life would be subsumed under reason, and man would be in harmony with God. Thus the confidence gained during the Enlightenment that all was essentially well with man remained, but now it was asserted that man must bring about some kind of change in his manner of life in order to be fully justified in this confidence. The changes advocated by Rousseau and Lessing, however, lay in opposite directions. For Lessing salvation lay in reason, while for Rousseau it lay in nature and in man's willingness to submit to it. These two directions, which have been called Rationalism and Romanticism, form the background for the thinking regarding Easter faith and history until the rise of Liberalism in the middle of the nineteenth century.

I. Rationalism

A. Gotthold Lessing

In considering Rationalism it is convenient to begin with Gotthold Lessing (1729-1781). At the age of seventeen, Lessing was sent by his father, an orthodox Lutheran minister, from his home in Berlin to Leipzig, there to study theology and prepare for the ministry. But Lessing soon found himself more intrigued by the theater than by theology and began to write plays and essays on literary criticism. Debt forced him to return to Berlin, where he remained for six years. From 1755 to 1769 he wandered from place to place while continuing to write, mostly for the theater. During this period he composed his most famous play, *Minna von Barnhelm*. However, his interest was gradually shifting from the theater to theology, and when in 1769 he became the librarian at Wolfenbüttel for the Duke of Brunswick, he found the leisure he needed to devote himself almost exclusively to theology.

At Wolfenbüttel Lessing obtained a 4000-page manuscript entitled *An Apology for the Rational Worshippers of God*, written by Hermann S. Reimarus, a professor of oriental languages at Hamburg, who had died in 1769. Reimarus had written this, not for the purpose of publishing it, but simply to relieve his feelings of skepticism with regard to orthodox Christianity. Between 1774 and 1778 Lessing published seven excerpts from this work without revealing its author. He called them the *Anonymous Wolfenbüttel Fragments*, and declared that he had been quite unable to discover how and when they came into the Duke's library. To understand this deception of Lessing's, we must remember how close was the connection between church and state in the Germany of those days, and how the power of government would be unleashed to ostracize anyone who openly denied the essentials of orthodoxy. Hence, to give the heresy hunters a false lead, Lessing hinted that these fragments might be the product of a certain J. L. Schmidt, an obscure Deist who had died a quarter of a century before. Lessing himself never revealed the author, but the conviction steadily grew that Reimarus was the man. This conviction was confirmed in 1814 when Reimarus' son informed the librarian at Göttingen that his father was indeed the author.

Lessing sought to maintain a semblance of orthodoxy by attaching to the fifth fragment (in which Reimarus had denied the resurrection of Jesus by pointing to the apparent discrepancies in the Gospel accounts) three paragraphs in which he appeared to disagree with Reimarus. "How much could be said in reply to all these objections and difficulties!"[3] exclaimed Lessing. But then he proceeded to say that even if the objections could not be answered, the truth of Christianity would stand, for the Christian religion did not depend upon arguments regarding historical details in the Bible but rather upon the knowledge of Christianity that one has in his heart. Instead of thinking of Reimarus' arguments as destroying the faith of the Christian, Lessing replied that "for the Christian, Christianity is simply a fact, the Christianity which he feels to be true and in which he feels blessed. When the paralytic feels the beneficial shocks of the electric spark, does it worry him whether Nollet or Franklin or neither of them is right?"

This statement makes it clear that Lessing believed that the basis for the Christian faith did not depend upon the objective facts of history. This depreciation of history provides the clue to why Lessing had wanted to publish these fragments. He wanted to show that the basis for Christianity lay in the soul rather than in history. The last and most important fragment, "On the Intentions of Jesus and his Disciples," contained what

[3] H. Chadwick (ed.), *Lessing's Theological Writings*, pp. 17f.

was really the first attempt in the history of thought to reconstruct the New Testament in terms of historical explanations that did not depend upon the supernatural but simply upon the normal range of human behavior.

According to Reimarus, Jesus' intention was to establish the earthly Messianic kingdom predicted by the Old Testament. When he went to Jerusalem, he hoped that by cleansing the temple and excoriating the Pharisees before the multitudes, he would arouse a popular insurrection against the religious leaders and be acclaimed as the Messiah. But the plan went afoul and Jesus was crucified by the Pharisees for his indiscreet actions and remarks. Jesus' followers were disheartened until they remembered a strand of Jewish teaching (extant in the Talmud and in Justin Martyr's *Dialogue with the Jew Trypho*) that the Messiah must come twice, first to suffer and then to reign in glory with unlimited power. The disciples had seen what a profitable and easy life preaching had been during their time with Jesus, and so they decided to continue this life by preaching that Jesus had risen from the dead and would soon return. Consequently, they rushed to the tomb, removed the body of Jesus, and hid it where it could never be found. Then they began to preach that Jesus was risen, and to prove this they employed many Old Testament arguments and pointed to the change that had occurred in their own behavior. But as proof of their worldly ambitions, they had their first converts lay all their possessions at their feet.[4]

Such a reconstruction removed any idea of a supernatural intervention of God in history. Lessing published it because he wanted to show that religion did not have to depend on the report of what God had done for men in history, but on the reason that all men already possessed in their own souls. This disjunction between history and reason became explicit

---

[4] C. Voysey (ed.), *Fragments from Reimarus*, pp. 84-119. Reimarus' reconstruction of New Testament history never gained general acceptance because it failed to explain how, if the disciples were perpetrating what they knew to be a fraud, they were yet willing to suffer and die for Jesus.

in the writings he composed during the last three years of his life.

In reply to J. D. Schumann, who tried to refute the *Fragments* by making the traditional appeal to the fulfilled prophecy and miracles of the Bible, Lessing wrote an essay entitled, "On the Proof of the Spirit and of Power" (1778).[5] This title came from Paul's statement in I Corinthians 2:4, "My speech and my message were . . . in demonstration of the spirit and power," and had been used from Origen onwards as the proof text for saying that Christianity's validation rested upon spirit (fulfilled prophecy) and power (miracles). Lessing's purpose in this essay was to disprove this traditional approach. But true to his policy of trying to avoid ostracism by conceding all that he could to orthodoxy and denying what he could not concede in a way that to the unsuspecting would seem to be an affirmation, Lessing asserted that the miracles of Christianity did indeed occur, and that these miracles persuaded those witnessing them to believe. But he departed from tradition by saying that fulfilled prophecies and miracles lost their power the moment they were reported to others as happening. Lessing argued that an historical truth was not capable of logical demonstration, and, since reported miracles are historical truths, the truth of Christianity could not be demonstrated by them. "Accidental truths of history can never become the proof of necessary truths of reason" (53). This famous statement of Lessing has rung down the corridors of theological thought to the present day.

Lessing declared, for example, that he believed the historical fact that Alexander the Great had conquered Asia in a short time. However, because this was a merely historical fact, he could not, on the basis of it, risk anything whose loss would be irreparable to him. Lessing also affirmed the historical fact that Jesus rose from the dead and therefore declared himself to be the Son of God. But Lessing refused to base a belief in the deity of Christ upon the fact that he could not find any historical objection against the resurrection, for

[5] Chadwick, *op. cit.*, pp. 51-59.

to argue from the resurrection to Jesus' deity was to argue
from an accidental fact to a necessary truth, and this was a
metábasis eis allò génos (shifting of categories). The gap between accidental truths of history and necessary truths of
reason Lessing pictured as "the ugly broad ditch which I
cannot get across, however often and however earnestly I
have tried to make the leap" (55).

We must not be misled by Lessing's affirmation of the
resurrection. It must be viewed in the light of his strategy of
conceding to orthodoxy what was nonessential for his argument, in order to preserve some chance of convincing people
of his basic point. Søren Kierkegaard, who seventy-five years
later found in Lessing a great inspiration for his philosophy,
observed that Lessing was speaking by way of "concession"
when he said that he did not deny the miracles and fulfilled
prophecies of Scripture.[6] To affirm that Jesus rose from the
dead means nothing when it is also affirmed that, being an
historical event, this could provide no basis for faith today.
But what Lessing was really saying was that all that happens
in history, whether one is an eyewitness of it or not, is accidental and therefore cannot be the basis for believing an
eternal truth, a truth so vital that its loss would be irreparable.

In the "Education of the Human Race,"[7] which appeared in
1780, Lessing makes it clear how he knows an eternal truth.
Having moved beyond the Deistic notion that the world and
man as he is at present are satisfactory, Lessing looked for
ultimate fulfillment for humanity at a point in the future. "It
will come! The time of perfecting will assuredly come!" (96)
Retrogressions may occur along the way, but Lessing was
sure that man would ultimately exemplify the fact that he is
essentially in harmony with God. Man has always been endowed with divine reason, but lacking experience and training
he lived contrary to it and succumbed to idolatry and sin.
Then God began to educate him, first through the Old Testament economy in which man learned to live according to the

[6] S. Kierkegaard, *Concluding Unscientific Postscript*, p. 88.
[7] Chadwick, *op. cit.*, pp. 82-98.

35

outward forms of virtue by the inducement of earthly rewards, and secondly through the New Testament economy when man was taught the inward attitude of virtue by the promise of the true life that was to come after this present, earthly one. The third and final stage will come when man is led (apparently by certain gadflies like Lessing) to infer, from the direction in which God has been moving man, the ultimate goal at which he is to arrive: virtuous living for the sake of virtue alone. During this process the truths of reason were given to men by means of revelation in order that they might be stimulated to own up to them, but "revelation gives nothing to the human race which human reason could not arrive at on its own" (83). "God has permitted and caused the pure truths of reason to be taught, for a time, as truths of immediate revelation, in order to promulgate them the more rapidly, and ground them the more firmly" (94). These "pure truths of reason" are "the better conceptions of the divine Being, of our nature, of our relation to God" (95). Hence the ultimate basis for truth is reason, which has been intuitively in the human soul from the beginning. Operating on this basis, Lessing felt he could come to know necessary, eternal truths without concerning himself with history, for he was already on the right side of the "ugly ditch" that separates the accidental truths of history from the necessary truths of reason. Consequently, it was of no moment whether Reimarus was wrong or not, for so long as one receives the blessing of Christianity when he is stimulated to own up to the reason that resides in his soul, he has all that he needs.

B. Immanuel Kant

The great philosopher Immanuel Kant followed Lessing in making a radical disjunction between faith and history. In his *Religion Within the Limits of Reason Alone* (1793),[8] Kant constantly distinguished between the religion of practical

---

[8] I. Kant, *Religion Within the Limits of Reason Alone* (tr. and ed. by T. M. Green and H. Hudson).

reason, whose precepts are known to all men through the categorical imperative heard from the depths of the soul, and historical religions that, while having many different forms, are essentially only approximations of this one religion of reason. These historical religions are necessary for bringing about the acceptance of the one pure religious faith of reason, for because of the peculiar weakness of human nature there is a need for historical religions with all their trappings of miracles, institutions, a founder, dogmas, and special regulations, to awaken men to heed the categorical imperative.

According to Kant, the categorical imperative provides every man with the knowledge of the perfect man. Kant also affirmed that an historical record of the perfect man, Jesus Christ, is found in the New Testament. However, this perfection of Jesus which lay in his inner disposition could not be made manifest to others directly but only mediately through his teachings and actions. Since the knowledge of this inner disposition came by inference from his empirical words and actions, there would always be some room to doubt whether Jesus really was controlled by perfect motives in the inner reaches of his soul and was not just putting on a front of perfection. Nevertheless the categorical imperative, which we all possess, demands that we put the best construction on things so that we see in Jesus his ultimate perfection (59).

Thus, like Lessing, Kant regarded the empirical stuff of history to be incapable, in and of itself, of conveying eternal truth, for such could be known only from the depths of one's own soul. He alluded to Lessing's figure of the wide ditch by asserting that between an objective fact (such as would exist in an historical report) and a concept in the mind there is no mediating analogy, "but rather a mighty chasm the overleaping of which leads at once to anthropomorphism"(59). Indeed, for Kant Lessing's ditch had become a chasm, for Kant found the historical report of the supernaturalness of Jesus—his virgin birth, miracles, and resurrection—to be a definite hindrance to reason. Such things discouraged the living of the moral life, because "the elevation of such a holy person above all the frailties of human nature would rather, so far as we can see, hinder the adoption of the idea of such a person for our imitation" (57). The resurrection of Jesus is particularly detrimental to the life of reason because it implies that reason cannot finally subsist in and of itself but must ever be dependent upon a material body for its existence (119). Thus "an attempt to discover in Scripture that sense which harmonizes with the *most holy* teachings of reason is not only allowable but is deemed a duty" (78). Consequently, the supernatural features of the historical record must be reinterpreted to conform to the demands of reason before the best construction could be put on Jesus' motives so that he could become a stimulus to awaken men to reason.

C. *Heinrich Paulus*

Several of Kant's followers, anxious to maintain Jesus as one suitable for human imitation, applied Rationalism to New Testament scholarship. The most representative example of this movement was Heinrich Paulus, professor of theology at Heidelberg from 1811 to 1851. In the introduction to his *Life of Jesus* (1828) he revealed the influence of Kant when he said that he hoped this method of explaining away the miracles in the Gospels would not deter his readers from seeing that "the truly miraculous thing about Jesus is Jesus himself, the purity and serene boldness of his character, which is, notwithstanding, genuinely human, and adapted to the imitation and emulation of mankind."[9]

Paulus argued that the miracles existed only in the minds of the evangelists, who, like the Jews of that time, attributed all phenomena to the immediate action of God. Nevertheless, the Gospel texts preserved certain details that provided the clue for their natural explanation. The resurrection of Jesus was really nothing more than a resuscitation. Jesus' loud cry just before he was thought to have died showed how much strength he really had left. When Jesus was removed from the

[9] Quoted by A. Schweitzer, *The Quest of the Historical Jesus*, p. 51.

cross, he was not really dead but in a deathlike trance. The bloodletting that was produced by the spear thrust, the coolness of the tomb where he was laid, the spices with which Joseph embalmed him, all worked to bring Jesus out of this trance. He exchanged the grave clothes for those of the gardener, and so it was that Mary Magdalene mistook him. Jesus summoned what strength he had left to meet with his disciples, and during the next forty days he tried to recuperate, and garnered what strength he had for his brief meetings with them. But then he realized that death was near. There happened to be a cloud on a mountain where he and his disciples were and this provided him with a chance to make a grand exit. He walked away from his disciples and into this cloud and then went off somewhere and died. But the disciples believed that he had ascended into heaven.

This rationalistic procedure, however, obviously failed to make Jesus an example to be imitated. It pictured him as an impostor who deliberately deluded his disciples into thinking he was a supernatural person. Hence, in Paulus the full implications of Rationalism became evident. What man should know about God and what duty God required of man found no support whatsoever in the Jesus of history. He could not be emulated so long as he was viewed in the supernaturalistic terms of the four Gospels, and the attempt to explain away this supernaturalism made Jesus an impostor. According to Rationalism, therefore, man could find in history no support for building a system of ethics. Instead, he must look away from history and concentrate his attention upon the categorical imperative of his own soul. There was no possibility of bridging the ugly chasm between history and faith, for history was in reality a detriment to faith.

II. Romanticism

Around the close of the eighteenth century the mood of Romanticism, already foreshadowed by Rousseau, became increasingly popular. Like Rationalism, this mood expressed a confidence, tracing back to the Enlightenment, that man had powers within his grasp which, if properly used, would enable him to find fulfillment as one who was essentially in harmony with God. But it revolted against the uniformity that Rationalism tended to impose on man with the emphasis on the categorical imperative which was the same for all. If man really was essentially in harmony with God, could not this harmony lie within the realm of a person's individual predilections, his desire to find his own fulfillment, his instinct to live, to be free, to create something particular? Why should these inner surgings be repressed and sacrificed on the altar of reason? Since the particularities of an individual correspond more to the flux and becomingness of history, it would seem at the outset that Romanticism would be more successful in finding a basis for faith in history.

A. *Friedrich Schleiermacher*

This philosopher and theologian became a great spokesman for Romanticism. His systematic presentation is set forth in his work *The Christian Faith,* which first appeared in 1828.[10] Schleiermacher insisted that religion was more than a mere morality, a fulfilling of one's duty toward his fellow man. For him religion was to love and serve God. The starting point for the knowledge of God was in the feeling of absolute dependence. This feeling arises not only from the knowledge that one is determined by his environment, but also to some extent from the freedom one has to control his environment, for even this freedom is something that has been given to us (§ 4.3). Thus in every aspect of his being, man is entirely dependent. It is from this feeling of absolute dependence that one receives the knowledge of God as the "Whence" of all things (§ 4.4).

When a man rebels against the fact that he is absolutely dependent, he experiences pain in his soul, which is an evidence of sin (§ 66). But when he acquiesces to his depend-

[10] F. Schleiermacher, *The Christian Faith.*

ence, he enjoys the knowledge of God. In the earlier and popular expression of his thinking, Schleiermacher had declared that even a longing for immortality was a rebellion against one's finitude and thus a negation of true piety.[11] In his systematic theology he is more guarded, declaring simply that while "there is a way of denying the survival of personality in following which we may be more deeply pervaded by the God-consciousness than if we accepted it," yet it is possible to have a belief in immortality and still be pious if we value the afterlife simply because it provides an unimpeded knowledge of God (§§ 158, 163).

Jesus Christ was the one who, though having the same environment and nature as other men, was unique in that he lived fully in accord with his absolute dependence. As a result a community came into existence and still continues that, in mutual fellowship in looking to Jesus Christ, finds in his example a redemptive power to live as absolutely dependent (§ 11). This power is not derived from believing in the miracles that Jesus performed or in his purported resurrection. Just as the disciples experienced the power of Jesus before they had any thought of his rising from the dead, so also "faith in Jesus as Redeemer develops out of a total impression [of his life]" (423). In fact, miracles must be denied, for if God did break into the natural flow of things, then we could not have a feeling of absolute dependence from the nature that surrounds us, for this nature would never be a perfect expression of God until it had been invaded by the supernatural (179). Consequently, the power that Jesus had and imparts to men through the church is not miraculous but natural. It is not a power that remedies the defects of nature, but it is the natural power of a natural man enabling natural men to own up to their absolute dependence on nature. The divine element in Jesus must be regarded "as an action of human nature, grounded in its original constitution and prepared for by all its past history" (64).

[11] F. Schleiermacher, *On Religion: Speeches to Its Cultured Despisers,* pp. 99f.

It would surely seem, under Schleiermacher's system, in which Christ is so much a part of history and in which nature, past and present, provides the knowledge of God, that Lessing's ditch had been bridged. But as we trace the development of this approach through Hegel to Strauss, we find that such is not the case.

B. Georg F. W. Hegel

Despite certain differences, the philosopher Hegel should also be considered in connection with Schleiermacher, for he too saw the whole world as the expression of God. For Hegel, God was conceived of as "spirit," as that which is pure identity and incapable of change. But spirit existing in and for itself implies a duality in which spirit is able to stand over against itself and look at itself. That aspect of spirit which transcends itself is universal in that it is able to view all of itself, but that aspect which is transcended can and does express itself in particulars. However, even a particular manifestation of spirit can transcend itself and see its universality. Spirit thus exists in a triad that is suggestive of the Christian trinity: "Father," spirit in its universal form, "Son," spirit in its particular form, and the "Holy Spirit," arising as the particular, transcending itself, and finally viewing itself as the universal. Hence the true meaning of God, or spirit, comes to light, for spirit is to be defined as "absolute reflection within itself in virtue of its absolute duality."[12]

Man himself finds a place within this concept of spirit, for he corresponds to that second, particular manifestation of it. But man can be a unity with God when he learns to exist as true spirit, that is, when he learns to stand over against himself and to view himself as spirit—as being of infinite value and having an eternal destiny; in short, when he learns to view himself as having the freedom that is appropriate to God.

Hegel viewed the history of the world as the process by which the world, comprising the physical phenomena of na-

[12] G. Hegel, *The Philosophy of History*, col. 306a.

ture and the psychical impulses of man, comes to express its freedom and oneness with God. Man's understanding of himself as free has come about in three stages: in the oriental world the despot saw himself as free, but because no one besides him was also free, this freedom manifested itself in capriciousness rather than in the good. The next higher level of freedom came in the Graeco-Roman world, where the aristocracy governed itself as a democracy. Here there was some freedom gained, but it was imperfect because not all men were understood as free. Ultimate freedom, however, was finally realized under the monarchy of the German nation of Hegel's time. That which led to this ultimate freedom was Christianity. According to Hegel, the salvation of the world came in the particular person of Jesus Christ (303b). Jesus Christ was the first man to view his own spirit as capable of having identity with God, for he said, "Blessed are the pure in heart, for they shall see God." He also saw that this oneness with God was to be enjoyed despite all sufferings inflicted by nature and by men who had not yet learned of their freedom, for those who nevertheless persisted in viewing themselves as manifestations of the spirit would enjoy the glory of God. Therefore Jesus was willing to persist in his teaching even though it meant so arousing the anger of the Pharisees that they would kill him.

It was necessary for Jesus to die because by so doing it became evident that he had attained the freedom and infinity of spirit "by stripping himself of his finiteness and surrendering himself to pure self-consciousness" (308a). The death of Jesus also served a necessary function by stripping away his visible aspect so that the disciples and early church were subsequently able to think of him in terms fully appropriate to the spirit (306b). Thus was launched the great idea of Jesus that as man viewed himself as an infinite spirit he would realize his potential as a part of God. Men themselves are to appropriate this idea and accomplish Jesus' own history; however, Jesus himself remains unique. "The appearance of the Christian God," affirmed Hegel, "can occur only once, for

God is realized as subject, and as manifested subjectively is exclusively one individual" (306b). But how Hegel could say that Jesus was unique is difficult to ascertain, because all men are to reduplicate Jesus by understanding their spirit as the expression of God. The only possible way that Jesus could be unique in Hegel's system is that he manifested this God-consciousness as a single individual, whereas his followers have done this in an ever larger group that always gains its inspiration from Jesus, the first to live in this way.

When Jesus launched the idea of true freedom that was ultimately to bring about the redemption of the human race, this idea became a part of history and thus had to go through the process of thesis, antithesis, synthesis. The spirit of Christ that became embodied in the early church found its antithesis in the barbarism that swept over the Roman empire. Then a synthesis developed as the Roman church, which continued to embody the spirit of Christ, demanded allegiance from the secular states which had overcome barbarism. But this new synthesis was imperfect because the secular states did not render their allegiance to Rome through freedom but by way of compulsion. Thus it was necessary for a new antithesis to appear in which the secular states became swallowed up in the ecclesiastical church, which by that time had become utterly worldly. Thus spirit could no longer find its expression in the institutional church and, having to exist in and of itself, it emerged in a form that was no longer subservient to the positivistic religion implied in the Christian church, but was purely the expression of the idea which Jesus launched. This new form was the German monarchy of Hegel's day, which considered the church an integral part of the state. The state, therefore, was now the expression of that unity with God which spirit implies.

But even here there remains one more measure of waltz time. This idea that had come to realization under the German monarchy of Hegel's day had its antithesis in the particularity of the German nation. But now that Hegel had spelled out its meaning in conceptual form, he had transcended the particular, and through his philosophy spirit had fully manifested its inherent deity. Thus it becomes clear how Hegel could say that "reason is the sovereign of the world . . . . The history of the world presents us with a rational process" (156b).

Hegel felt that accurate and scientific knowledge about God could only be had when one thought and spoke as a metaphysician. For him the language of the New Testament was the pictorial language of human imagination as it sought to express ultimate reason. Consequently, the New Testament emphasis on the resurrection of Jesus was only an imaginative way of expressing the continuation of the idea that Jesus had taught. Hegel explained the rise of belief in the resurrection as follows: Gradually the disciples' grief over the death of Jesus subsided, and the spirit and image of his pure manhood rose, as it were, out of the grave. But along with this spirit there was the memory of his physical presence with them. "What was wanting in the divinity present in the loving community [of Christians] . . . was an image and a shape. But in the risen Jesus, lifted up heavenward, the image found life again, and love found the objectification of its oneness."[13]

Thus it would seem that Hegel, like Schleiermacher, was not troubled by Lessing's ugly ditch, for God was to be found in the becomingness of history. Like Schleiermacher, Hegel could not acknowledge a supernatural intrusion of God into the course of history, for the necessity for such an intrusion would imply that ordinary history is imperfect and hence no longer adequate for presenting the rational process which is God. The implications of Hegel's thinking for finding in history a basis for faith become evident in the thinking of David Strauss.

C. David Strauss

In his *Life of Jesus* (1835) David Strauss made it clear that he was beginning his investigation with the explicit presupposition that all events in history are equally amenable to the

[13] G. Hegel, *On Christianity: Early Theological Writings*, p. 292.

law of cause and effect.[14] Thus, along with Schleiermacher and Hegel, Strauss excluded the possibility for the supernatural explanation of the Jesus of the Gospels. But Strauss did not try to explain away the supernatural element in the Gospel records by such far-fetched explanations as the rationalist Paulus. Rather, following the lead of Hegel, he theorized that it arose from the tendency of the disciples to depict in imaginary terms the great idea that they had learned from Jesus, that man can conceive of himself as an expression of the divine. Strauss sought to support this approach by historical argumentation. What historical fact had caused the early church and the Gospel writers to use their particular imagery for embellishing the life of Jesus with the supernatural? The answer, Strauss felt, was the Messianic hope of the Jewish people, which had been kept alive through the writings of the Old Testament.

In his consideration of the resurrection of Jesus we find the best example of Strauss' methodology for explaining the supernatural, for he affirmed that "all the other miracles in the history of Jesus could be adduced as a consequence of the [disciples' faith in the] resurrection" (85). Strauss asserted that the death of Jesus had "for the moment" completely destroyed the disciples' faith that Jesus was the Messiah, and therefore they fled back home to Galilee. But there in the freer air, where they were safe from the fear of the Jews and where they had been with Jesus, the conviction that he was the Messiah began to reassert itself. This meant that they had to solve the problem of how he could be the Messiah and yet be crucified as a criminal. For the Jews of that day the answer to all such problems was to be found in the Old Testament. The disciples found in such passages as Isaiah 53 and Psalms 22 the theme of suffering, which they ascribed to Jesus as the Messiah. Thus it is that Luke 24:32 says that their hearts burned within them as they realized that Jesus, the Messiah, must first suffer and then be glorified in heaven. Then they reasoned that this

---

[14] D. Strauss, *The Life of Jesus*, pp. 79f.

46

very burning in their hearts was nothing less than the risen Jesus himself, communicating with them. This impression increased in intensity until some of the more emotional actually had hallucinations of Jesus appearing to them. The power of suggestion from these caused the rest also to have hallucinations (742).

The disciples then realized that since Jesus was truly risen his tomb must be empty, and indeed Psalms 16:10, "Thou wilt not suffer thy holy one to see corruption," and Isaiah 53:10, "Thou wilt prolong his days," certainly taught an empty tomb. In Galilee the disciples were not reminded of the occupied tomb of Jesus which, had they seen it, would have again plunged them into despair. But when the courage and conviction of the disciples had reached a sufficient level to return to proclaim the gospel in Jerusalem, "it was no longer possible by the sight of the body of Jesus either to convict themselves or to be convicted by others" (743). Strauss conceded that the fifty days between Easter and Pentecost was too short a time both for the occupied grave of Jesus no longer to have a convicting effect and for the disciples to become enthusiastic enough to preach, but here again he claims that the author of Acts made the day when the disciples first preached Pentecost simply because he wanted the announcement of the new law to coincide with the anniversary of the day when the old law was given at Sinai. Strauss actually felt that the time which had elapsed between the death of Jesus and the commencement of the disciples' preaching was much longer (743f.).

Thus for Strauss the resurrection, like all the other miracles that are a reflection of resurrection faith, is a myth, i.e., the idea of the essential oneness of God and man clothed in concrete and supernatural terms. But, Strauss reasoned, if all men are potentially able to be one with God and if history is so constituted that men will actually come to live according to this potentiality, then why should one insist, as did Hegel, that there was anything special about Jesus? Strauss queried (779f.):

47

If reality is ascribed to the idea of the unity of the divine and human natures, is this equivalent to the admission that this unity must actually have been once manifested, as it never had been, and never more will be, in one individual? This is indeed not the mode in which Idea realizes itself; it is not wont to lavish all its fulness on one exemplar, and be niggardly towards all others. . . . It rather loves to distribute its riches among a multiplicity of exemplars. . . . Is not unity of the divine and human natures a real one in a far higher sense, when I regard the whole race of mankind as its realization than when I single out one man as such a realization? Is not an incarnation of God from eternity a truer one than an incarnation limited to a particular point of time?

Thus Strauss made crystal clear what was implicit in Schleiermacher and Hegel: if Jesus be a part of the history of the world in the same way that every other man is, then whatever salvation he achieved could be achieved by other men who exerted themselves to the same degree as did Jesus. Jesus, therefore, is simply one of the many who have lived according to their divine potential. Despite all their efforts to the contrary, Schleiermacher and Hegel had actually considered Jesus as nothing more than an exemplary expression of human capability. Consequently, as Strauss pointed out, the knowledge of God was not summed up in Jesus but was reflected in the whole of human history. Indeed, Jesus had helped men to see that they were one with God, but he had not done this by pointing to himself or even to history as a sensible, empirical fact from which this knowledge could be gained. Rather, he had caused men to realize an idea that was already resident within their minds. Strauss declared (780f.):

But mind having once taken occasion by this external fact [of Jesus], to bring under its consciousness the idea of humanity as one with God, sees in the history only the presentation of that idea: the object of faith is completely changed; instead of a sensible, empirical fact, it has become a spiritual and divine idea, which has its confirmation no longer in history but in philosophy. When the mind has thus gone beyond the sensible history, and entered into the domain of the absolute, [history] ceases to be essential; it takes a subordinate place, above which the spiritual truths suggested by history stand self-supported; it becomes a faint image of a dream . . . and does not, like the idea, share the permanence of the spirit which is absolutely present to itself.

Hence Schleiermacher, Hegel, and Strauss take their place with Kant and Paulus on the same side of the ugly ditch as Lessing, for in reality they, too, found the ultimate basis for truth in an idea that they shared with all men, rather than in some particular point of history. History was simply the place where the mind, by a process of selection and arrangement, finds illustrations of the idea that could be grasped without history. And because truth was found in the mind rather than in history, Jesus, who is a part of history, ceased to be the crucial source for truth.

CHAPTER THREE

Nineteenth Century Liberalism

David Strauss had indeed carried the thought of Schleiermacher and Hegel to its logical conclusion, but the Christian world could not be content with such a line of thought. While much of the Christian world of that day did not want to accept all the implications of embracing a positive, historical religion, neither could it bring itself to divest Jesus of all uniqueness. Strauss had been accepted as a professor at the University of Zürich, but the outcry against his *Life of Jesus* was so great that the University fulfilled its contract with him, not by letting him teach, but by giving him a lifelong pension.

Although the work of Strauss was the logical outcome of the philosophy of Hegel, yet it had not fully followed the historical method. Strauss had not, for example, been completely convincing in his preference for Matthew as the most reliable Gospel. A truly historical consideration of the life of Jesus from the vantage point of positivistic historiography could not be made until it could be determined which of the Gospels, or which strands of tradition in the Gospels, were primary and which were secondary. In 1835, the very year Strauss published his *Life of Jesus*, Karl Lachmann set forth in his "De ordine narrationum in evangeliis synopticiis" an argument for the literary priority of the Gospel of Mark. Lachmann observed that the differences between the Synoptic Gospels were really not so great as it might appear. Indeed, the diversity was great when one compared Matthew with Luke, but if one compared Matthew with Mark and then Luke with Mark, one found that Matthew and Luke never disagreed in their sequence of events as over against Mark. Therefore Lachmann concluded that both Matthew and Luke had used Mark as a source when they wrote their Gospels, and hence Mark was a better historical source than either Matthew or Luke.

In 1838 C. G. Wilke, in his *Der Urevangelist*, strengthened the case for the priority of Mark by advancing two further arguments: (1) the verbal similarity is much greater when Matthew and Luke are compared with Mark than when they are compared with one another; (2) almost all of Mark is reproduced by both Matthew and Luke. In the same year C. H. Weisse made still another contribution to the argument in his *Die evangelische Geschichte kritisch und philosophisch bearbeitet* by contending that if the graphic details of Mark had been the work of an epitomizer, they would have contained more embellishments, but since they are so simple and artless, they must have been an original composition.

Weisse also advanced a line of argument that made evident another strand of tradition which, like Mark, was primary. Matthew, he suggested, was the combination of both Mark and a collection of the sayings of Jesus. Luke was composed on the basis of Mark and these sayings as contained in another version of Matthew. Hence the sayings of Matthew, which have been commonly denoted as "Q," and Mark comprise the two sources which were closest to Jesus.

Thus the work of Lachmann, Wilke, and Weisse had shown which sources in the Gospels were best suited, from the canons of the historical method, for giving an historical view of Jesus. Since Mark was comprised mostly of reports of what Jesus did, it came to be regarded as the primary source for the chronological sequence of Jesus' ministry. Q, which comprised Jesus' sayings, came to be regarded as the primary source for his thinking and motivation. Christian thinkers who could not accept Strauss' total destruction of Christianity as an historical religion based on Jesus, now began to work with these primary sources. Since these sources had gained their reputation through historical reasoning, they were more reliable than Strauss had admitted, and thus they presented the possibility of escaping his position and maintaining the Jesus of history as crucially significant for faith. This possibility was exploited in numerous "lives of Jesus" written between 1860 and 1900. These many writers were convinced that on the basis of Mark and Q they were able to counteract the negative conclusions of Strauss in which the Jesus of the Gospels was obscured by the mythical thinking of the early Christians. Albert Schweitzer singled out H. J. Holtzmann's "life of Jesus" as the classical example of this approach. "Scarcely ever," declared Schweitzer, "has a description of the life of Jesus exercised so irresistible an influence as that short outline . . . with which Holtzmann closes his examination of the Synoptic Gospels. This chapter became the creed and catechism of all who handled the subject during the following decades."[1] An examination of Holtzmann's concluding chapter will show how nineteenth-century Liberalism attempted to make the Jesus it found in history important for faith.

I. H. J. Holtzmann's "Life of Jesus"[2]

Holtzmann began his summary of the life of Jesus with some very laudatory remarks about the superiority of the Gospel of Mark. Mark is closer to the real Jesus than either Matthew or Luke because here the real individual named Jesus of Nazareth appears with a minimum of distortion arising from the religious ideas of the disciples. Matthew and Luke reveal their dogmatical bias by beginning with the virgin birth of Jesus, but in Mark Jesus appears simply as "Jesus from Nazareth" (Mark 1:9). "Nowhere does the human Jesus emerge in such a recognizable fashion as in the Gospel of Mark" (475).

---

[1] A. Schweitzer, *The Quest of the Historical Jesus*, p. 204.
[2] H. Holtzmann, *Die synoptischen Evangelien.*

Furthermore, the Gospel of Mark is the source for the indispensable chronological framework of the ministry of Jesus. Luke disturbed this framework by his interpolation found in 9:51–18:14. No orderly progression is discernible in Matthew either, because in chapters 5-7 Jesus publicly declares himself to be the Messiah, while in later chapters he wants to keep this a secret. But in Mark all is orderly. According to Holtzmann, Mark shows in chapters 1-9 seven stages by which the ministry of Jesus encompassed a progressively larger territory. Then, from chapter 10 onwards, the disciples began to realize the peculiar way in which Jesus was to be the Messiah: rather than setting up an earthly, political kingdom, he would go to Jerusalem to die.

While Mark provides us with the basic sequence of the events of the ministry of Jesus, it is the sayings of Jesus found in Matthew which give us a clue to his inner motives. To be sure, these sayings are cluttered up with certain apocalyptic ideas, but Holtzmann quickly dismissed these by arguing that since they contradict each other they stem from the disciples, who shared these apocalyptic ideas with all Jews of that time (458). But when these sayings were culled out, the pure sayings of Jesus remained, and these showed Jesus' basic purpose and the motivation for his actions as recorded in Mark. From his baptism onwards, Jesus was conscious of a special mission from God, and no circumstance deterred him from this conviction.

The purpose of Jesus was not to establish an earthly kingdom (as Reimarus had asserted), for "to try to establish a theocracy within the Roman empire would have been the work of a fanatic" (482). Neither did Jesus expect to have a part in an apocalyptic intervention of God into the ordinary sequence of events. To be sure, the term "kingdom of God" had an apocalyptic meaning in the book of Daniel, but Jesus could not have used this term apocalyptically because he spoke of the kingdom of God as having already commenced with his ministry (458). He believed that the kingdom of God would come as the impact of his life and teachings fashioned a new humanity that loved God and lived righteously.

It was this purpose of Jesus which accounts for the course of his ministry. At the outset he was increasingly popular with the multitudes. However, they soon became disenchanted with him when they realized that he was not interested in delivering them from the tyranny of Rome. Furthermore, the ethical teachings of Jesus were so pure that they tended to hold people at bay. They likewise exposed the hypocrisy of the Pharisees so unmercifully that they soon realized that their influence would be destroyed if Jesus were not killed. Jesus decided to bring all this hatred to a climax by going to Jerusalem. He knew that he would die there, but he nevertheless decided to go because he felt that his willingness to die for righteousness would be the best way to impress his life and teachings upon men. "Jesus saw that, immediately resulting from his death, an event would take place, whose result for the disciples and the whole human race would be the beginning of the kingdom of God" (409). Jesus' prediction of his resurrection and second coming was simply a way of saying that his death would bring about a transformation of human society into the kingdom of God. Jesus' words at the Last Supper indicate his confidence that his shed blood "would bring a new mankind into union with God" (410).

Such a life provided a strong incentive for men to imitate it. So perfect was this example of Jesus that Holtzmann said, "No one will want to find another example like it in the history of the developing God-consciousness of man" (459). Since this supreme example was the Jesus of history, it was argued that Christianity was not just an idea but was dependent upon its historical founder.

But what of the supernatural element in the life of Jesus that caused Strauss to regard the Gospels as myths? To consider this supernatural element as a myth was impossible for Holtzmann, for he acknowledged forthrightly that the moral example of Jesus exists "only in the closest, most indissoluble connection with the accounts of the miracles" (510). Therefore he could not count these miracles as merely human ideas lacking an historical foundation without making the moral example of Jesus also just an idea. But neither could Holtzmann find an historical basis for these miracles by lighting upon some facet of the text that could be construed as providing a natural explanation for them, for Rationalism's attempt to do this had cast a shadow on the moral example of Jesus.

Holtzmann therefore attempted to assert the historicity of the miracles in a way that would, if anything, strengthen the picture of the moral example of Jesus. He regarded the Gospel of Mark as representing the miracles in a way that was generally superior to the other Gospels. Mark does not stress the agency of angels in performing miracles; rather, he represents the miracles as stemming from the "incomparably mighty self-understanding of Jesus and the peculiar energy of his inner being" (508). This was especially true in the case of the healing miracles, for when Jesus performed them Mark makes it particularly evident that there was an inner connection between moral and spiritual sickness (498). Jesus healed men because of the impact of his moral purity on them. His command for the sick to exercise faith meant that if one would be physically well, he must repent of spiritual sickness (510).

However, Holtzmann had greater difficulty in explaining how the nature miracles—the feeding of the five thousand, the stilling of the waves, and the walking on the water—were the result of Jesus' moral purity and zeal. He even admitted that such miracles could be "more easily explained as ingenious, sublime pictures of ideal truths" (499)—which was, of course, very close to Strauss' way of explaining the miracles. Nevertheless, they were not myths, because they had a basis in historical fact. To avoid the approach of the Rationalists, Holtzmann argued that it was impossible to discount the possibility that Jesus performed certain remarkable changes in nature, because modern knowledge had not yet advanced to the point where it could list all of the possible natural happenings.

Consequently, Holtzmann was confident that he had main-

tained an historically valid picture of the moral example of
Jesus by handling the supernatural in a way that either
strengthened this moral picture or, at least, did not detract
from it or its historicity. He confidently asserted that "the
Synoptic Gospels allow themselves to be regarded fully in
terms of scientific norm" (513). Then he chided the theologians who, by insisting on the supernatural, became involved
in such fruitless dogmas as the sinlessness and deity of Jesus,
when the purely scientific approach could reveal him as a
reality of eternal worth (513).

But Holtzmann himself was not purely scientific, for at one
point in his argument he made the fatal admission that one
must hold a dogmatic presupposition in order to agree to
his historical re-creation of Jesus. He declared that there
was something unique about Jesus. The inward power of
Jesus' Messianic consciousness was "something lying beyond
our experience," and "it implies a power for the understanding
of which our ordinary experience offers no key" (476). In
fact, Jesus was so unique that the historian could only agree
to the picture of Jesus presented by the Gospel of Mark
"through a way of understanding that is already controlled
and winged by a principle of religious faith" (500). Thus,
despite all the historically valid arguments for the priority of
Mark and Q, despite all the ways in which Holtzmann based
his picture of Jesus upon these two sources, despite his claim
that his investigation was "purely scientific," the resulting picture of Jesus could only be seen by those who already possessed a commensurate religious faith.

It is noteworthy that along with this stress on the uniqueness of Jesus, Holtzmann admitted that a more satisfactory
explanation for the nature miracles could be found if it were
possible to establish the resurrection of Jesus simply through
an unbiased historical investigation (500):

> Insofar . . . as our whole second group of miracles [the nature
> miracles] rests upon the presupposition of a superhuman energy
> by which Jesus was able to control external nature, it seems that
> the final climax of these miracles is to be found in the resur-

rection; and our whole investigation could be unified around the question as to what status an impartial, historical investigation of this preeminent possibility might have.

In other words, if the resurrection could be established, Holtzmann would not be embarrassed either by the nature miracles or by the uniqueness of the character of Jesus, which is so without parallel in human experience that one must have a religious faith in order to accept it. If the resurrection could be established by historical investigation, his methodological procedure would be historical from beginning to end and would not depend upon a religious presupposition. However, he had limited himself to the Synoptic Gospels in this early work of his, and he felt that the resurrection narratives in the Synoptics were too conflicting to be of use for historical investigation. I Corinthians 15:1-11, on the other hand, might be more promising for proving the resurrection (501). But Holtzmann did not try to follow out this possibility at that time.

> *Note.* Holtzmann did take all the New Testament data of the resurrection into account in later years when he taught New Testament theology at Strassburg from 1874 to 1904. The results of these labors are found in his book on New Testament theology.[3] But from this it is evident that he did not regard the resurrection as historically credible. Holtzmann reasoned that when Jesus had died, the disciples had no hope that he would rise again, because even though Jesus had predicted his death, it was inconceivable to them that the Messiah should die. So they anointed his body and placed a large stone over the tomb (I, 379f.). But Peter continued to have a desperate feeling of remorse over having denied Jesus, and the need to alleviate this led him to have a vision of Jesus as risen (I, 431). His experience prompted the other disciples to have similar hallucinations. In order to justify their belief as Jews that Jesus was the Messiah, the disciples then gleaned from the Old Testament verses which could show that the Messiah must first suffer and then be glorified. Armed with these, they were able to preach that Jesus was the Messiah (I, 341f.).

[3] H. Holtzmann, *Lehrbuch der Neutestamentlichen Theologie,* 2 vols.

Thus Holtzmann never came to believe that Jesus rose from the dead. Rather, to the end he continued to base Christianity upon the moral purpose of the historical Jesus, which was steadfast even unto death (I, 423).

II. *The Theology of Liberalism*

Alongside the numerous lives of Jesus which appeared from 1860 onwards, there arose a theology of Liberalism that spelled out the ideas that were implicit in these reconstructions of Jesus' life. The theology of Liberalism was set forth chiefly by Albrecht Ritschl and his followers.

A. *Albrecht Ritschl*

Albrecht Ritschl, professor of theology at Göttingen from 1864 until his death in 1889, set forth his system of thought chiefly in the third volume of his study of the doctrines of justification and reconciliation.[4] For Ritschl all theology centered in Jesus Christ and, like Holtzmann, he criticized Strauss for reducing Jesus to one among other great men. For Ritschl Jesus was absolute because he was convinced that he had the God-given vocation of founding the kingdom of God. Indeed, as a Jew of his time, Jesus spoke of this kingdom in apocalyptic terms, but the primary idea of this kingdom, Ritschl affirmed, was purely moral and ethical. In the life of Jesus "that universal human morality of which the kingdom of God shall be the perfect realisation preponderates" (469). It was by living so unswervingly for his vocation, despite his suffering, the calumnies of the Jews, and finally death itself, that Jesus "reconciled" men to God the Father. This steadfastness of purpose to do the will of God made it evident that a man need not be enslaved to nature and death, which are at enmity with God, but is, instead, able to live contrary to nature and do the will of God, and thus demonstrate a recon-

[4] A. Ritschl, *The Christian Doctrine of Justification and Reconciliation.*

ciliation with God. For Jesus death was an ascent to an eternal life with God, where one is set free from the burden of the transitory world (360), and so his obedience even to death shows that God loves men even though they die. Therefore they should remain steadfastly engaged in their God-given vocation, for in this way the kingdom of God will be realized on earth.

Indeed, all mankind should learn to imitate Jesus; nevertheless, Jesus will always remain unique because he was the one who founded the whole kingdom of God, whereas others have only particular vocations to carry out as it develops (450f.). Others may, to be sure, imitate Jesus quite fully, but unlike Jesus, who did it alone without following a model, they must always do it through an inspiration received from him (462). For Ritschl Jesus thus becomes so exclusively important for religious knowledge that such knowledge can only consist of what has become meaningful to Christians through the influence Christ has had over them, through the community which he founded. The Christian, therefore, should not raise the question of whether Christ was pre-existent (451), nor should he speculate as to whether Jesus actually had superhuman powers to control nature (456). Such ideas are theoretical, and the believer needs no knowledge of Christ beyond that which is valuable for him in terms of enabling him to persist in his vocation.

How then did Ritschl understand the way in which one gains knowledge of Christ? To this question he answered simply (2f.):

> Authentic and complete knowledge of Jesus' religious significance—His significance . . . depends on one's reckoning oneself part of the community which he founded. . . . We can discover the full compass of his historical actuality solely from the faith of the Christian community.

Thus, like Holtzmann, Ritschl made historical knowledge dependent upon a prior faith in Christ, and so, for both of these men, Lessing's ditch remained unbridged, for history could only speak when faith was present. However, the emphasis placed upon history by the two foremost successors of Ritschl, Adolf Harnack and Wilhelm Herrmann, may indicate that they were trying to overcome a weakness in his thinking. Harnack, of course, is known as one of the greatest church historians. But it was Hermann who, as a theologian and professor at Marburg, expended great efforts to make history more important for faith within the basic outlines of Ritschl's thought.

B. Wilhelm Herrmann

So strong was Herrmann's insistence on the importance of history for faith that he said that if Christianity could not base itself upon the historical Jesus, it was nothing more than a subjective mysticism. In one of his most important works,[5] Herrmann declared, "We Christians know only one fact in the whole world which can overcome every doubt of the reality of God, namely, the appearance of Jesus in history, the story which has been preserved in the New Testament" (59). This story produces such certainty because it tells of one who lived completely for the establishment of the kingdom of God, a society comprised of those who have unbounded confidence in God and boundless love toward their fellow men. Jesus not only taught the kingdom of God, he lived for it. His sinlessness and his complete identification with the ethical ideal of the kingdom shine through every page of the Gospels and most completely in the fact that Jesus lived for righteousness to the extent of being willing to die for it. By so identifying himself with God, Jesus became the representative of God, and as such he remains unique in history, for no other man has even come close to imitating him. We might be tempted to think, therefore, that since Jesus is so unique in his sinlessness, the God whom he represented could only condemn sinful men. But Jesus showed that this was not the case, because he ate with publicans and sinners and patiently bore with his disciples as they made their first faltering steps

[5] W. Herrmann, *The Communion of the Christian with God.*

toward living for the kingdom of God. Since Jesus persevered in this way even to death, he must have been completely assured of the absolute triumph of the kingdom of God over all sin, and since he was so completely identified with God in his life, we can be assured that the kingdom of God will indeed triumph in our lives and in the world. This was Herrmann's way of arguing that the historical Jesus makes one certain of God and of the ultimate triumph of righteousness.

This picture in the Gospels of the sinlessness of Jesus was, in Herrmann's thinking, so sure a foundation that it could not be disturbed by any conclusions to which historical criticism might come in its consideration of the Gospels. Even though some historian were to conclude that the Gospel narratives were a legend, this very legend, setting forth as it does the sinless person of Jesus, would make it possible for him to "have his eyes opened to see the consistent and clear portrait of a Personal Life that has no equal" (84). Thus there is the perfection of a human life in the Gospels even if their historical foundations were completely destroyed.

Neither would this picture of Jesus be disturbed if the miracles which accompany it were disproved. One might think that the resurrection of Jesus is essential for the certainty and comfort that life, rather than death and the decay of nature, was the ultimate end of things. But according to Herrmann, such comfort would have a frail foundation, for it would depend upon an historical record mediated through witnesses, which knowledge could never have more than an approximate certainty. Thus a faith based on the resurrection would always be in jeopardy. Furthermore, a faith depending upon an historically mediated knowledge is possible only to those who either are learned enough to be themselves historians or who blindly submit to the authority of the historian, whereas a true faith must be equally the possibility for all (76). According to Herrmann, this true faith becomes possible simply when one is confronted with the inner life of Jesus. "The traditional record of Jesus may appear doubtful, but the essential content of that record, namely, the inner life of Jesus, has the power to manifest itself to the conscience as an undeniable fact" (235f.).

Though this inner life is mediated by witnesses who lived at another time in history, yet it is accepted by men today as an "undeniable fact" because of the categorical imperative that exists in the heart of every man. However, before one will find in Jesus the certainty of God and of the triumph of righteousness, this moral consciousness must be awakened. "We do not grasp the fact that the Gospel records bring us, until the enrichment of our own inner life makes us aware that we have touched the Living One" (74). This enrichment comes by entering fully into our historical and social relations as human beings. We do not find that which answers fully to our innermost being in the world of nature surrounding us but rather in fellowship with other human beings. "If we simply endure our relationship to other men, instead of living it, then the personality within us, to which God desires to reveal himself, remains dormant, and we do not see the facts through which God alone can reveal himself to us" (65). "All specifically human life," declared Herrmann, "rests absolutely upon the assumption that men know they are unconditionally bound to obey the law of duty. Now we find that law in the God whose influence upon us is seen in no other experience so clearly as in the power the Person of Jesus has over us. . . ." (103). It is in this Gospel tradition that one comes to meet the "Personal Spirit" who constantly confronts us in our everyday life and the manifestations of whose work are "all around us" (83). It is this "Personal Spirit" who confirms the truth of the claim made by the Gospel tradition that Jesus is the Saviour of the world. We must first improve our relations to this "Personal Spirit," and then it will confirm to us the truth of the inner life of Jesus and the consequent certainty that God exists.

One cannot read Herrmann without admiring his efforts to show how the Jesus of history is essential for believing that there is a God who will cause righteousness to triumph. If

Herrmann teaches us nothing else, he should show us how important it is for faith to have a basis that is in history and outside of ourselves. But it is apparent that Herrmann was unsuccessful in grounding Christianity in history, for the history that he claimed as the basis for faith could not stand by itself as history but could only be confirmed by a faith awakened to the categorical imperative. This prior understanding of what constituted the categorical imperative determined what aspect of the Gospel records was confirmed as valid and valuable. Like Ritschl, he asserted that the only valid religious knowledge was what could be accepted as valuable. Religious knowledge was confirmed by a value judgment, rather than by the historical method. Herrmann declared that Lessing was right in saying that it was impossible "to attach religious conviction to a mere historical decision" (72).

But incontestable facts of history have a way of making themselves finally heard, even though the would-be hearers insist they could never be valuable. During the period of Liberalism's ascendancy, which was approximately 1860 through 1900, the historical method continued to be applied to the Gospel records, with the result that certain facts about the Jesus of history became unmistakably clear. These facts made it impossible for Liberalism, with its presuppositions, any longer to make a pretense of finding its basis in the Jesus of history.

III. The Clash with History

It was the historical investigations of Johannes Weiss and Wilhelm Wrede that made the Liberal interpretation of the life of Jesus impossible. Weiss showed that it was impossible to understand the kingdom of God primarily in ethical terms; Wrede showed that it was impossible to regard the Gospel of Mark as virtually free from the author's own theological bias unless one were willing to concede that Jesus was indeed supernatural.

A. *Johannes Weiss*

The son-in-law and former student of Albrecht Ritschl and a teaching fellow at Göttingen, Johannes Weiss published in 1892 a work on the kingdom of God motif in Jesus' preaching. In the preface of the second edition (1900)[6] he paid the following tribute to his old teacher: "In the school of Albrecht Ritschl I have become convinced of the peculiar significance of the theological concept of the kingdom of God which formed the organizing center of his theology." However, a comparison of the eschatological teachings of Jesus with the Jewish apocalypticism of that time had convinced Weiss that the Liberal interpretation of the kingdom of God was quite foreign to Jesus' usage of the term. Weiss did not feel that it was wrong for theologians to give new meanings to concepts found in the New Testament, but he did feel that the difference in meanings should always be made clear (7).

Ritschl had taught that for Jesus the kingdom of God had already begun to manifest itself in his ministry in so far as the disciples had come to live the ethical life, and that this kingdom, through powers already existent in the world, would result in the triumph of righteousness. But Weiss insisted that such a view came from imposing the presuppositions of Kant upon the New Testament (64). When, however, one allowed the teachings of Jesus to speak for themselves, it became clear that for Jesus the kingdom of God was impending but had not yet made its appearance. During his earthly ministry, Jesus did not conceive of himself as a Messiah who was establishing the kingdom of God, but rather as one who was preparing men for that supernatural intervention of God when his kingdom would be established. In the future, when he was glorified, Jesus would assume the role of the apocalyptic "Son of Man" described in Daniel and Enoch and be instrumental in actually establishing the kingdom (24). In the thinking of Jesus, the kingdom of God

[6] J. Weiss, *Die Predigt Jesu vom Reiche Gottes.*

was something completely supramundane, which stood in complete contradiction to this world. This means that one cannot speak of the kingdom of God in the thinking of Jesus as being a development of something that is already existent in this world. Therefore on the basis of these conclusions, the dogmatical, religious, and ethical application of the concept of the kingdom of God in recent theology, which has completely removed it from all eschatological and apocalyptic concepts, is unjustified (49f.).

However, there were times when Jesus did speak of the kingdom of God as a present reality (e.g., Matt. 12:28), but at such times he did not mean that men, on their part, were coming to realize the Lordship of God, but that the power of Satan, who is pre-eminently the cause of evil, was being broken "by the work of Jesus" (21). But such statements, rather than signifying the actual appearance of the kingdom, were in reality "moments of exalted prophetic inspiration, when he was overcome by the conviction of a [future] triumph" (21).

These teachings of Jesus regarding the kingdom of God were, according to Weiss, inseparably connected with a peculiar consciousness that Jesus had of his own mission, which was completely foreign to the popular reconstruction advanced by Liberalism. "The Messianic consciousness of Jesus, as it is expressed in the name 'Son of Man,' partakes fully of the transcendental, apocalyptic character of Jesus' concept of the kingdom of God and cannot be separated from it" (61). From his baptism onwards, Jesus had the conviction that he had been selected to be the judge and ruler of the future kingdom of God, and for him this conviction was natural, for he felt himself to be the Son of God and living in God in a way that is beyond anything comparable in human experience (60). Such a person would escape being a fanatic only if he actually enjoyed such a relationship to God that it would be natural for him to speak of God as entrusting everything to him so that after his death he would come again in the clouds of glory to establish the kingdom of God (62).

So contrary was Jesus to anything in ordinary human experience that Weiss concluded that the only idea in the teaching of Jesus which could have any worth for modern man was his emphasis on the fatherhood of God (66f.). The rest of what he taught had become extraneous because men were now accustomed to think of a humanity of God developing from this present world, rather than from the entirely new one which Jesus proclaimed.

The bases for Weiss' conclusions were the result of sound historical investigation. Faced with such conclusions and remaining true to its premises, Liberalism could no longer find a basis for itself in the Jesus of history.

B. *Wilhelm Wrede*

The second decisive attack against the Liberal re-creation of Jesus came from Wilhelm Wrede, a professor of New Testament in Breslau, in his treatment of the Messianic secret first published in 1901.[7] Whereas Weiss had focused attention primarily upon the apocalyptic framework of the teachings of Jesus, Wrede was concerned mainly with the question of Jesus' Messianic consciousness, and in particular with the question of why, in the Gospel of Mark, there is the emphasis that Jesus should keep his Messiahship a secret until after his resurrection, as in Mark 9:9: "And as they were coming down the mountain, he charged them to tell no one what they had seen, until the Son of man should have risen from the dead." Why did he forbid the demons to announce that he was the Son of God? Why should he keep the miracles he had performed a secret? Why should he have spoken in parables to the multitudes and have given their meaning only to his disciples?

Wrede emphasized that, according to Mark, the answer was that Jesus was the Son of God and the Christ, who could not be publicly manifested as such until his resurrection, the event which would justify applying these titles to him. Because Mark regarded Jesus as supernatural, he also depicted him as knowing that he would die and rise again. Mark understood God to be at work in all that Jesus said and did, and

---

[7] W. Wrede, *Das Messiasgeheimnis in den Evangelien.*

therefore he pictured Jesus as being motivated in a way that finds no analogy in human experience. "The motive for the behaviour of Jesus does not result from what is peculiarly human, or what stems from human goals or drives. Rather [in the understanding of Mark] it is a divine purpose, which lies beyond human understanding, which forms the single, comprehensive motivation for explaining Jesus" (131). Thus Wrede argued that the Marcan representation of Jesus, rather than presenting "the human Jesus" (to use the words of Holtzmann), depicts a figure that is so completely divine that "this Gospel sets forth no historical view of the real life of Jesus" (131). The Gospel of Mark, except for a few incidental details, is not history but theology.

Wrede came to the conclusion that Mark's picture was unhistorical by making a choice between three alternatives. If Jesus really was as Mark set him forth, then he was either supernatural or demented. An ordinary person conceiving of himself as Jesus did and behaving accordingly would be considered insane. But since Wrede did not want to regard Jesus as insane, and could not regard him as supernatural, he took the third alternative that the Marcan picture of Jesus was not a representation of Jesus as he really was, but was, instead, a picture of Jesus composed from the theological presuppositions of the early church.

How, then, did the church come to write the Gospel of Mark? Wrede answered that Jesus, during his lifetime, never claimed to be the Messiah. But when he died the memory of him continued to make such an impression on the disciples that they began to think of him as one who had to suffer and die in order to redeem. If he is the redeemer, then he surely must reappear. This meant that he was alive and therefore risen from the dead. Regarding him as having risen, they came to think of him as the Messiah. Thus Wrede declared that "to date the Messiahship of Jesus from the resurrection was not a thought of Jesus himself, but rather of the early church" (218). This newly conceived faith of the early church then found it only natural to go back into the life of

Jesus and explain it all from the vantage point of the resurrection. "The previous life of Jesus took on the hue of the day of Easter, from the moment that the brilliance of this day shone back on that life" (228). In representing Jesus, therefore, this Gospel recalls how he had indeed never made any public claim to be the Messiah because the Messiahship was to become known only at the resurrection. It was because of the conviction of the resurrection, therefore, that Mark set Jesus forth in such purely supernatural, theological terms.

Hence Wrede, like Weiss, had shown that it was impossible for Liberalism, with its presuppositions, to find a support for its theology in the Gospel of Mark. The chief way that it had been able to escape the mythicism of Strauss had been through the supposition that, since Mark was the earliest Gospel, it was therefore least historically suspect and presented Jesus in a way that did not set him off too far from humanity. But Wrede dashed this possibility to the ground, for he showed that the Gospel of Mark is completely permeated with a theological understanding in which Jesus is set forth as supernatural and unique. Wrede's solution was that this was the creation of the early church. But to say this was to return to the position of Strauss, from whose clutches Liberalism had tried so hard to free itself. His position had been reasserted because Liberalism had failed in its attempt to find any one part of the Gospels that was not tainted by the supernatural and would thus set forth a "human Jesus" who would serve as its support. The idea of the supernatural permeated every Gospel so thoroughly that no human Jesus could be found there.

The three alternatives which Wrede faced can actually be reduced to two: either Jesus was indeed supernatural, or the idea of this supernaturalness was the product of human thought in which either Jesus thought he was the apocalyptic Son of God or the early Christians thought him to be such. Corresponding to these two alternatives there emerged two great names in the history of New Testament thought, Martin Kähler, the professor of New Testament and systematic theology at Halle, and Albert Schweitzer, who was then a young assistant minister in Strassburg. Schweitzer forthrightly asserted that the Gospels were the product of human thought: they reflected Jesus' mistaken conviction that he was to play a role in the apocalyptic coming of the kingdom of God. Martin Kähler, however, insisted that Jesus actually was what the Gospels represented him to be, the one who was declared to be the Son of God by his resurrection from the dead.

IV. The Two Alternatives

A. Martin Kähler

It was not Weiss and Wrede who led Kähler to take the supernatural alternative. Weiss' book had scarcely appeared in 1892 when Kähler delivered before a pastors' conference a lecture in which the very alternatives that arose from the work of Weiss and Wrede appear in the title of the published work: *Der sogenannte historische Jesus und der geschichtliche, biblische Christus* (*The So-called Historical Jesus and the Really Historical, Biblical Christ*).[8] The two German words for the adjective "historical" in this title are taken from the two German words for "history," *Historie* and *Geschichte*. Kähler employed these words in order to distinguish between two ways of knowing history: *Historie* is known through an application of the historical method, with its underlying presupposition that nothing can be known in history except what is capable of bearing an analogy to ordinary human experience, while *Geschichte* is history known in some other way, depending on the particular theologian in question. In his lecture Kähler asserted that the Liberal "lives of Jesus" were largely fiction because they had sought after the Jesus of the Gospels by means of *Historie*. Jesus should instead be known by *Geschichte*, for *Historie* reduced Jesus to human analogy, whereas *Geschichte* would allow one to know Jesus as the Biblical

[8] The page references in the text are those of the second edition (1896) edited by E. Wolf, 1956.

writers understood him, that is, as the supernatural Son of God who rose from the dead and ascended into heaven. Thus, by the use of these two words for history, Kähler set forth the alternatives that the historical considerations of Weiss and Wrede were soon to force upon Christian thought.

Like these men, Kähler posed the problem of the Messianic consciousness of Jesus, for he said that one must either "deny the mental health of Jesus, or accept him in the way the New Testament sets him forth, namely, as the unique Son of God" (61). Kähler rejected the Liberal re-creations of Jesus because of the contradiction that was implied when Liberalism stressed Jesus as the unique revelation of God and yet explained him in terms which excluded the supernatural. How, he inquired, could Jesus give us a revelation from God if he is to be understood on the basis of analogies drawn from ordinary human experience? "We must either dispense with a revelation from God [which Liberalism really does], or there must be another Christ set forth than that of . . . the approach of historical theology, which depends on testing sources and controlling everything by analogies" (37). Therefore, these Liberal "lives of Jesus" were on a *"Holzweg"* (a road ending nowhere) (18).

To find the real Jesus, the New Testament must be approached from the starting point of its writers, namely, that Jesus had actually risen and ascended to heaven. Whereas in Liberalism the question of the resurrection of Jesus was either ignored, depreciated, or considered merely the disciples' attempt to do justice to Jesus' moral perfection, with Kähler the resurrection became the very place where one must begin in order to know Jesus. The disciples were convinced that Jesus was the glorified Lord, "not because his earthly life had made such an impression upon their soul, but because the resurrection first placed this earthly life in its proper perspective and gave it its implicit and appropriate content."[9] Thus, while in Liberalism the historical Jesus was always sought behind the Gospels as something to be found when the veil

---

[9] M. Kähler, *Der sogenannte historische Jesus und der geschichtliche, biblische Christus* (2nd ed., 1896), p. 106.

of their dogmatic coloring was drawn aside, Kähler asserted, "The resurrected Lord is not the historical (*historisch-*) Jesus behind the Gospels, but the Christ of apostolic preaching, which is the content of the whole New Testament."[10] Just as it was the risen Jesus who, though the Holy Spirit, enabled the evangelists to preach him as risen in their presentation of him in the Gospels, so it was also the risen Jesus whom the apostles preached in their epistles. Both the Gospels and the epistles are equally the setting forth of the risen Jesus (63f.), although the Gospels have the unique function of showing that the risen Jesus was the Word who had become flesh (34f.). Thus the truly historical (*geschichtlich*) Jesus is the resurrected Lord, and consequently the Gospels do not give us a distorted picture of him as he was during his earthly ministry when they set forth his miracles, his apocalypticism, and his Messianic consciousness, for during that ministry he was the Word made flesh who would rise from the dead and ascend into heaven.

Another reason why Kähler was opposed to the view of Jesus gained by *Historie* was that to know such a Jesus one must either be an historian himself or be dependent upon someone who was. True to the Pietistic tradition, Kähler asserted that each individual must be equally capable of gaining knowledge of Jesus from the Gospels himself. "Dogmatics is a matter of judgment concerning matters which are accessible to every Christian" (37).

But while faith was not determined by the judgments of the learned historian, it was anything but a subjective conviction for Kähler. The sinlessness of Jesus presented in the New Testament was in such sharp contrast to the sinfulness of mankind that one should be persuaded not only that Jesus was more than a mere man, but that even the New Testament picture of him could not be the product of human imagination.

We know the picture of Jesus from our childhood, and we live in a civilization whose best aspects stem from the picture

[10] Wolf (ed.), p. 41.

of Jesus, and which are a reflection of his incomparable glory. But still, as we compare ourselves with Jesus, he is foreign to us. And yet he is so lifelike [in this picture], so real, that it is as though we had seen him before us. This picture is not the idealizing poetry of the human spirit; in this picture the very being of Jesus himself has left its imperishable stamp upon us (58).

Herrmann, it will be remembered, also argued for the truth of Jesus from the impression made by his sinlessness. But when Kähler used this argument, he meant something quite different. For Herrmann, this sinlessness was something which was known from the Gospel accounts divorced from the idea of the miraculous and the resurrection. Kähler, however, in the ensuing debate which he had with Herrmann, insisted that the New Testament emphasis on the sinlessness of Jesus is based on the fact that Jesus is the supernatural, risen Lord (40f., note a). To see this sinlessness one must, according to Kähler, see the Jesus of the epistles as well as the Gospels, and not just from the Gospels as Herrmann would have it (67f., note b). Kähler asserted that the ultimate reason for faith in Jesus is Jesus himself, as he confronts us in his revelation in history. Herrmann, on the contrary, said that while faith was strengthened by the Jesus of history, Jesus could not be the final ground for faith, for faith is dependent ultimately on nothing but faith itself (64f., note a). Thus for Kähler it is Jesus himself who authenticates himself as one is confronted by the New Testament, and, accordingly, faith avoids the option of either being based upon the authority of a learned historian or being a subjective leap.

Kähler did not, however, regard historical arguments as altogether vain. They were useful in gaining understanding of the cultural and historical background of the Gospels (26f.). Furthermore, for Kähler historical argumentation demonstrated that the faith of the early Christians was centered in Jesus as risen rather than in a person conforming to human analogy.

When we ask at what point in their discussions the historians deal with the certainty [of the early church that Jesus is the risen Lord], we find that they begin . . . with the experience of Paul. They ascertain the unwavering faith of the early church as far as they can determine the testimonies and traces left by those early witnesses (40f.).

One wonders whether, for Kähler, the resurrection was the only possible explanation for this faith. But since such a line of reasoning would make faith dependent upon the ability of the learned historian, Kähler was content to say that faith finds a sufficient basis in the sinlessness of Jesus set forth in the New Testament.

B. *Albert Schweitzer*

The very same day that Wrede's book was published there appeared a book by Albert Schweitzer with a very similar title: *Das Messianitäts- und Leidensgeheimnis. Eine Skizze des Lebens Jesu* (The Secret of the Messiahship and the Passion. A Sketch of the Life of Jesus).[11] This book sought to solve the same problem as Wrede's, for Schweitzer queried, "Why was the Messiahship a secret to Jesus? To explain this means to understand his life" (6). But Schweitzer attempted to answer this question, not by understanding the theme of the Messianic secret as a creation of the early church, but as an actual conviction which led Jesus to act as he did. From the moment of his baptism onwards, Jesus was conscious of enjoying a complete solidarity with God. He was convinced that he was the one who was to be God's agent for preparing men for the kingdom of God, and that when it was established by a cataclysmic, supernatural work of God, he would rule as God's representative. Wrede had declared that it was impossible to explain why Jesus, if he were conscious of being the Messiah, should want to keep it a secret. But Schweitzer produced an explanation.

Jesus sought to ready men for the kingdom of God, which he was convinced would appear very soon. But the kingdom of God and of the Messiah were inseparable. When the king-

[11] The English translation appeared in 1914 under the title *The Mystery of the Kingdom of God.*

dom of God was established, the Messiah must appear and vice versa. Jesus was convinced that he was the Messiah who would be manifest at the establishment of the kingdom of God. But since the kingdom had not yet appeared, he therefore did not act or teach publicly as one who was the Messiah.

> Jesus' Messiahship . . . was a secret, inasmuch as it could be realised only at a definite time in the future. It was a conception which could be formulated fully only in his own consciousness. Wherefore the people could not understand it—and need not know anything about it. It was enough if by his word and his signs he might convert them to faith in the nearness of the kingdom, for with the coming of the kingdom, his Messiahship would be manifest (186).

It was only to the disciples that he revealed his secret, when toward the end of his ministry he was convinced that the kingdom of God would be established when he died. He also confessed his Deity and Messiahship to the high priest, and for this confession he was condemned to death.

Five years later Schweitzer published his monumental work *Von Reimarus zu Wrede.*[12] His interpretation of the life of Jesus was valid, argued Schweitzer, because it avoided the inconsistencies and difficulties of both Weiss and Wrede. Weiss was correct in seeing the preaching of the impending apocalyptic kingdom of God as the key for understanding Jesus' teaching and his Messianic consciousness. But Weiss had erred in not providing any explanation for the policy of secrecy. Wrede, on the other hand, had made the theme of secrecy the key to the Gospel history. But in supposing that the theme of secrecy arose from the fact that Jesus was thought of as the Messiah only from the resurrection onwards, Wrede was faced with a great difficulty in explaining Jesus' confession of his Messiahship to the disciples at Caesarea Philippi and to the high priest. Why did Mark even mention these if his purpose was to show that Jesus wished his Messiahship to be kept a secret until the resurrection?

[12] The English translation appeared in 1910 under the title *The Quest of the Historical Jesus.*

74

However, everything falls into place when one understands that the theological idea that controls the thinking of the author of Mark was actually the thought that controlled Jesus himself. "After all, why should not Jesus think in terms of doctrine and make history action, just as well as a poor Evangelist Mark can do it on paper under the pressures of the theological interests of the community?" (348) If Mark, as Wrede would have it, was really convinced that Jesus believed himself to be the Messiah and yet wanted it kept a secret until it would be meaningful in terms of the resurrection, why could not Jesus have had the very same conviction and consequent mode of behavior? Truly believing that he was the Messiah who would be made manifest at the coming of the kingdom, he would tell this to his close disciples, and being convinced that he must die in order to bring in the kingdom, he would also confess this to the high priest.

Schweitzer's approach had the greater advantage because it asked nothing more difficult to conceive of than Wrede asked, while at the same time it avoided Wrede's difficulties. But Schweitzer's approach raised the question of whether, in having this conviction regarding himself, Jesus was justified or deluded. To say that he was justified would involve accepting supernaturalism. To say that he was deluded would reject supernaturalism but it would involve something else: a rejection of any worth that Jesus might have for the human race, for of what value are the thoughts of a deluded, apocalyptical fanatic? Schweitzer chose the alternative of saying, in as nice a way as possible, that Jesus was deluded (368f.):

> Jesus, in the knowledge that he is the coming Son of Man, lays hold of the wheel of the world to set it moving on that last revolution which is to bring all ordinary history to a close. It refuses to turn, and he throws himself upon it. Then it does turn; and crushes him. Instead of bringing in the eschatological conditions, he has destroyed them. The wheel rolls onward, and the mangled body of one immeasurably great man, who was strong enough to think of himself as the spiritual ruler of mankind as to bend history to his purpose, is hanging upon it still. That is his victory and his reign.

The best thing which Schweitzer could say about Jesus was that he was "heroic." But Schweitzer had to confess that the way in which the historical Jesus expressed his heroism was not "a help but perhaps an offense to religion" (399). In fact, "the spiritual life of our own time seems like to perish at his hands, for he leads to battle against our thoughts a host of dead ideas . . . and himself destroys again the truth and goodness which his Spirit has created in us, so that it cannot rule the world" (2). Consequently, it is this historical Jesus who must be set aside. "It is not Jesus as historically known, but Jesus as arisen within men, who is significant for our time and can help it. . . . The abiding and eternal in Jesus is absolutely independent of historical knowledge and can only be understood by contact with his Spirit which is still at work in the world" (399).

With such statements it becomes clear that Schweitzer had not only returned to but had gone beyond the position of Strauss. Strauss had found ultimate truth, not in the individual Jesus of history, but in "the idea of Christ existent in humanity." Schweitzer had found it in "the spirit of Jesus," to which, apparently, every man had access. But whereas Strauss had found nothing offensive in Jesus himself (for Strauss he epitomized the oneness of God with man), Schweitzer regarded the historical Jesus as destructive of truth and goodness. Hence as Schweitzer took his place on the faith side of Lessing's ditch by declaring the Jesus of history to be an offense to religion, he went beyond any of his predecessors by removing his religious convictions as far as possible from the history side of that ditch.

Thus in Schweitzer the conflict between the Enlightenment and the New Testament became unmistakably clear. The Enlightenment had declared that all men were essentially in harmony with God and could achieve fulfillment by availing themselves of the powers they already possessed. The New Testament, whose apocalypticism and supernaturalism had become crystal clear through the historical method, said that man was at odds with God and that something must be done in order to remedy the situation. This remedy had been accomplished in history in the person of Jesus Christ and in his resurrection, for in Jesus Christ God had worked to accomplish man's redemption. The mood of the Enlightenment was the conviction that no man needed to go beyond himself to find fulfillment. The New Testament set forth a religion in which God had accomplished man's redemption at a particular place and time in history, so that man, in order to be redeemed, had to look beyond himself to what God had done at this place in history. It was no wonder, then, that Schweitzer, remaining true to the Enlightenment, had declared that the historical Jesus was an offense to religion and that redemption was to be found in a universally working spirit. Thus, Lessing's ditch remained unbridged in Schweitzer because his faith was in no wise compatible with the historical religion of the New Testament.

If men could have gone on being content with themselves, no doubt the thinking of Schweitzer and the ideals of the Enlightenment would have continued to be predominant. But the twentieth century, which had just dawned, was about to witness a catastrophe which caused many to have serious doubts that man had any right to feel confident that he was in harmony with God.

CHAPTER FOUR

Dialectical Theology

THE IMPLICATIONS OF THE ALTERNATIVE WHICH SCHWEITZER had chosen became even clearer in the person of Ernst Troeltsch, professor of theology at Heidelberg from 1894 to 1914. Troeltsch declared that since the historical method had shown that the religion of the New Testament was based essentially on the idea of a supernatural, apocalyptic intervention of God in history in the person of Jesus Christ, it was no longer acceptable to men who were confident that all was basically well with man and the world. Modern man could not accept a particular religion, a religion which looked to one person in history as the source of salvation for the rest. Rather, man was to conceive of himself as being saved by a process which was occurring throughout mankind as a whole.[1] Troeltsch was convinced that this process would inevitably continue: "Whatever is life and truth at present will be maintained or will return and will not come to be regarded as untruth by anything that will come" (49).

Troeltsch was not simply expressing his own private convictions when he claimed that the best of his contemporary culture would never pass away. Rather, such confidence was the mood of his time and of his nation. Germany felt she must win the war that broke out in August, 1914, in order to maintain the *Kultur* that she had developed since the eighteenth-cen-

---

[1] E. Troeltsch, *Die Bedeutung der Geschichtlichkeit Jesu für den Glauben*, p. 6.

tury Enlightenment. Thus when Adolf Harnack, one of Germany's leading theologians, spoke to an assemblage of American citizens in Berlin on August 11, 1914, a week after Belgium had been invaded, he said: "Our *Kultur* is the most precious possession of humanity . . . and we will pledge our wealth and our blood to the last drop for this *Kultur*."[2] Harnack declared that this *Kultur* was threatened by the Russian hordes, whose way of life was entirely different because they "could not tolerate the light of the eighteenth century" (228).

It was this same confidence in German *Kultur* that led ninety-three German intellectuals to sign a petition on October 3, 1914, entitled "An die Kulturwelt," which endorsed the war policies of Kaiser Wilhelm II and even those which included the killing of Belgian civilians and the destruction of the library at Louvain, with its priceless treasures. This petition concluded by saying: "We will fight this war to the end as a people of *Kultur*, to whom the legacy of a Goethe, a Beethoven, and a Kant is just as holy as its hearth and soil." Among the signatures that were affixed were those of Wilhelm Herrmann and Adolf Harnack,[3] who had talked so much about imitating Jesus' love and willingness to die for the establishment of the kingdom of God. Possibly these signatures were motivated by the conviction that the level of civilization the German nation had achieved was to be equated with the advance of the kingdom of God and hence should be maintained at any cost, even the committing of such unspeakable atrocities in Belgium. At least this was the way Karl Barth, then a young pastor in Switzerland, interpreted these signatures. For him the day when this document was published was a "black day." "Among the signatures," he recalled in later years, "I found to my horror the names of nearly all my theological teachers whom up to then I had religiously honored. Disillusioned by their conduct, I perceived that I should not be able any longer to accept their ethics and dogmatics, their

---

[2] A. Harnack, "Rede zur deutsch-amerikanischen Sympathiekundgebung," *Aus der Friedens- und Kriegsarbeit*, p. 288.

[3] *Frankfurter Zeitung*, October 4, 1914, p. 2.

biblical exegesis, their interpretation of history, that at least for me the theology of the 19th century had no future."[4]

I. Karl Barth's New Theological Direction

Disillusioned with Liberalism, Barth thereupon set about writing a commentary on Romans, whose first edition appeared a few months before the close of World War I. In this commentary Barth pursued a course of theological thought which was diametrically opposed to the confidence of the Enlightenment and Liberalism that man was essentially in harmony with God. Barth had found inspiration in the thinking of the Danish philosopher Søren Kierkegaard, who at about the middle of the preceding century had taken sharp issue with the philosophy of Hegel and its assertion of a continuity between God and man. In the foreword to the second edition Barth said,

> If I have a system, it is limited to a recognition of what Kierkegaard called the "infinite qualitative distinction" between time and eternity, and to my regarding this as possessing negative as well as positive significance: "God is in heaven, and thou on earth."[5]

To understand Barth's new theological direction it is necessary to recall something of the main outlines of Kierkegaard's thought. He opposed Hegel's assumption that man and the world were in such harmony that the antithesis between them could be brought together in a synthesis of "both-and." Hegel claimed that he had overcome the contradiction between the God who "is" and history which is "becoming," but Kierkegaard insisted that "being" and "becoming" were such mutually exclusive terms that a rational synthesis was not possible and that man was therefore left with an "either-or" decision. To say that God, in Christ, had become man was a complete

---

[4] K. Barth, "Evangelical Theology in the 19th Century," *Scottish Journal of Theology Occasional Papers*, No. 8 (1959), 58.
[5] K. Barth, *The Epistle to the Romans*, p. 10.

paradox, which man could not grasp by reasoning or by any invention of his imagination, for such an idea is "a folly to the understanding and an offense to the human heart."[6]

How then, according to Kierkegaard, had men ever come to know Christ as God? The disciples who had walked with Jesus had come to know the God-man, though their nearness to Christ was not the reason but only the occasion for this knowledge. The reason for their knowledge was that God enabled them to believe and know what was otherwise absurd. Likewise today people come to this knowledge through a divine miracle performed on the occasion of hearing the testimony that stems from the original disciples. However, since this testimony is only the occasion for knowledge and not its cause, it need be no more detailed than the simple statement that "we have believed in such and such a year that God appeared among us in the humble figure of a servant, that he lived and taught in our community, and finally died" (87). But the ability to accept this report is not something man possesses; it is a gift of God. "Faith is itself a miracle, and all that holds true of the Paradox [of the Incarnation] holds true of faith," for "how else could faith have the Paradox for its object, and be happy in its relation to the Paradox?" (53)

Thus whereas Hegel, in continuing the confident spirit of the Enlightenment, had taught that man was an expression of the spirit of God so that he could comprehend God with his own spirit, Kierkegaard asserted that there was a disjuncture between God and man that could only be bridged by a work of God. For the remainder of the nineteenth century, while the confident spirit of the Enlightenment continued to hold sway, Kierkegaard's philosophy enjoyed very little popularity. But World War I showed Barth the inhumanity that man, sometimes under the pretense of serving God, was capable of showing to his fellow man, and thus he saw in the philosophy of Kierkegaard an understanding of man that seemed more realistic than Hegel's. Drawing upon Kierkegaard's philosophy,

[6] S. Kierkegaard, *Philosophical Fragments,* ed. by D. Swenson, p. 86. The next two page references in the text are to this work.

Barth set forth a system of theological thought that was in direct contradiction to Liberalism.

In *The Epistle to the Romans* Barth asserted that God and the world were incapable of being in a harmony that the powers of human reason could grasp. The kingdom of God, instead of being an ethical society embodying man's deepest moral insights, was something "on the other side of morals" and "beyond all human possibilities, whatsoever they may be."[7] The life of Jesus was not an exemplification of any human possibility except that of death, and in dying Jesus made it clear that God had said "No!" to all the possibilities in this world.

But this "No!" of God that is heard in the death of Christ is accompanied by the "Yes!" which is heard in his resurrection. However, this "Yes!" that opens up the knowledge of the kingdom of God, of Jesus as the Christ, and of God as revealed in Jesus, does not enter into this world so as to become a part of it in any way, for everything in the world stands opposed to God. Thus Barth declared that the fact of the resurrection of Jesus did not depend upon whether the tomb was open or closed.[8] Likewise, there was no connection between such facets of the resurrection as the appearances listed in I Corinthians 15 and the resurrection itself, for "if the resurrection be brought within the context of history, it must share in its obscurity and error and essential questionableness."[9] Instead, in the resurrection the new world of the kingdom of God had gone no further than simply touching the old world of man "as a tangent touches a circle, that is, without touching it" (30). Thus by use of the figures of the tangent and the circle, Barth was able to say that the resurrection was "the non-historical event *par excellence*" (204), and yet declare that it took place outside the gates of Jerusalem in the year A.D. 30 (30).

How then does one gain knowledge of the resurrection, which is so distinct from all other historical events that it

[7] Barth, *The Epistle to the Romans*, p. 159.
[8] K. Barth, *The Resurrection of the Dead*, p. 135.
[9] Barth, *The Epistle to the Romans*, p. 204.

cannot even be inferred from the resurrection appearances? Barth answered that we must become "new men" and that we have an indication of what this means only when we come to the end of ourselves. Actually, "we can only believe in what is new, and moreover, our capacity reaches no further than to believing that we believe" (150). Just as the resurrection of Christ could not become in any wise a part of this present world, so faith in the resurrection could not be predicated of man as he is. Thus the harmony between God and man which had so characterized the theological thought of the preceding century-and-a-half was now discarded, and in its place Barth put the idea of such a discontinuity between the two that man could not know God except by dying to himself and to every involvement in this world.

Under such a system it is obvious that history known by the historical method could have no function in the establishment of faith, for such knowledge is a part of the world. Historical investigation is only "preliminary" (7) to the basic task of getting to the heart of things. In carrying out this basic task in the study of Romans, one should not rely upon history but upon a "creative energy" which enabled one "with intuitive certainty" (7) to break down the walls which separate the first from the twentieth century, so that both the writer and reader are confronted with the heart (*die Sache*) of Romans. For Barth this *Sache* was the wholly other God, who confronts man in Jesus Christ (10). Paul was confronted with Christ as he wrote Romans, and the reader must place himself in the same position if he is to understand it. The words of Romans are simply Paul's attempt to express this existential confrontation, whereas Jesus Christ himself lies beyond these words. Thus while the historical method threw light on the meaning of the words which Paul used, it did not lead to the knowledge of Christ. Barth therefore released himself from subservience to the historical method by declaring that Romans was not to be understood from its historical context but from the vantage point of Jesus Christ. In this way Barth felt free to preach the Word of God. He reminisced (9):

I myself know what it means year in and year out to mount the steps of the pulpit, conscious of the responsibility to understand and interpret, and longing to fulfil it; and yet, utterly incapable, because at the University I had never been brought beyond that "awe in the presence of history" which means in the end no more than that all hope of engaging in the dignity of understanding and interpretation has been surrendered.

This minimizing of the historical method naturally aroused great protests. Adolf Jülicher, in a review, maintained that Barth was guilty of "violating holy documents . . . out of pride in his own spirituality." Adolf Schlatter declared that through Barth's treatment of Romans, "it had ceased to be an epistle to the Romans."[10]

In 1923 Adolf Harnack directed to Barth a letter of fifteen questions entitled, "To the Despiser of Scientific Theology amongst the Theologians."[11] In the fourteenth question Harnack asked how it was possible to arrive at anything but a dreamed-up Christ if one refused to study the Gospels by means of the historical method. To this Barth replied that one came to certainty regarding Christ only through "a faith which God had aroused" (13). Harnack then asked whether this knowledge of Christ, which came solely from God, found any support at all in Jesus, the historical person (17). Barth answered that the historical reality of Christ is not the "historical" (*historisch*) Jesus but rather the Christ whom the New Testament witnesses as risen. "This is the evangelical, historical (*geschichtlich*) Jesus Christ, and any other apart from this witness and apart from this revelation is no longer known" (23f.).

Such a statement makes it obvious that Barth found the terminology of Kähler (*historisch* and *geschichtlich*) helpful in applying the philosophy of Kierkegaard to theology. Barth could find much in Kähler that would accord with his new theological course. In fact, in terms of the two alternatives that remained at the close of the nineteenth century, Barth

[10] Quoted by W. Kümmel, *Das Neue Testament,* pp. 473, 554.

[11] K. Barth, *Theologische Fragen und Antworten,* pp. 7-9. Continuation of this dialogue is found on pp. 9-32.

had taken that of Kähler rather than the one chosen by Schweitzer. But there is a difference between Barth and Kähler that should be noted. For Kähler, the reason for believing the resurrection was the matchlessness of Jesus that shines through the entire New Testament witness.[12] Human reason was capable of acknowledging that the life of the Jesus presented in this witness contrasts sharply with man as he is, and yet expresses the idea of what man ought to be. Thus man could come to know the truth of Christ by reason. But Barth declared that faith was completely the work of God and did not depend on any arguments acceptable to human reason. Like Kähler, Barth wanted to stress the supernaturalness of Jesus, but he did not want to see it as being continuous with anything that pertains to man and this world.

This difference between Kähler and Barth helps to clarify what is meant by the term "Dialectical Theology," which is so often used for the theology which arose under Barth. Hegel had a dialectic of a thesis and an antithesis which were brought together in a higher synthesis, but in the Dialectical Theology of Barth God and the world were an antithesis which could not be synthesized because God could come no closer to touching the world than a tangent can to touching a circle. Barth's theology was "dialectical" in the sense that it dealt with opposites of a "yes" and "no" variety.

Dialectical Theology gained many adherents in the years following World War I. The theologian Alan Richardson of England has termed Barth a "prophet who (in his own metaphor) 'rang the bell' in his *Römerbrief* in 1919 and caught the attention of a disillusioned generation, which no longer looked upon the world through the rose-tinted spectacles of Romantic Liberalism."[13] Despite the critics, there were several from the younger generation of theologians, such as Friedrich Gogarten, Emil Brunner, and Rudolf Bultmann, who joined with Barth to give impetus to this new movement. Through their combined efforts a periodical called *Zwischen den Zeiten* ap-

[12] See Chapter 3, pp. 71f.
[13] A. Richardson, *The Bible in the Age of Science*, p. 89.

peared in 1922 and for eleven years was the chief organ for the new Dialectical Theology.

During the early 20s Dialectical Theology also received considerable help from a new approach in interpreting the Biblical text which was called *Formgeschichte* (Form Criticism). First applied to the study of the Old Testament by Hermann Gunkel and then to the New Testament by K. L. Schmidt in *Die Rahmen der Geschichte Jesu* (1919), Form Criticism viewed the writings of the Bible as products of the religious life of the group in which they originated. Thus the individual parts of the Synoptic Gospels achieved their present form through the usage to which they were put in the early church. The Gospel narratives are not reports rendered by neutral observers of how Jesus spoke and acted before his death and resurrection, but rather are so much a part of the Easter faith of the early church that they were used in its preaching, worship, and catechetical instruction. Therefore one is not interpreting the Gospels according to the intention of those responsible for their present form if one seeks within them a kernel of purely "historical truth" about Jesus that is not tainted by dogmatic notions. One must view them from the vantage point of their intention to witness to the resurrected Christ. This new direction for interpreting the Gospels fit in perfectly with Dialectical Theology and its emphasis upon understanding the New Testament from the vantage point of Jesus as risen. Thus Form Criticism was of no little service in helping the new theology to gain ascendancy.

But despite the advantages in its favor, Dialectical Theology soon encountered difficulty from disagreement within its own ranks. Just as in Kierkegaard there had been the emphasis both on the existential predicament of man and on God's revelation to him in Jesus Christ (without ever showing how the two could really get together), so some of these theologians came to stress the human side of the antithesis while Barth came to stress the divine side. Through the years the thinking of Bultmann, with its interest centered upon how man can receive revelation, has become the great alternative to the thinking of Barth, with its stress on the revelation that comes from God. Therefore the subsequent history of Dialectical Theology can be understood by following the debate which has been carried on between Barth and Bultmann and which, interestingly, has centered to a large extent on the resurrection of Jesus Christ.

II. The Barth-Bultmann Debate over the Resurrection

This debate has gone through two phases. In the first phase, which took place during the 20s, Bultmann disagreed with Barth on the matter of the methodology by which Scripture was to be interpreted, but asserted that he was basically in agreement with him theologically. The second phase began with Bultmann's essay on demythologizing, which appeared in 1941 and showed that the hermeneutical disagreement of the 20s could only result in a theological divergence as well.

A. The Hermeneutical Debate

In 1922 Bultmann reviewed the second edition of Barth's *The Epistle to the Romans* and declared that "in the main I am in agreement with Barth."[14] Then two years later he published an article entitled "Liberal Theology and the Most Recent Theological Movement,"[15] in which he made it clear that he joined Barth in his stand against Liberalism and the Enlightenment with its assumption of an essential harmony between God and man. Like Barth, Bultmann saw the disjunction between God and man as complete. "God signifies the total abolition of man" (18). Bultmann also stood with Barth in his answer to Harnack that a knowledge of Jesus obtained from the historical method was no revelation from God (4).

[14] R. Bultmann, "Karl Barths 'Römerbrief in zweiter Auflage,'" *Christliche Welt*, 36 (1922), col. 371.
[15] R. Bultmann, *Glauben und Verstehen*, I, 1-25.

However, along with these statements regarding his basic agreement with Barth, there appeared criticisms of the methodology by which Barth interpreted Scripture. Bultmann agreed with Barth that a proper interpretation of the Biblical text came only when one pressed beyond the grammatical and historical details to the basic concern or subject matter (*die Sache*) of the passage and allowed everything to be controlled and understood from its vantage point. But Bultmann complained that Barth assumed that everything in the text was so *equally* capable of bearing witness to the *Sache* that he was virtually saying that the text was plenarily inspired.[16] For Bultmann all the text was not equally the expression of the *Sache*, for in some places Paul gave a pure expression of it while in others it was beclouded by all kinds of alien ideas inherited from Judaism, Hellenism, and certain unsophisticated aspects of the primitive Christian faith.[17]

Barth's answer appeared in the preface to the third edition of *The Epistle to the Romans*. He acknowledged that he regarded all parts of the text as equally good expressions of the *Sache*. But he also agreed with Bultmann that the influence of the worldly ideas of Hellenism and Judaism on Paul could surely be seen in Romans. However, in distinction from Bultmann he declared that not just some but all the words of Romans were equally influenced by the world and were equally alien to the *Sache*. All of Romans must be controlled and understood in "relation to this subject-matter (*Sache*) which is—the Spirit of Christ."[18] For Barth the *Sache* was something completely beyond the text of Romans and outside of human experience. It was a part of that revelation which a man could know only as he died to himself and the world and became a new man in Christ. For Bultmann, on the other

[16] Bultmann, "Karl Barths Römerbrief . . . ," col. 372. Incidentally, in Barth's first edition of the *Römerbrief* (1918) he acknowledged that, had he to choose between "the historical-critical method of Biblical investigation and the venerable doctrine of Inspiration, I should without hesitation choose the latter . . ." (p. 1).

[17] *Ibid.*, col. 373.

[18] Barth, *The Epistle to the Romans*, p. 17.

hand, this *Sache* was closer to the text; in fact, in some places Paul's own words were themselves an adequate expression of it.

This hermeneutical difference between Barth and Bultmann became clearer when Bultmann replied to Barth's *Die Auferstehung der Toten*, published in 1924.[19] This book by Barth was an interpretation of First Corinthians from the vantage point of the theme of the general resurrection of the dead, which is found in the fifteenth chapter. Barth regarded the term "the resurrection of the dead" as expressing the miracle which God performed in revealing himself to men. Hence it was the basis upon which Paul sought a solution for all of the problems at Corinth. But this miracle of revelation found its full expression in the resurrection of Jesus.

Barth's understanding of the resurrection of Jesus had undergone no change since the writing of *The Epistle to the Romans*. It was "a historical, divine fact, which as such is only to be grasped in the category of revelation and in none other" (138). Since the resurrection could be known only by revelation, Barth argued that Paul's purpose in speaking of it in I Corinthians 15:1-19 was not to give any historical verification for this event but rather to show that the message which he had preached to the Corinthians was the same as that of the primitive church. There could be no thought of an historical argument in this passage because it contains such a theological and unhistorical matter as "Christ died for our sins" and that he was raised "according to the Scriptures" (132f.). The resurrection appearances of verses 5-8 are not cited as proofs but are, along with the resurrection itself, articles of faith which express the miracle of God's revelation to man (133). Not even the fact of the five hundred brethren who saw the risen Jesus and were still living was cited as a proof of the resurrection. This was mentioned to show that one who has seen God's power in the resurrection of Jesus does not, by the fact that he has died, cease to benefit from the resurrection (142ff.). Finally, verses 12-18 base

[19] K. Barth, *The Resurrection of the Dead.*

the resurrection of Jesus upon such an historically unverifiable matter as the future resurrection of the dead (133).

Bultmann objected that to interpret I Corinthians 15:1-19 as containing no attempt to give historical arguments for the resurrection of Jesus was false exegesis. Why did Paul stress that the five hundred brethren were *still* alive if his purpose was to assert that the resurrection continues to be meaningful even if one has died?[20] Bultmann agreed with Barth in wanting to understand the resurrection of Jesus as something that did not establish any continuity with this world and therefore could not be known by the historical method. But he felt that Paul had tried to argue for the resurrection from the world. "I can only understand I Corinthians 15:1-9 as [Paul's] attempt to make credible the resurrection of Christ as an objective historical event" (54).

As for the resurrection of the dead, Barth interpreted Paul as saying that it was not a future and final event in the sense of that which marked the end of history. According to Barth, "The last *things* are not, as such, *last* things."[21] An event in history, even though it was supernatural, could not be the basis of all history and existence, for such an ultimate event must be that which lies totally outside of history and thus is capable of embracing all history and existence. Indeed, Paul does use the future tense in speaking of the "resurrection of the dead," but allusions to the future are only "parables" (103) in which Paul struggles to set forth the concept of the resurrection of-the dead as the beginning and foundation of all history.

Thus, for example, the mystery according to which at the last trump the dead shall be raised and the living shall be changed in a twinkling of an eye signifies the divine call given to man to find his life in God, and this call comes in the indivisible moment of time which divides the past from the future (287f.). Furthermore, Paul's declaration in I Corinthians 15:54 that the mortal body shall put on immortality

[20] R. Bultmann, "Karl Barth, 'Die Auferstehung der Toten,'" *Glauben und Verstehen*, I, 54.

[21] Barth, *The Resurrection of the Dead*, p. 104.

90

means the present enjoyment of the victory of Jesus over death (209-211).

Bultmann was so sure that this was not what Paul meant that he expostulated, "I can only regard all this as a violent handling of the text."[22] But all would be well, he declared, if Barth would agree that Paul's fidelity to the basic subject matter varied from place to place so that he could be considered wrong at certain points. According to Bultmann it is apparent where Paul expressed the *Sache*. These are the places where he spoke of the resurrection as a *present* reality, or when in speaking of the future state he described it in terms which could apply equally well to the present, as in Philippians 1:23 and I Thessalonians 4:17, where the future is a "being with Christ" (64). Bultmann felt that for Paul resurrection faith was a moment-by-moment experience of "peace with God" (Rom. 5:1), or a moment-by-moment sense of the sufficiency of Christ (I Cor. 1:30). When this faith was expressed purely, it did not speak of some new, future existence; whenever Paul departed from this he erred, because he was letting Hellenism or Jewish apocalypticism influence him (64).

Thus, since Bultmann allowed one group of Paul's statements to stand in judgment over another group, the *Sache* was so within reach that it could be expressed in the text. For Barth, however, the *Sache* was so far above the text that all parts of the text were an equally good but nevertheless imperfect expression of it. Since interpretation was to be carried out from the vantage point of this transcendent *Sache*, Barth was not bound to follow the text slavishly. If Paul was struggling to express the *Sache*, why should the interpreter be subject to Paul and not rather join with him in this struggle, and say things that to the interpreter were a better way than Paul's of expressing the *Sache*?

The contrast between Barth's *Sache*, at a far remove from the text, and Bultmann's, which was in the text, indicated the great divergence between these men even during this early

[22] Bultmann, "Karl Barth, 'Die Auferstehung der Toten,' " p. 63.

period. Since God and man could not get together in Dialectical Theology, it was inevitable that one's attention must be concentrated either on man or on God. Bultmann chose to center his attention upon man, whereas Barth had centered his attention upon God. This divergence became more pronounced as the years passed. The basis upon which Barth was finally able to carry out the writing of his systematic theology helped to make his position more consistent and explicit.

In 1927 Barth had made his first attempt to construct a systematic theology with his writing of *Die Lehre vom Worte Gottes* as the first part of his *Prolegomena zur christlichen Dogmatik*. However, four years later he wrote another book which discredited the orientation of its predecessor and declared itself to be, at last, the proper beginning for systematic theology. In the foreword to this first half-volume of *Die kirchliche Dogmatik*, Barth confessed that in his first attempt he had been unclear whether revelation began with the Word of God or with human existence, because it borrowed so heavily from the existentialism of Kierkegaard. Thus it had left open the door to the anthropocentric thinking of Schleiermacher, Ritschl, and Herrmann. Insofar as it had let itself be nourished by existentialism, it had made the Word of God subservient to existentialism and had failed to let theology be nourished solely from its source in the Word of God.[23]

Free from any dependence on knowledge derived from human experience, the criterion of Christian language was now to be "the essence of the church, which is Jesus Christ, God in his gracious approach to man in revelation and reconciliation" (I/1,3). This shift in Barth's thinking is reflected in the change in the title of his theology from "Christian Dogmatics" to "Church Dogmatics." For Barth the adjective "Christian" connoted the human and experiential aspect of Christianity, whereas "church" connoted the Word of God which stands over against men and is to be believed because it is the faith of the church. Thus Barth had broken all ties

[23] K. Barth, *Church Dogmatics*, I/1, ixf. Henceforth references to the *Church Dogmatics* will be given simply by volume and page.

with anything which might control his theology from the human side of the dialectic.

B. The Theological Debate

With the passage of time Bultmann's position also became more consistent and explicit. The fact that he began his famous essay on demythologizing[24] with a discussion of the situation in which man finds himself in this present era shows how important a role man played in his thinking. Modern man, declared Bultmann, finds that it is both senseless and impossible to accept the world view of the New Testament, which was that of a pre-Copernican age in which man thought of heaven as above the sky and of hell as beneath the earth. Neither is it possible to believe in miracles, since the great advances of science have come solely from the postulate that the universe is a closed system in which all that happens results from prior causes. "It is impossible," asserted Bultmann, "to use electric light and the wireless and to avail ourselves of modern medical and surgical discoveries, and at the same time to believe in the New Testament world of demons and spirits" (5).

> *Note.* Bultmann felt compelled to prefer the world view upon which science proceeds to that of the New Testament, not through any dogmatic preference but simply because science finds confirmation from facts which are determined and controlled by the critical method. Indeed, this modern world view may undergo modifications in the future, but it will only do this through discoveries which stem from the use of the critical method. The world view of the New Testament, on the other hand, finds no confirmation from an application of the scientific method.[25]

Modern man also finds it senseless to adhere to the world view of the New Testament because, regardless of whether

---

[24] R. Bultmann, "New Testament and Mythology," *Kerygma and Myth*, I, 1-44.

[25] See R. Bultmann, "Zum Problem der Entmythologisierung," *Kerygma und Mythos*, II, 181.

he understands himself in naturalistic or idealistic terms, he knows that he is above nature and is responsible to organize his life so that he becomes the master over nature. But the New Testament as it stands hinders a responsible mastery over nature, for in its world view man is constantly liable to interference from supernatural powers. These powers do not work directly upon the spirit of man so as to increase his ability to act responsibly in gaining a mastery over nature, but rather are viewed as benefiting man via nature. For example, the New Testament regards the blessings of redemption to be mediated through the resurrection of the dead body of Jesus. But, objected Bultmann, "If that is the way God makes life available for man, God's action is inextricably involved in a nature miracle." Modern man cannot accept this world view of the New Testament "because it regards man's essential being as nature and redemption as a process of nature."[26]

Bultmann was nevertheless convinced that the New Testament is so true that its message is unique and absolute. But modern man cannot possibly accept it as true until he is brought to realize that the New Testament sets forth its message in the imagery of a myth. By "myth" Bultmann means "the use of imagery to express the otherworldly in terms of this world, and the divine in terms of human life, the other side in terms of this side" (10, note). To talk of the purpose of the world, the meaning of human existence, or how to be delivered from bondage to nature is to talk of the "otherworldly," the "divine." As men grope for words to speak of such things, they often resort to concepts and imagery drawn from within this world. Such language is very apt to put the reader on a false scent by causing him to interpret it literally instead of figuratively, and thus to miss the point completely. But the moment one realizes that the important thing in a myth is not its imagery but the understanding of existence that it enshrines, it becomes highly relevant as a possible interpretation of the meaning of existence.

[26] Bultmann, "New Testament and Mythology," p. 8.

The New Testament likewise becomes relevant when the purpose of its mythical language is understood as having this function, and for those who have faith it becomes a book with an absolute claim upon man. In doing away with this mythical language one need not, as with the old Liberalism, strip away the husk of the mythical and dogmatic elements of the New Testament in order to reach the kernel of its truth. Rather, one need only see the purpose of all its mythical elements and then reinterpret them as an expression of the meaning of existence.

The mythical language of the New Testament borrows from Jewish apocalypticism, Oriental Gnosticism, and Hellenistic mystery cults, and sets forth a dualism in which man is regarded as being under Satanic power, which can only be broken by the greater power of God. The imagery that expresses this dualism is itself useless, but the meaning of human existence which it implies, that is, the existentialist interpretation of this imagery, is highly relevant. In fact, the only question that remains is whether this interpretation is true. Bultmann has the faith to believe that this existential interpretation of the New Testament is the final truth for all men.

A demythologized and reinterpreted New Testament sets forth an understanding of human existence as either authentic or unauthentic. Even though the New Testament writers did draw some ideas from Gnosticism, they never accepted the Greek idea that sin was caused by the soul being imprisoned within an evil, material body. Rather, according to Paul, sin arose from the "flesh," a term which for him meant all that was embraced within the sphere of the visible, concrete, tangible, and measureable reality. The sensualist lives for the flesh when he seeks pleasure from material things. One also lives for the flesh when he exerts himself in the hope of receiving a tangible reward from this sphere. Such a life involves one in anxiety, because there is always the possibility that death will sever one from the world. Thus to live for the "flesh" or the "world" results in becoming more bound to it and to nature and less able to live in responsible freedom.

This anxiety and resultant bondage hinder one from loving others, for if one is anxious, he is more concerned about himself than others. This living for the "flesh," with the concomitant bondage to nature, anxiety, and self-centeredness, is unauthentic living.

But the New Testament also speaks of truly authentic life, the life of faith. In such a life we look not to the things which are seen but to the things which are unseen; we look to God, the unseen, intangible reality, who confronts us as love so that we have the forgiveness of sins and are free from the shame and guilt of the past. This love also frees us from a fear of the future and of death, for if God loves us, we may "open ourselves freely to the future" (19). To be open to the future is "eschatological existence" (20). This existence does not give a promise of a future redemption and deliverance from physical death, for such a promise would bring blessings through a change in nature and thus dampen one's ardor to exert his responsibility to control nature at the present. Instead, "eschatological existence" causes one to live in full responsibility for the present moment. Living thus in the moment with a wholeheartedness made possible by freedom from fear of the future or regret for the past, one devotes his full energies of the moment to responsible living, and thus knows authentic life.

But the New Testament declares that this transition from unauthentic to authentic living is possible only through faith *in Christ*. At this point Bultmann posed the question of whether it was necessary also to demythologize this New Testament emphasis that authentic living is possible only through the historical event of Jesus Christ. The existentialist philosopher Martin Heidegger had done just that. Though Kierkegaard, from whom Heidegger borrowed, had received his understanding of existential, authentic living from the New Testament without getting rid of Christ, Heidegger had set forth the New Testament concept of existential living as altogether possible apart from Christ. Bultmann candidly confessed his great debt to Heidegger (who was his colleague at the University of Marburg from 1921-28), but charged him with a grave error in presuming to think that a man could attain to authentic living by his own self-assertion. All self-assertiveness leads to self-glorying, which turns one toward the flesh and away from God and thus defeats the very effort to live authentically. Heidegger's great mistake was that he had failed "to see that self-commitment can be received only as a gift from God" (29). A man will achieve authentic living only when he sees that there must be an act of God from without to deliver him from his self-assertiveness and has faith to accept the claim of the New Testament that this indeed happens in Christ.

The New Testament sees the cross and the resurrection as the act of God in Christ by which we are brought into authentic living, but "it is beyond question that the New Testament presents the event of Jesus Christ in mythical terms" (34). There is no doubt that there was an historical figure named Jesus, but the presentation of him as pre-existent, as born of a virgin, as a doer of miracles, as omniscient, and finally as resurrected and ascended—this is mythical language which arises from the attempt to set forth the significance of Jesus as an event of salvation. This being the case, "we can dispense with the objective form by which these myths were cast" (35) and concentrate on the eschatological meaning denoted by such language.

There are many ways in which the New Testament writers strove to convey what the cross of Jesus meant to them. The cross was the place where there was forgiveness and where the power of sin was broken. But it was more than this, for according to Colossians 2:15 the cross represented an open triumph over the principalities and powers. This is mythical language which really means that the cross of Christ has the cosmic significance of standing in judgment against all that is involved in this tangible, visible world. Understanding the cross in this way excludes thinking of it in terms of factual statements as the place where we receive forgiveness and are released from the power of sin. Instead, it becomes the means by which we hear the imperative to undergo crucifixion with Christ, to cease to live for the temporal world and to trust God. The cross then ceases to be "just an event of the past which can be contemplated in detachment, but is the eschatological event in and beyond time, for as far as its meaning for faith is concerned, it is an ever-present reality" (36). The cross of Christ, then, is understood as "a permanent historical fact [*ein geschichtliches Geschehen*] originating in the past historical [*historisch*] event which is the crucifixion of Jesus" and which through "the preaching of the cross as the event of redemption challenges all who hear it to appropriate this significance for themselves, to be willing to be crucified with Christ" (37).

As for the resurrection, the only thing historical about it is the Easter faith of the disciples, in which they had come to appropriate the cross as an eschatological event.

> The resurrection itself is not an event of past history. All that historical criticism can establish is the fact that the first disciples came to believe in the resurrection. . . . The historical event of the rise of Easter faith means for us what it meant for the first disciples—namely, the self-manifestation of the risen Lord, the act of God in which the redemptive event of the cross is completed (42).

This faith, leading to the apostolic proclamation and resulting in the founding of the church, which through proclamation and faith has existed ever since, is the eschatological event which makes the cross the permanent "fact," the existential challenge, that has confronted men through the ages as well as today. This eschatological event began with the person of Jesus of Nazareth and has continued wherever there has been faith. Hence Bultmann can conclude his essay by saying that "the agent of God's presence and activity, the mediator of his reconciliation of the world unto himself, is a real figure of history. Similarly the word of God is not some mysterious oracle, but a sober, factual account of a human life, of Jesus of Nazareth possessing saving efficacy for man" (44).

But in saying that Jesus has saving efficacy for man, Bultmann is not saying that any facts about Jesus (any *Was*) are essential for faith. Were certain facts about Jesus an essential part of proclamation, then proclamation would depend in part on the objective world from which a man must be freed in order to live authentically, and thus such facts would only enmesh a man further in the world. Rather, only the fact that he did exist (the *Dass*) is essential, for otherwise authentic living would be impossible since a man would be shut up to his own self-assertiveness. Bultmann appeals not to any proof but only to faith in asserting the finality of the Christian message, for "it is precisely its immunity from proof which secures the Christian proclamation against the charge of being mythological" (44). If Christianity could be proven, then it would depend upon this visible, tangible world and would therefore be unable to deliver men from this sin, which consists in dependence upon this world.

A look at Bultmann's system as a whole reveals that it is based upon the assumption that there are two kinds of knowledge: that which is gained by inference from the objective world, and a knowledge of authentic living that is known only in the moment when it is lived. Bultmann began his argument for demythologizing by appealing both to scientific knowledge and to the knowledge which alone (according to his premise) can enhance responsible living in defiance of nature. Of these two kinds of knowledge it is apparent that the latter is his decisive argument for demythologizing. The presuppositions of existentialism—not the discoveries of science —comprise the real reason for demythologizing the New Testament. This must be done, not because science has proven that hell is not under the earth, but because the New Testament sees salvation as tied up with certain facts that have to do with this world, such as the historical cross and the physical resurrection. Since a mere fact encourages detached contemplation and unauthentic living, it must be reinterpreted as an imperative. Thus Bultmann said,

> If the challenge of demythologizing was first raised by the conflict between mythological cosmology of the Bible and the modern scientific world view, it at once became evident that the

99

restatement of mythology is a requirement of faith itself. For faith needs to be emancipated from its association with a world view expressed in objective terms, whether it be a mythical or a scientific one.[27]

However, science and existentialism represent one of the great tensions in Bultmann's thinking. On the one hand he has historical and scientific knowledge that comes to him from the objective world of facts, and on the other hand he has an existential knowledge that depends in no wise upon the world. Bultmann has made great contributions to an historical understanding of the New Testament, and yet all this knowledge has nothing to do with the existential knowledge which exists in authentic living. In fact, objective knowledge can so distract from existential knowledge that it becomes impossible to live authentically. Existential knowledge must be stripped of all the remnants of the objective knowledge of the world or it will not save one from the world. It is at this point that Heinrich Ott, who is now the successor to Karl Barth at the University of Basel, has made one of the most penetrating criticisms of Bultmann, for he has asked how one who is living by existential knowledge should orient himself toward the objective knowledge of the world, or, to put it in other words, where does objective knowledge fit into one's total knowledge?[28]

This disjunction between the knowledge that is from God and that from the world is inevitable to those who begin with the premise that revelation must be wholly other and contrary to this world. When there is no rapprochement between the world and revelation, it is difficult to see how knowledge of both the world and revelation can reside in one knowing subject. It would appear that Dialectical Theology carries with it the threat of schizophrenia.

With the publication of Bultmann's manifesto for demythologizing, his system of thought, based on the human side of the dialectic, became clear. It was the sixth book of the

[27] R. Bultmann, "Bultmann Replies to His Critics," *Kerygma and Myth*, I, 210.

[28] H. Ott, *Geschichte und Heilsgeschichte in der Theologie Rudolf Bultmanns*, p. 11.

Church Dogmatics (III/2), published in 1948, that contained Barth's reply to Bultmann's essay on demythologizing. During the sixteen years that had passed since the first half-volume of the *Church Dogmatics* had appeared, Barth had written enough (3300 pages) to make clear the position he was now holding since making a complete break with existentialism. One must understand something of the "new Barth" in order to appreciate the stance from which he answered Bultmann.

Barth's shifting of his theological foundation from such existential language as "the qualitative distinction between eternity and time" simply to Jesus Christ as the concrete revelation of God was accompanied by an emphasis in which the resurrection of Jesus became even more central in Barth's thinking. It was during the forty days of the post-resurrection appearances of Jesus that God was fully revealed to man (I/2, 114). These appearances were the full revelation of God because they revealed God's grace to man. Christ had had to die upon the cross for man's sin; nevertheless, in Christ God manifested himself during these forty days to sinful men, and this was nothing less than an act of sheer grace. This full revelation is not identical with Scripture itself, for the Bible is only a witness to these appearances. The Old Testament witnesses to them by anticipating them and the New Testament by remembering them (I/2, 114). Not even the Scriptural records of these post-resurrection appearances are identical with this revelation, for their account of what happened is confused, and as they attempt to state this event in human language they "stammer" (I/2, 115). Consequently, the resurrection appearances are the "Archimedean point" (I/2, 117) upon which all the Biblical witness rests. The revelation of God during these forty days is so complete and final that no further revelation will ever come to supplement it. The appearances of the forty days are "a present without any future . . . an eternal presence of God in time" (I/2, 114).

Such words that make the resurrection pervade all of time could lead one to think that the later Barth, like the earlier one, cannot speak of a future resurrection of the dead. However, as Berkouwer has noted, "the definitive character of the resurrection has increasingly come to the fore in Barth's thinking as the triumph which is still to be made manifest."[29] Thus, while Barth speaks of the resurrection of Jesus as a time which needs no future, as having no "eschatological intention" (I/2, 117), yet it is also "completely eschatological in intention," for "if we confess that Christ is risen and risen bodily, we must also confess to our own future resurrection" (I/2, 117).

Barth acknowledged that this emphasis upon the future was in definite contrast to his earlier days, concerning which he confessed (II/1, 635),

> When I came to expound a passage like Rom. 13:11f. ("Now it is high time to wake out of sleep: for now is our salvation nearer than when we believed . . .), in spite of every precaution I interpreted it as if it referred only to the moment which confronts all moments in time as the eternal "transcending meaning" of all moments in time . . . . But . . . I missed the distinctive feature of the passage, the teleology which it ascribes to time as it moves towards a real end.

Thus, in expounding I Corinthians 15, the Barth of later years clearly affirmed that the final end that will occur with the resurrection of the dead is "a historical and therefore a temporal event" (III/2, 624).

However, Barth continued as in his earlier days to interpret Scripture from the *Sache,* which was wholly above the text. The only difference was that now this *Sache* was explicitly the revelation of God in Christ during the forty days following Easter. Even the future resurrection of the dead must be understood from this vantage point, and since the resurrection of Jesus has no eschatological intention, this future resurrection of the dead must be understood as nothing more than the resurrection of Jesus himself. In speaking of the full revelation that came during the forty days, Barth said, "Revelation remains revelation and does not become a revealed state. Revelation remains identical with Christ . . ." (I/2, 118). Consequently, the future resurrection of the dead cannot itself be

[29] G. Berkouwer, *The Triumph of Grace in the Theology of Karl Barth,* p. 203.

any revelation supplementary to that in the appearances of the resurrected Jesus. Rather, it must simply reveal the glory of his resurrection.

This glory was fully revealed to those who saw Jesus after Easter, but these were but a small number in comparison with the whole human race. However, the appearances of the forty days point to the time when this glory will be revealed fully in all creation. At this time the love of God, which is manifested so fully in the resurrection, will be visible in every corner of creation and at every moment of creation's existence. When this universal manifestation takes place, time will have ceased. There will then be a "present without a future," just as before creation there was a "present without a past." At this time "the secret of Calvary will be revealed as indicated in the forty days" (III/2, 624). Also there will be an eternalizing both of creation as a whole[30] and of human beings as individuals. This eternalizing does not involve a changing of creation or of individuals but, rather, a manifestation to them of the love of God made evident in the forty days of the post-resurrection appearances. At this time an individual's unchanged life will be revealed "in all its merited shame but also in all its unmerited glory" (III/2, 633). Hence, in the Christian hope "there is no question of a continuation into an indefinite future of a somewhat altered life . . . [but, rather,] an 'eternalising' of this ending life" (III/2, 624).

Thus Barth remained true to his dictum that "revelation must remain identical with Jesus Christ" so that, when the love of God manifested in the forty days after Easter is shed on all creation, the only change which creation undergoes is that the light of the love of God shines upon every aspect of it.

> *Note.* The latest statements of Barth on this subject indicate no deviation from this position. Indeed, in IV/3, 928, Barth does speak of the renewed creation as "maintaining its own light, and bearing witness to God in this renewed form in which it is conformed to the image of the Son of God."

[30] In III/3, 89f. Barth declares that even the wingbeat of a fly in some ancient geological age will be preserved.

Such words would seem to indicate that creation undergoes an inherent change when it is eternalized. But it must be remembered that Barth does not regard anything in the created world as inherently bad. The world is the best of all possible worlds (III/1, 385). Even death is an inherently good thing that will also be eternalized. The evil in the world, which is overcome by the redemption of Christ, is that power of *das Nichtige*, that threat of evil which seems to exist as men look at the death, sorrow, and misery of the world and forget Christ. When creation is eternalized, the light of Christ will be unmistakably evident everywhere and consequently, creation, without undergoing any inherent change, will appear as it should have all along, because the threat of *das Nichtige* has been removed. In this way it will have and maintain its own light and thus be conformed to the image of the Son of God.

Thus in the new Barth man does look forward to this final triumph. Where this applies to human beings, it is the "resurrection of the dead." It is significant, however, to point out how this deviates from New Testament teaching, which declares that the resurrection of the dead involves an *inherent* change in the individual. According to the New Testament the change will be so great that mortality will be exchanged for immortality, weakness for strength, dishonor for glory (I Cor. 15:52ff.). The resurrection body of the believer will be fashioned like unto Christ's glorious body (Phil. 3:20-21). But in Barth no such inherent change can occur, for it would mean that revelation had extended itself beyond Christ to include something in the created world. And Barth must remain true to his principle that "revelation remains identical with Christ" (I/2, 118).

Thus it is evident how seriously the new Barth carried out his promise to base everything on "Jesus Christ [who is] God in his gracious approach to man in revelation and reconciliation" (I/1, 3). But the stress on this is so great that revelation never really bridges the gap between God and man, but remains with God, who is conceived as standing over against man. Gustav Wingren has remarked that Barth "begins with the Word directed to men . . . which never can become man's possession or quality in himself."[31]

[31] G. Wingren, *Theology in Conflict*, p. 25.

This emphasis on God and the events of redemption as standing over against man must be kept in mind in order to understand Barth's reply to Bultmann's essay on demythologizing, which reply appears in III/2 of *Church Dogmatics*, particularly pages 442 through 447. Barth's basic criticism of Bultmann was that the latter understood the resurrection as occurring only when there was faith in response to the *kerygma*. "On Bultmann's view," declared Barth, "the Easter history is merely the first chapter in the history of faith, and the Easter time the first period in the age of faith," and "Jesus himself had not arisen" (III/2, 445). For Barth, on the contrary, "Jesus himself did rise again and appear to his disciples. . . . Hence the disciples were not alone with their faith. It was established, awakened and created by God in this objective encounter" (III/2, 445). Thus, whereas for Bultmann objective facts were detrimental to faith, for Barth the resurrection viewed as an objective event was the very basis of faith. However, for Barth the objective event of the resurrection was not known by the historical method but in another way. He reproached Bultmann for rejecting the resurrection because it could not be known by the historical method:

> It is sheer superstition to suppose that only things which are open to "historical" [*historisch*] verification can have happened in time. There may have been events which happened far more really [*viel sicherer wirklich*] in time than the kind of things Bultmann's scientific historian can prove. There are good grounds for supposing that the history [*Geschichte*] of the resurrection of Jesus is a pre-eminent instance of such an event (III/2, 446).

Here Barth uses the two German words for history, *Historie* and *Geschichte*, in a contrasting way. In III/1, 78ff. Barth had made very clear that events which were *Geschichte* were just as historical as those which are *Historie*. *Historie* is, according to Barth, all that has taken place in the past but which stems from causal connections with the rest of creation. *Geschichte* is the broader term. It includes those events which are *Historie* as well as those which are the result of the immediate working of God, such as creation and the resurrection. History itself, in fact, is *unhistorisch* because as a whole it stems immediately from God. But no miracle can be completely *unhistorisch*, for, taking place as it does within the created world, it always has some relation to this context. Thus even the resurrection has "a tiny 'historical' [*historisch*-] margin" (III/2, 446). But it is basically *Geschichte*, since it was the result of the immediate working of God. Hence there can be no doubt that Barth affirms the historicity of the resurrection of Jesus.

To be sure, he terms the resurrection a "saga" or "legend," but he assigns these names to distinguish it from a myth. According to Barth, a "saga" or "legend" points to an event that did occur, but whose details are of such a nature that it cannot be verified by the historical method. Much of the Bible consists of sagas and legends which cannot be verified historically simply because there are no independent records of the same events which could act as their control. The Easter story is also a saga-legend because it is impossible to harmonize the Easter accounts as an historian would, and thus determine the chronological sequence of all that took place. But these saga-legends are not myths, because there is unquestionably an historical event that is behind these records. "The Easter story is differentiated from a myth, both formally and materially, by the fact that it is all about a real man of flesh and blood" (III/2, 452).

How then does Barth gain knowledge of this event apart from the historical method? When a man comes to have faith in the resurrection, it is because he, very much like the original disciples, has been confronted with the risen Jesus through the preaching of the joyous message of Easter. According to the New Testament, "this faith . . . was made possible only by the resurrection itself" (III/2, 446). It was just as hard for men to accept the idea of the resurrection in New Testament times (the Greeks on the Areopagus laughed at the thought) as today, but when a man does believe it, it is simply the miracle of the resurrection appearances repeating themselves in an individual case.[32] In this way Barth insisted, as over against Bultmann, upon the objectivity of the resurrection of Jesus.

Since the way in which each interpreted the resurrection depended on the way in which knowledge of it was derived, it is not surprising that, in the last round of the debate, attention again became centered upon the question of hermeneutical procedure. Barth had made the knowledge of the resurrection available only through the work of the resurrected Lord, whereas Bultmann had determined, from an existential analysis of man, the form this knowledge would take. As the debate continued, the discussion focused upon the question of knowledge. Bultmann's reply to Barth's remarks in III/2 came in an essay entitled "Das Problem der Hermeneutik," first published in 1950.[33] Here he complained that Barth was "interpreting the pronouncements of Scripture by means of an imported body of abstract categories" (260) when he spoke of an event in history that could be established with more certainty than anything the historian can establish. The thought of such a history was considered "abstract" by Bultmann because he did not see how it could be possible to differentiate such faith from a blind acceptance involving a sacrifice of the intellect (261). Bultmann also objected that, in Barth's system of knowledge, a man must believe in the resurrection by "appealing to an imperative of truthfulness, which is of a higher or different kind from that forbidding us to consider anything true, which contradicts the truths actually presupposed in the understanding I have of the world—the understanding which is the guide for all my activity" (261).

In defense of his own position, Bultmann acknowledged that he also came to the New Testament with a special method of interpretation. But he argued that his procedure was legiti-

[32] In IV/2, 149, Barth states in greater detail the way knowledge of the resurrection is possible: "Because the resurrection takes place in the majesty and will and act of God, the knowledge of it cannot derive from the knowing man, but only from the one who is revealed in it."

[33] Parenthetical page references refer to the English edition, published in 1955. *See* Bibliography.

mate because he avoided setting up a system of knowing that had no bearing upon man as he is. "I am trying to proceed methodically," declared Bultmann, "while in the case of Barth I can perceive only arbitrary assertions" (261).

"Prior understanding" (*Vorverständnis*) was the crucial term for Bultmann's method of interpretation. He reasoned that interpretation of a text was only possible on the basis of a prior understanding. One can understand what another tells him about animals that live in a foreign land or about the founding of a kingdom in the past because there are similar things in one's experience that make possible the comprehension of things that would otherwise be unknown. "In the same way the comprehension of records about events as an action of God presupposes a prior understanding of what may in my case be termed the action of God—let us say, as distinct from man's action, or from natural events" (257). For Bultmann an act of God could only be that which enhanced authentic living. He believed that every man has an intuitive understanding of authentic living, which becomes evident whenever one queries concerning the meaning of life. The New Testament, when it is demythologized, becomes meaningful to men, for then they are no longer troubled by the concept of miracle, and what they have in its place accords with their prior understanding of what it means to live authentically. Thus Bultmann claimed that, in distinction from Barth, his method of interpretation was relevant to men as they are, and did not ask them to believe things which were contrary to the world they knew.

Barth's answer to this essay appeared in 1952 with the publication of IV/1 of *Church Dogmatics*. In the foreword Barth replied to Bultmann's complaint that he had an arbitrary and abstract methodology by asserting that his methodology left him free to hear what God might want to say to him. "Bultmann's hermeneutical suggestions can become binding on me," said Barth, "only when I am convinced that by following them I would say the same things better and more freely."

There followed in 1952 a pamphlet entitled "R. Bultmann:

Ein Versuch ihn zu verstehen."[34] Here Barth not only reiterated the superiority of his hermeneutic because of the freedom it gave him to heed what God said, but criticized Bultmann because his hermeneutic forced God, from the outset, to speak only in a certain way. Barth asked how a methodological principle could be correct which allowed one "to barricade himself" behind the limits of one's own understanding "in order to protect oneself against the Word of God. . . . How can we listen to the New Testament if we are always thrusting some *conditio sine qua non* between ourselves and the text? . . . Surely it would be better to cultivate as flexible and openminded an approach as we can, instead of donning the existentialist strait jacket?" (124) Barth agreed that the New Testament must become meaningful to man, but that this was possible only through the working of the Holy Spirit, for "it is only through the Holy Spirit that the Old and New Testaments can be appreciated as a testimony to the Word of God" (126f.).

With this pamphlet the Barth-Bultmann debate on the resurrection ended. It was impossible for either man, taking the position that he did, to say anything further to the other. In the years since 1953 Barth has continued to be adamant in his rejection of Bultmann, though Bultmann has held out hope that Heinrich Ott can effect a rapprochement.[35] Ott himself asserts that the difference between Barth and Bultmann is not beyond repair. He sees the possibility for a rapprochement in the fact that both are seeking to formulate the way in which the Word of God can be understandable to man. So desirous is Bultmann of making the Word understandable that he has sacrificed its objectivity and analogy to other events in the world so that it might be relevant to man's existential predicament. Barth, on the other hand, has stressed its objectivity. This means that it bears no analogy to anything

[34] This article appeared in English under the title, "Rudolph Bultmann: An Attempt to Understand Him," *Kerygma and Myth*, II, 83-132.

[35] R. Bultmann, "Autobiographical Reflections," *Existence and Faith*, p. 288.

in this world and therefore can become understandable and meaningful to men only through the enabling of the Holy Spirit. Ott feels that these differences could be resolved and that theology would enjoy a significant advance if it could be realized that language is the link by which objects are made meaningful to men.[36]

Under Ott's approach there would be both the emphasis of Barth upon the objectivity of the God who reveals himself in Christ, and an attempt to maintain Bultmann's emphasis by making the language about this objective event meaningful to men in their needs. Such, of course, would be a happy solution to the Barth-Bultmann controversy. But a question that would have to be settled is where the control for this language would lie. With Bultmann it lies so fully on the side of the existential needs of man that these needs exercise a fatal control over it. The only place where this need to demythologize does not change the language of the Bible is in the fact (the *Dass*) that Jesus did exist. But in so doing Bultmann is saying, in effect, that the "ugly ditch" between history and faith remains, and that revelation must bypass history in order to become acceptable to men. With Barth, on the other hand, the control for revelation lies so completely with the God who reveals himself that revelation does not become any fixed datum of history but, rather, takes place only when God chooses to reveal himself. The Bible functions only to witness to this revelation that can always occur, and its meaning is to be understood in terms of this revelation, and not vice versa. Consequently, though Barth asserts that revelation has taken place in history, it is not controlled by history, that is, by the Biblical record of the past, but by revelation itself. Thus he is saying, in effect, that revelation cannot be conveyed by history but must come directly to a man from God. Barth, therefore, takes his place with Lessing on the revelation side of the ditch.

The third alternative would be to regard an historico-gram-

[36] H. Ott, "Objectification and Existentialism," *Kerygma and Myth*, II, 306-335.

matical exegesis of the Bible as the control for our knowledge of God, a knowledge that is indeed relevant to our ultimate needs. If such an alternative were possible, it would surely be the ground for a reconciliation between Barth and Bultmann. Hermann Diem, the professor of theology at Tübingen, has complained that Barth and Bultmann "no longer meet on the ground of exegesis, where alone the rights and wrongs of this argument can be thrashed out."[37] But more important, such an alternative would amount to the bridging of Lessing's ugly ditch and hence to the acknowledging of Christianity's claim to be an historical religion by handling this religion in a way that is consistent with this claim.

[37] H. Diem, *Dogmatics*, p. 105.

CHAPTER FIVE

The New Quest of the Historical Jesus

EVEN BEFORE THE CLOSE OF THE BARTH-BULTMANN DEBATE, the conviction began to emerge that the basic history of Christianity must play a more crucial role for faith. Representatives of both the Barth and Bultmann schools could be heard telling of the need to give history a greater role in transmitting revelation. The first article to appear in the *Zeitschrift für Theologie und Kirche,* when its publication was resumed after World War II, was written by a member of the Bultmann school, Gerhard Ebeling, professor of theology at Zürich, under the title "The Significance of the Historico-Critical Method" (1950). He asserted, "It is vital to clarify . . . the theological relevance of critical-historical work on [Scriptural] texts and events."[1] Even in 1950 Hermann Diem, who has generally followed the approach of Barth and acknowledged the hermeneutical circle in which one interprets Scripture as he hears the Word proclaimed, declared that unbelievers should be allowed to interpret the Bible simply by the universally accepted historical and philological presuppositions, for otherwise "the teaching of Holy Scripture would not only be suspicious to those who stand outside the church but would also be theologically false."[2]

It is interesting to notice how far such thinking had advanced over the mood of nineteenth-century Liberalism.

[1] G. Ebeling, *Word and Faith,* p. 58.
[2] H. Diem, *Grundfragen der biblischen Hermeneutik,* p. 4.

112

The proponents of Liberalism had been able neither to recognize that the historical method had final control over the knowledge of Christianity nor that the Easter faith so apparent in the New Testament was the essential basis from which to interpret it. With the arrival of Dialectical Theology and Form Criticism, however, it became generally accepted that the New Testament could be understood in no other way than from the vantage point of the Easter faith of the early church. But now, without there being the slightest inclination to set Easter faith aside as less than central for the New Testament, the feeling became evident that the results of a critical and historical investigation of the New Testament should be made more relevant for Easter faith. This feeling has become most evident in a movement which has been called "the new quest of the historical Jesus."[3] This movement, receiving its initial impetus from the followers of Bultmann, has brought repercussions from the whole world of theological scholarship. But since this new quest is primarily a response to the preceding Dialectical Theology, attention will be focused upon certain representatives of the Bultmann school and then upon Hermann Diem, who follows in Barth's tradition.

I. The New Quest in the Bultmann School

To understand how Bultmann's students came to inaugurate this new quest, it is necessary to go back a bit and consider how Bultmann himself handled the question of the historical Jesus in his "life of Jesus" written in 1926.[4] The first impression one gains from the foreword of this book is that Form Criticism had caused him to be skeptical about the possibilities of getting back to Jesus himself. Indeed, this book on Jesus was an application of the conclusions Bultmann had reached in his *History of the Synoptic Tradition,* a monu-

[3] Cf. the title to James Robinson's book, *A New Quest of the Historical Jesus.*

[4] Subsequent page numbers refer to an English edition published in 1958. *See* Bibliography.

mental work on Form Criticism that appeared in German in 1921. In the foreword to *Jesus and the Word,* Bultmann declared that there were two basic traditions in the Synoptic Gospels, the Hellenistic and the Palestinian. Of these two, the Palestinian was the earlier, but even within this tradition there were layers to be distinguished "in which whatever betrays the specific interests of the church or reveals characteristics of later development must be rejected as secondary" (13). However, even when the oldest layer is found, "there is the possibility that its contents are also the result of a complicated historical process which we can no longer trace" (13). Indeed, in this earliest layer of tradition "Jesus is named as the bearer of the message; [and] according to overwhelming probability he really was." But "whoever prefers to put the name of 'Jesus' always in quotation marks and let it stand as an abbreviation for the historical phenomenon with which we are concerned, is free to do so" (14).

To the historian seeking unshakeable ground, such talk would seem to make the writing of a book about Jesus quite problematical. But Bultmann's ultimate concern was not simply to find out what happened but, rather, to enter into a "dialogue" with history. For Bultmann history ceases to be objective to the extent that one examines it in a detached and dispassionate manner. But it becomes highly objective and "speaks" to one coming to it with a sense of need and asking existential questions: "History . . . speaks only when one comes seeking answers to the questions which agitate him. Only by this attitude can we discover whether an objective element is really present in history and whether history has something to say to us" (4f.).

It is because of this view of what makes history "objective" that Bultmann was not greatly troubled by the fact that he could not, with certainty, go beyond the oldest layer of the Palestinian tradition and find the Jesus of history. Rather, the Palestinian tradition "meets us as a fragment of tradition coming to us from the past, and in the examination of it we seek an encounter with history" (14). If we come to this earliest tradition, not with a feeling of complacency but driven by the desire to answer life's most pressing questions, then this tradition will stand over against us and speak to us. Thus Bultmann's purpose in writing his book on Jesus was to bring his reader to "a highly personal encounter with history" (6). From this it becomes evident that Form Criticism was not the primary reason that it was difficult for Bultmann to find the Jesus of history. The real problem was that Bultmann was not sufficiently motivated to press through the difficulties to the Jesus of history, for his goal as an historian was simply to have an encounter with others of the human race who had left records of their answers to life's most pressing questions.

> *Note.* Some other prominent Form Critics have written "lives of Jesus" but have not been noncommital about the possibility of breaking through church tradition to know something about Jesus himself. There are, for example, Martin Dibelius' *Jesus* (1939)[5] and K. L. Schmidt's encyclopedia article on Jesus Christ,[6] in which they have said quite a bit about the Jesus of history.

But there was still another reason why Bultmann felt no ultimate need to get back to the Jesus of history. His book on Jesus had been written to make possible an encounter with history and perhaps even with the Jesus of history. But such an encounter was wholly distinct from having an encounter with the Christ of faith by way of Christian proclamation: "Just as in my book on Jesus there is no thought of setting forth a Christian proclamation, so also is it impossible for one to encounter the historical Jesus in Christian proclamation."[7] To have an encounter with the Christ of faith was the really desirable thing and, consequently, there was a lack of interest that kept both Bultmann and his followers from writing another "life of Jesus" for almost thirty years. It was not until

[5] The first English translation appeared in 1949. *See* Bibliography.

[6] K. Schmidt, "Jesus Christus," *Die Religion in Geschichte und Gegenwart*, 2nd ed., III, cols. 110-151.

[7] R. Bultmann, "Zu J. Schniewinds Thesen," *Kerygma und Mythos*, I, 133.

the publication in 1956 of Günther Bornkamm's *Jesus from Nazareth* that such a book was again written by a member of the Bultmann school.

However, in all fairness to Bultmann it should be pointed out that the separateness between the Christ of faith and the Jesus of history was not absolute. For Bultmann it was the Jesus of history who helped give rise to the Easter faith of the early church. Bultmann began his book on New Testament theology by saying, "The message of Jesus is a presupposition for the theology of the New Testament. . . ."[8] Other influences, such as Gnosticism, Jewish apocalypticism, and Easter faith, had made their contribution also, but none of them would have given rise to the church, with its proclamation of the Christ, without the fact of the historical Jesus. The early church deified Jesus and counted him as their Messiah, not because he actually was this in fact but because this was their way of saying that Jesus was decisive for their Christian message. Their ultimate concern in all the theological language with which they spoke of Jesus was to stress that without the fact (the *Dass*) that Jesus had given to their faith, there would be no faith. The faith of the early church, then, presupposed in part the *Dass* of Jesus. As the original believers had come to faith through the *Dass* of Jesus, so subsequent believers came to faith by the fact that they were confronted by someone who proclaimed this faith. Hence Bultmann could even say that the Word of God that was in Jesus becomes incarnate whenever one who has the faith that ultimately began with Jesus proclaims the Christian message, for "the incarnation is an event which is continually being re-enacted in the events of proclamation."[9]

However, the Jesus of history supplies nothing more than the original fact that helped get faith started. The knowledge that comes from faith in the Christ (the *Was*) stems in no wise from anything that was in history. Thus, if historical considerations have no more importance for faith than to point to

[8] R. Bultmann, *Theology of the New Testament*, I, 3.

[9] R. Bultmann, "Bultmann Replies to His Critics," *Kerygma and Myth*, I, 209.

Jesus as the original "that" implied in all subsequent preacher-hearer encounters, and if the really vital thing that is said in these later encounters stems from Easter faith, which has no grounds in history whatsoever, then the door is almost fully open to the charge that the Christ of faith is a myth—an idea that can be thought but that lacks any basis in this world. However, since for the Bultmann school faith itself cannot be grounded in history without ceasing to stimulate authentic living, the only way this school could protect faith from being a myth was to find more connection than a mere fact between the historical Jesus and Easter faith. This is what it has tried to do in its new quest of the historical Jesus.

A. Ernst Käsemann

The paper read by Ernst Käsemann[10] at the 1953 conclave of "old Marburgers" is considered as the real beginning of the new quest. Käsemann charged that Bultmann's insistence that Christianity be seen wholly in terms of the Easter faith of the early church could only imply "a Christian faith that is understood as faith in the exalted Lord, for whom the historical Jesus, as such, had no constitutive significance" (126). He also stated that, unless a connection could be established between the Jesus of history and the Christ of faith, the door was open to a docetism in which God no longer revealed himself in history but had simply become a myth comprising the Easter faith of the early church (141).

To support a new quest for the historical Jesus, Käsemann argued that the early church, simply by virtue of the fact that it wrote the Gospels, found it necessary to include within its *kerygma* this Gospel history in order to make its faith in Christ consistent with Jesus as a person of history. Käsemann insisted that the Christian message, therefore, loses a vital aspect if, as Bultmann would have it, it does not speak of the Jesus of history. But Käsemann realized that since the Gospels

[10] E. Käsemann, "Das Problem des historischen Jesus," *Zeitschrift für Theologie und Kirche*, 51 (1954), 125-153.

117

were written by those who had Easter faith, it was difficult to get back through that faith to see Jesus as he really was. The only way this can be done is to look for certain things in the Gospels which cannot be explained by any parallels found in the faith and practice of the early church of that time or in the Judaism and Hellenism from which particular parts of the church borrowed ideas. Käsemann believed that certain contexts in which the theme of the absolute authority of Jesus was found could not be explained as being the expression of any part of the primitive church. The declaration of Jesus that his authority was greater than that of the Mosaic law surely could not have stemmed from the Jewish wing of the church (144f.). Likewise, his contempt for the purported boundary between the holy and the profane, which came to light when he ate and drank with publicans and sinners, could definitely find no parallel in a branch of the church which borrowed some ideas from the Hellenistic mystery cults (146f.). Finally, since the early church itself had a high regard for John the Baptist, its Easter faith could not account for the Gospel records (e.g., Matt. 11:11-12) in which Jesus declared that John the Baptist was a part of the old aeon and virtually out of the kingdom of God. Therefore the authority of Jesus, as set forth in the Synoptic Gospels, can be explained by none of the historical forces which were at work in the early church. Judaism, Hellenism, and even Easter faith itself are not sufficient to account for this aspect of Jesus and, therefore, historical reasoning points back to Jesus himself as the source of this sense of ultimate authority. By means of the historical method, then, there emerges a Jesus who claims such an absolute authority that "both before and after Easter he revealed himself to the disciples as the Lord, in that he placed them before the immediate presence of God where they enjoyed the freedom and responsibility of faith" (152).

Thus, according to Käsemann, history known through the historical method had something to say that was relevant for faith, but a further investigation of his thought shows that faith still plays the decisive role for providing knowledge.

Without faith the historical method merely sets forth facts regarding the past that are devoid of any unity of meaning. From the following statement it becomes apparent that Käsemann tried to leave as much room as possible for the historical method (*Historie*) to function in providing interpretation, although in the end it is the interpreter who supplies the needed meaning:

> History [*Historie*] becomes historically [*geschichtlich*] relevant, not through tradition as such, but through interpretation, not simply by establishing what happened, but through understanding events of the past which have become and remain as objective facts. . . . History [*Historie*] possesses historical [*geschichtlich*] significance only to the extent that it, through questioning and answering, brings its question and answer into our present situation and thus finds those who are desirous of interpreting it—those who hear and represent its question and answer for our present situation (130).

It was by exercising this interpretive capacity with regard to the history of Jesus that the early church was able to gain a message to preach. In the same way, men today, who have become released from the world by the freedom that faith gives, are able to look to the Jesus of history and see his absolute authority as answering to their faith:

> The absolute authority of Jesus corresponds to the freedom of faith, and for this faith the history of Jesus recurs as the present history of the exalted and proclaimed Lord and yet as the earthly history in which the claim and comfort of the Gospel is found (153).

Thus for Käsemann faith must first exist and then one is able to see in the history of Jesus that which corresponds to his faith. In this way Käsemann succeeded in making something that might be known about the Jesus of history relevant for faith, and thus brought faith and history into a closer connection than they had enjoyed with Bultmann.

B. Ernst Fuchs

Whereas Käsemann had found in Jesus' teaching that which stemmed unquestionably from Jesus himself, Ernst Fuchs, in

119

an article first published in 1956 entitled "Die Frage nach dem historischen Jesus," singled out an aspect of Jesus' behavior in the Gospels as being historical and relevant for faith.[11] This was that Jesus ate and fellowshipped with sinners. Fuchs argued that this theme was less likely to be a product of Easter faith than Jesus' teaching, because the church, in stylizing its tradition about Jesus for its edificatory and evangelistic purposes, was less apt to change tradition regarding what Jesus did than that regarding what he said (156).

For Fuchs this aspect of Jesus' behavior found a real parallel in Easter faith. To him a demythologized Easter faith meant that "in the very God from whom a man feels that he must flee, one has found a refuge whom he now loves" (151). Since the Gospels were written from the vantage point of a post-Easter Pauline faith, they must be read accordingly, and thus a certain theme in the Gospels comes to stand out as most relevant to this faith:

> When we continue our inquiry into faith in the Pauline sense of faith in the gracious God, we are able to ignore for the moment what tradition in the Synoptic Gospels tells us about Jesus and what happened to him and simply establish what Jesus himself . . . has said about our relationship to God (153).

Thus faith singles out Jesus' emphasis on a man's relationship to God as so pertinent to faith that it becomes, as it were, "established" by this faith.

Jesus emphasized that God was gracious toward sinful men. He ate and drank with sinners to depict the fact that God loved those who were apparently banished from him. This brought Jesus into conflict with the self-righteous Pharisees, and to defend his conduct he gave the parable of the prodigal son. But Jesus was so convinced of God's grace that, rather than simply talking about it, he preferred to live out this truth by loving sinners and assuming the role of God's representative to them.

Jesus had seen what had happened to John the Baptist, who had acted as God's representative and preached the coming

---

[11] E. Fuchs, *Zur Frage nach dem historischen Jesus*, pp. 143-167.

of the kingdom. John had been put to death, and Jesus knew that his actions would so evoke the wrath of the religious leaders that they would put him to death also. And indeed, Jesus died before the gates of Jerusalem because the leaders "opposed the idea that he, as a mere man without any official capacity, could have the right to act the part of God and, without any proper theological training, exemplify God's gracious purpose in his own behavior" (155). By deciding to live and die in this way, Jesus inspired his disciples to live in the confidence of God's grace and act as God's representatives. In so doing, they implicitly acknowledged the greatness of Jesus, and the very faith by which they repeated his decision became an Easter faith in which they spoke of Jesus as risen from the dead. "One could only venture to believe in the resurrection of Jesus when one dared to imitate Jesus and accept God's grace as God's *true* will and persevere in this even to death" (165). Hence it came about that the early church preached Jesus and the resurrection, and from this vantage point of Easter faith they wrote the Gospels. Thus the Gospels retain the fact that Jesus behaved as one who assumed the role of God's representative.

Today as men come to the Gospels, they can know that this behavior was anterior to Easter faith even though it is so parallel to it, because historical reasoning leads to the conclusion that, as the church expressed its faith, it would not have changed the actions of Jesus as much as it changed his words. Therefore Fuchs declared, "The so-called Christ of faith is, in fact, no different from the historical Jesus" (166). But while Easter faith traces its origin back to the Jesus of history, this faith depends more upon itself than upon Jesus, for it ever remains a venture (*Wagnis*) in which one dares to live as Jesus did. He does not provide a sure foundation on which one may rest; rather, he may inspire one to live as he dared to live. However, the Jesus of history is, in Fuchs, closer to Easter faith than he was with Bultmann, for the venture one makes in faith finds a parallel in what Jesus also ventured to do.

121

C. Günther Bornkamm

The next major proponent of the new quest of the historical Jesus was Günther Bornkamm, with his book *Jesus von Nazareth* (1956).[12] Like Käsemann and Fuchs, Bornkamm regarded the unmatched authority of Jesus as both historically valid and relevant for Christian faith and proclamation. Käsemann had stressed the authority of Jesus as it was manifested in his teaching, and Fuchs as it manifested itself in his behavior, but Bornkamm declared that this authority "was equally recognizable in his words and in his deeds" (61).

This authority manifested itself in Jesus' teaching in the fact that he did not, like the Rabbis, base his authority on the Scriptures. The authority of Jesus was not derived; rather, it was immediately in his person and was fulfilled in him. This immediate authority also expressed itself in the simplicity of Jesus' teaching. He did not have to go far afield to find illustrations for his messages. The material for his parables came from the everyday life of the particular group to which he was speaking, and thus even in the material that illustrated the message of God, Jesus confronted the people with God as an immediate fact. This authority also manifested itself in Jesus' actions. As he responded to individuals and groups from every part of the spectrum of human types and personalities, Jesus remained himself. He never put on different personages for different situations, for what he really was, was always immediately before men.

Bornkamm termed this authority of Jesus as the "immediate present" (*unmittelbare Gegenwart*).

> This directness, if anything, is part of the picture of the historical Jesus. He bears the stamp of this directness right from the very beginning. The immediate present is the hallmark of all the words of Jesus, of his appearance and his actions, in a world which . . . had lost the present, because it lived between the past and the future, between tradition and promises. . . (58).

[12] The English, *Jesus from Nazareth*, appeared in 1960. Subsequent page references refer to this edition.

This essential characteristic of all of Jesus' ministry has a great relevance for Christian faith today, for to the Christian it conveys "the essential mystery of Jesus' personality and influence [*Person und Wirkung*], as understood by faith" (60). Thus Bornkamm made a quality about the historical Jesus relevant for faith—a thing which Bultmann could not bring himself to do.

The question then arises how Bornkamm was able to regard this "immediate present" as actually stemming from Jesus before his death, and not simply as a quality which Easter faith ascribed to him. Bornkamm argued that this "immediate present" is so striking and powerful that faith could not change it. Despite Easter faith, this "immediate present" of Jesus "is still distinguished by an authenticity, a freshness, and a distinctiveness not in any way effaced by the church's Easter faith" (24). Faith acknowledged and proclaimed this remarkable quality of Jesus in writing the Gospels. But faith was not strong enough to create it. "The person and work of Jesus, in their unmistakable uniqueness and distinctiveness, are shown forth with an originality which again and again far exceeds and disarms even all believing understandings and interpretations" (26).

Thus Bornkamm did not, like Käsemann and Fuchs, single out certain passages in the Gospels in which it could be argued that the material was so unique that it found no analogy in the faith of any branch of the church. To the contrary, the "immediate present" of Jesus pervades every aspect of the Gospels. Since Easter faith is not powerful enough to account for this quality of Jesus, it must trace back to Jesus himself.

Note. The similarity between this line of argument and the thinking of Wilhelm Herrmann and Martin Kähler should be observed, for both argued for the historicity of Jesus from the impact that his life makes upon one as he reads the Gospels. Bornkamm is actually closer to Kähler than Herrmann, for Herrmann believed that the life of Jesus did find analogy in a well-developed categorical imperative, whereas Kähler argued that human imagination was incapable of creating Jesus. Bornkamm's approach is also similar to Paul Althaus, who believes that historians have a well-developed "intuition" that enables them to know when they are face to face with a real, historical personage and not just an imaginative creation.[13] Thus, when one reads the Gospels, one knows he is face to face with a real Jesus.

But according to Bornkamm, the Easter faith of the church, like the "immediate present" of Jesus, also pervades every part of the Gospels. "We possess no single word of Jesus and no single story of Jesus, no matter how incontestably genuine they may be, which do not contain at the same time the confession of the believing congregation or at least are embedded in that confession."[14] Of course, this Easter faith of the early church arose from the resurrection of Jesus: "It is . . . certain that the appearances of the risen Christ and the word of his witnesses have in the first place given rise to this [Easter] faith" (183). It is this faith which led the church to project back into the life of Jesus such things as his performance of nature-miracles and the use of Messianic titles. Jesus himself, Bornkamm affirms, did not perform such miracles as the feeding of the 5,000 and walking on water. He was indeed a healer, but Bornkamm follows the approach of H. J. Holtzmann, who helped naturalize Jesus' healing miracles by saying that they depended on the faith of the one healed (130f.). Neither did Jesus apply to himself any of the Messianic titles reported in the Gospels (Chapter VIII).

Therefore, in the conclusion of *Jesus from Nazareth,* Bornkamm posed the question, "Are the [Gospels] giving [Jesus] an honor which the earthly Jesus, as we have seen, did not desire for himself?" (189) Bornkamm answered that Jesus during his earthly ministry, did not seek his own glory but was obedient even to the death of the cross. Consequently, he did not reveal his glory by the use of Messianic titles or the performance of nature-miracles. Nevertheless, all his actions and words were characterized by the quality of the "im-

---

[13] P. Althaus, *Das sogenannte Kerygma und der historische Jesus,* p. 40.

[14] Bornkamm, *op. cit.,* p. 14.

mediate present." When the apostles came to have Easter faith through the resurrection and glorification of Jesus, they recalled this quality that had been in Jesus and concluded that the glory God had now given to Jesus had been his, implicitly, all along. Thus "we understand why the [Gospels] have woven record and confession into one" (189). From the record came the quality of the "immediate present"; from faith came the knowledge of the glory of Jesus. Since this glory was implicitly his all along, it was only natural to project his use of Messianic titles and performance of nature-miracles back into his earthly ministry.

But while Easter faith projected the glory of Jesus' resurrection back into his earthly ministry, it did not, according to Bornkamm, project the theme of the "immediate present," for this theme in the Gospels stemmed from a quality that was openly manifest in Jesus before his death. Hence Christian faith, which is Easter faith, finds nurture and support from the impact of Jesus' "immediate present" found in the Gospels.

However, it should be noted that in Bornkamm's system faith must first exist before it can find support and nurture in this striking quality of the historical Jesus. The faith that the disciples had come to have through their fellowship with Jesus during his ministry was "broken down" at the cross to such an extent that it could only be rebuilt through the resurrection (173). Thus it was their Easter faith alone that enabled them to find relevance in their memory of the "immediate present" of Jesus. Hence it must follow that our faith, like that of the disciples, can only find relevance in the quality of the "immediate present" of Jesus *after we have Easter faith.* For Bornkamm, however, the resurrection that led to this Easter faith is something that is "removed from historical scholarship" (180). Therefore the faith that is really needed to find relevance in Jesus' quality of the "immediate present" must derive from something that can find no basis in history. It cannot derive from the quality of the "immediate present" that appears in the Gospels and, according to Bornkamm, stands there as an historical fact. Hence Bornkamm

125

takes his place alongside of Käsemann and Fuchs in finding in history some relevance for an already existent Easter faith, but stopping short of saying that history itself can engender this faith.

D. James Robinson

It is well to conclude this study of the way the Bultmann school has proceeded in its new quest with a consideration of James Robinson's *A New Quest of the Historical Jesus*.[15] Now a Professor of Religion at the Claremont Graduate School, Claremont, California, Robinson has, through years of European study and teaching, become imbued with its theological tradition. As an American he has earned his spurs in his grasp of continental scholarship, for Bultmann has spoken approvingly of the "methodical reflections"[16] by which Robinson has probed to the most basic presuppositions of this new quest. A consideration of Robinson makes clear the boundaries within which those who wish to remain generally within the Bultmann school can operate in seeking to bring history and faith into closer alignment.

The first four chapters of this book are devoted to a summary of theological developments since the nineteenth-century quest of the historical Jesus. The development of Form Criticism showed that the Gospels, far from being a dispassionate reporting of what Jesus said and did, were themselves an interpretation of the life of Jesus. Even Mark was the work of a man of faith to strengthen and inculcate faith in others. Thus, with the new approach of Form Criticism, it became quite impossible to disengage historical fact from theological interpretation. According to Robinson, historiography has also undergone a development since the last century:

[15] A revision of this book has appeared in German: *Kerygma und historischer Jesus*. Page numbers marked with an (*) in the text refer to the German revision.

[16] R. Bultmann, *Das Verhältnis der urchristlichen Christusbotschaft zum historischen Jesus*, p. 18.

The positivistic understanding of history as consisting of brute facts gave way to an understanding of history centering in the profound intentions, stances, and concepts of existence held by persons in the past, as the well-springs of their outward actions. Historical methodology shifted accordingly from a primary concern for recording the past *"wie es eigentlich gewesen"* [as it actually was], i.e., cataloguing with objective detachment facts in sequence and with proper causal relationships. Instead the historian's task was seen to consist in understanding those deep-lying intentions of the past, by involving one's selfhood in an encounter in which one's own intentions and views of existence are put in question, and perhaps altered or even radically reversed. (39).

With this new historiography it therefore became quite illegitimate simply to seek after the brute facts about Jesus, as was often the case with the old quest. But these very developments that had made the nineteenth-century quest for Jesus both impossible and illegitimate had actually opened the door to the possibility of a new quest. If, as Form Criticism had shown, the Gospels themselves were an interpretation of the life of Jesus for the purposes of faith, they must be an attempt to get at his deep intentions. The older "positivistic" historiography found it difficult to handle documents having such a purpose, but for the new historiography they were made to order. Hence the new historiography, joining hands with Form Criticism, could embark upon a new quest for the historical Jesus.

The British historian R. G. Collingwood is cited as a leading champion of the new historiography. A noted authority on Roman Britain, Collingwood made a major contribution to the philosophy of history in his *The Idea of History*, published posthumously in 1946. He not only stressed the past discovered by the historian, but also the historian's act in discovering the past, and felt that there was some sort of ontological relationship between the two. Thus he declared,

The activities whose history the historian is studying are not spectacles to be watched, but experiences to be lived through in his own mind; they are objective, or known to him, only because they are also subjective, or activities of his own.[17]

In accordance with his emphasis on the role of the historian, Collingwood also stated,

> The historian himself, together with the here-and-now which forms the total body of evidence available to him, is a part of the process he is studying, has his own place in that process, and can see it only from the point of view which at this present moment he occupies within it.[18]

Consequently, though Collingwood himself was not an existentialist but a neo-Kantian, nevertheless Robinson, along with others of the Bultmannian school, regarded him as coming to conclusions similar to theirs in their attempt to handle history existentially. Bultmann himself, in his 1955 Gifford Lectures, devoted considerable space to Collingwood and declared that he had said "the best that is said about the problem of history."[19] This is because Collingwood had not only seen that the historian is himself historically conditioned, but also that the very act in which he thinks history is itself a decision stemming from his own deep intentions, and therefore like the human actions that comprise the history that he is studying.

No one can deny the value in Collingwood's emphasis upon the relationship between history and the historian, nor that, in making this emphasis, historiography has made a significant advance. However, it may be going too far to suggest that this insight changes historiography so radically that it is now possible to reopen a quest for the historical Jesus that an older methodology could not carry through. Despite his new insight, Collingwood's task continued to be to "construct a picture of things as they actually were."[20] This is the goal of positivistic historiography, and Collingwood has continued to

[17] Collingwood, *The Idea of History*, p. 218.
[18] *Ibid.*, p. 248.
[19] R. Bultmann, *History and Eschatology*, p. 130.
[20] Collingwood, *op. cit.*, p. 246.

pursue it in spite of his emphasis on the role played by the historian himself in writing history. Furthermore, Robinson is perhaps going a bit too far when he charges positivistic historiography with being taken up only with "brute facts" and ignoring the profound intentions which have motivated the makers of history. Marc Bloch, whose positivistic method was considered in Chapter I, certainly made clear that his ultimate goal as an historian was to explain the behavior of people in history. Bloch said that to understand Luther, for example, one must "fathom his soul."[21]

Nevertheless, Robinson asserts that there is now an historiography so different that it justifies a reopening of the quest of the historical Jesus. It is this newer methodology that enables the historian to achieve an objectivity not possible under positivistic historiography. The older historiography thought that objectivity was gained simply by classifying particulars under categories that were generally accepted. But this was really a subtle form of subjectivity, for these very categories are a part of the western culture in which one lives and that has become a part of one's inner thought structure. Facts gained under such a system simply stimulate and reinforce one's a prioris and do anything but cause one to learn something new. Under this new historiography, however,

> Objectivity resides in a complete openness to what the creative historical event has to say. This involves a willingness to listen for underlying intentions and the understanding of existence they convey, with an ear sharpened by one's own awareness of the problems of human existence, and a willingness to suspend one's own answers and one's own understanding of existence sufficiently to grasp as a real possibility what the other is saying.[22]

Any method that will engender an openness and an ability to surrender one's own understanding so that one can grasp the deep intentions of those who lived in the past is certainly to be applauded. And surely since history is the study of

[21] M. Bloch, *The Historian's Craft*, p. 141.
[22] Robinson, *op. cit.*, p. 96.

what human beings have done in the past, an empathy for the problems confronting human kind will give one that sensitivity needed to understand why one acted as he did and thus have an encounter with him. However, it appears that Robinson is not entirely willing to be completely open to the past. In the English edition of his book the phrase "an ear sharpened by one's awareness of the problems of human existence" cites the prerequisite for an encounter with men of the past. But in the German edition this phrase is not quite so neutral. Here this prerequisite is termed "my own concern for the meaning of existence as prior understanding [*Vorverständnis*]" (117*). If one's sensitivity to the problems of human kind does more than give him empathy, if it involves a prior understanding of what is truly the meaning of life, then this prior understanding will make it difficult for one to hear what another is saying.

The term "prior understanding" is crucial in the Bultmannian vocabulary. In the preceding chapter it was shown that for Bultmann the prior understanding necessary to hear a word from God would not allow the possibility that God speaks through a fact which belongs to this objective world. "Prior understanding" knows that authentic living can only come when one turns his back upon the world and receives life from God. Robinson adheres very closely to this meaning of prior understanding. To him authentic living means "a basic renunciation of the struggle for existence" and an elimination of "all props controlled by man and as a result constantly available to him for securing his existence." In place of these things, man builds his existence "upon that which is beyond his control and available only as God's gift" (43f.).

Like Bultmann, Robinson believes that authentic existence cannot come by an act of self-assertiveness, but only by receiving existence as a gift, as it is proclaimed in the Christian message. Though this message is transmitted by human beings, it does not derive ultimately from the world but from God. It began when the apostles came to have faith that, though Jesus had died, yet God had not forsaken him, and hence God would not forsake them either if they lived, not for the world, but only for God. There was nothing in the world to convince the apostles of this; rather, the conviction was a work of God. What the apostles believed, they proclaimed; others came to believe it and preach it and thus the Christian message, the *kerygma,* has continued down to the present, and God has worked on the occasion of its proclamation to bring certain hearers to authentic existence. It is only through preaching that the *kerygma* is heard so that one can accept death to the world and life from God. Along with Bultmann, Robinson insists that the *kerygma* cannot be heard even when one, through historical methodology, discovers the deeper intentions of the Jesus of history and has an "I-thou" encounter with him, for this would mean that revelation could come through something that was a part of this world.

Nevertheless, in distinction from Bultmann, Robinson declares that the *kerygma* cannot remain so indifferent to history that it needs only the fact (the *Dass*) of Jesus' existence. "How," queries Robinson, "can the indispensable historicity of Jesus [for the *kerygma*] be maintained, while at the same time maintaining the irrelevance of what a historical encounter with him would mean, once this has become a real possibility due to the rise of modern historiography?" (88) Robinson is convinced that the new historiography has made it possible to have an encounter with the Jesus of history, and while this encounter is by no means the equivalent of receiving life and forgiveness from God through the *kerygma,* yet there must be a parallel between this encounter with the historical Jesus and the knowledge of Christ that one receives through the *kerygma.* If there be no parallel between them, then, Robinson argues, such a position (which is Bultmann's) cannot "fail to lead to the conclusion that the Jesus of the *kerygma* could equally well be only a myth, for one has in fact declared the meaning of his historical person irrelevant" (88). Therefore Robinson believes that the new historiography must be utilized to gain an historical encounter with the Jesus of history in order to

see if there was not indeed a parallel between the deep intentions of Jesus and the *kerygma*.

A new quest of the historical Jesus cannot limit itself to a
purely objective and critical research. Rather, it must make
evident Jesus' own understanding of existence, that is, this new
quest must be carried out in the realm of an "I-thou" relation.
Only then can the historical Jesus be compared with the *kerygma*
(118*).

But in following the new historiography to gain an "I-
thou" encounter with Jesus, Robinson cannot dispense with
the tried and proven methods of positivistic historiography.
Like Käsemann and Fuchs, he must use this approach in order
to find some strand in the Gospels that stems from Jesus himself and that could not be explained by Easter faith. To find
the deep intentions of Jesus, he must seek out certain sayings
"whose purity can be shaken neither by literary nor form-
critical investigations" (155*). He believes that these require-
ments are met by a certain group of Jesus' sayings that evince
a "polarity" in which "the message of Jesus exists essentially in
a statement concerning a present situation which is made in
view of an approaching eschatological future" (157*). An
example of such a statement is Matthew 21:31b: "The tax
collectors and harlots enter into the kingdom of God before
you." Here a basic question regarding existence in the present
is raised by reference to the eschatological event of the entry
of the kingdom of God into the world. But since the stress
in this saying does not fall upon the futurity, but rather upon
the fact of this event, it becomes evident that the point of
such a statement is that there is an existence to be received
from God that finds no support from this present evil
world. The world of the Jews of Jesus' time proffered no hope
to the tax collectors and harlots, but Jesus saw that by the
very fact that they were rejected by this world, they were
closer to receiving life from God than were the self-righteous
Jews.

Such a saying contains a dialectical understanding of existence that has a real parallel to the *kerygma* of the early

church. The point of the central assertion of the *kerygma*, that Jesus died and rose again (I Cor. 15:3-5), is not that certain events occurred in the past, but in the meaning that this has for the individual. Its point is that of "dying and rising with Christ," for Paul often used such language to describe the life he had come to live since hearing the Gospel (e.g., II Cor. 1:9; 6:8-10). Through the *kerygma* Paul had come to live from God rather than from the world.

Thus there is a real parallel between the essence of Easter faith and the deep intentions of the Jesus of history. However, the words of Jesus in the Gospels that express this deep intention cannot stem from the church's Easter faith, for the diversity of the forms expressing Jesus' deep intentions contrast sharply with the stylized language the church used to express its faith. It spoke simply of dying and rising with Christ, whereas Jesus indicated his deep intention in language ranging all the way from "He that exalts himself shall be abased" to "Blessed are the poor, for theirs is the kingdom of God." Therefore, since such language in the Gospels is not found in the language of the church, it stems from Jesus himself and not from the early church.

This method of argumentation is that of the positivistic historiography, which is based on the principle of analogy. Since the diversity of Jesus' language finds no analogy in the church, it therefore does not stem from the church but from Jesus himself. But true to the more recent insights of historiography, Robinson is not content simply to find some words that trace back to Jesus himself; he must have an encounter with the man whose deep intention gave rise to these words. Robinson sees from these statements of Jesus an indication of his deep intention to break with the present evil age and to live only for God. "The cross," says Robinson,

> must be interpreted as Jesus' climactic actualization of his message, "Repent, for God's reign is near." For this message means a radical break with the present evil aeon, which in turn involves the acceptance of one's own death to and in this world (89).

133

Hence one encounters in the historical Jesus one who accepted his own death to the world in order to live from God, who is transcendent to this world. From a mere historical encounter one may conclude, as did some of Jesus' contemporaries, that he was insane or possessed with a demon (Mark 3:22, 29). But faith convinces one that in Jesus' death there is a "transcendence" that is "the eschatological saving event in history" (89).

Faith finds no legitimization for itself and the *kerygma* in the encounter that it can have with the historical Jesus (77), for faith is weakened by any support that stems from "this present evil aeon" (44). For centuries faith in Jesus has been able to exist without any of the knowledge of the historical Jesus which modern historiography now provides us. But now for the first time after nearly 2,000 years there is historical knowledge about Jesus.

> These two avenues of access to the same person create a situation which has not existed in the church since the time of the original disciples, who had both their Easter faith and their factual memory of Jesus. They responded to this situation by intuitively explicating their memory until they found in it the *kerygma,* i.e., by "kerygmatizing" their memory (86).

Therefore, since the church now finds itself in possession of two avenues of knowledge to the same person, it must do as the original disciples and assimilate this knowledge into the *kerygma* and faith, for otherwise it will lay itself open to the charge that the Jesus it preaches and believes is a myth.

This is the way, then, that Robinson carries out his program of finding that which stems from Jesus himself and is assimilable to the *kerygma,* which is demythologized in the Bultmannian fashion. Since the essential thing in such a *kerygma* is a life that finds its support not in the world but in God, Robinson therefore singles out something in the life of Jesus for which the argument can be made that it stems from him and is also compatible with the *kerygma.* Robinson's "prior understanding" precludes his singling out something unique about the person of Jesus himself, even though the

New Testament *kerygma* stresses the function of Jesus to the extent of declaring that he "delivers us from this present evil age" (Gal. 1:4) and mediates eternal life from God (Rom. 6:23). If Robinson were open to what history has to say, he could see, if the facts warranted it, that the essence of Christian proclamation must always be Jesus himself. But with his prior understanding, he is not able "to suspend his own answers to history" sufficiently to hear such facts even if they did exist. With such an a priori, he finds it difficult to hear anything really new in his attempt to encounter Jesus. All he does is come up with a Jesus who talks suspiciously like a modern existentialist of the early Heidegger stripe.

> *Note.* Heinrich Ott has created some stir in the Bultmannian school by pointing out the implications for theology in Martin Heidegger's change of emphasis in recent years. Robinson himself, in the first volume of *New Frontiers in Theology*, has summarized the theological debate that Ott has initiated.[23] Robinson shows how Ott has attempted to "maintain that a position built upon the later Heidegger could lay claim to the early Heidegger with more appropriateness than can Bultmannian theology" (17). Whereas the earlier Heidegger emphasized the nothingness and the consequent vague sense of dread that surrounds the individual so that his only recourse is to will to live a truly authentic existence, Heidegger now emphasizes the marvel that one does indeed exist so that he can feel anxious in the midst of nothingness. In the later Heidegger, "Nothing, by pointing to the contingency of the beings, draws our attention to their being, so that the possibility of their not being functions as a veil through which we catch the surprising fact that they are" (19). Thus, unlike Descartes, who came to the knowledge of the beingness of the world around him by first establishing his own existence (*Cogito, ergo sum*), Heidegger has come to see first an ultimate being from which individual existences derive, and has thus rooted "objective thought in something more primal than a metaphysically understood subject" (21). A metaphysics that begins with Descartes "investigates beings in the light of their being. But it does not directly face the light itself [as the later Heidegger's thought enables one to do]" (21). Furthermore, the older metaphysics regards ultimate being as

[23] J. Robinson, "The German Discussion of the Later Heidegger," *The Later Heidegger and Theology*, pp. 3-76.

static, whereas the new Heidegger opens the door to being confronted with being as "happening." This understanding of being corresponds to the essential nature of language, whose words (as Heidegger's study of ancient etymological origins shows) arise from a confrontation with life, rather than from a detached contemplation of it. Hence, for Heidegger, "being is an occurrence of unveiling, a fate-laden happening upon thought" (40).

In such an approach, God can be the "fate-laden happening" that confronts one and gives rise to thought. Ott has followed out Heidegger's opening up of the possibility of God as the source of all beings. Thus there is "some material justification of Ott's present position as Barth's successor" (34), for Barth, too, makes his starting point in God.

On the other hand, Ott has been generally rejected by the Bultmannians (31). Bultmann fitted God into the earlier Heidegger as that which stands wholly over against the nothingness of the world and, without partaking of the world in any way as an objective entity, calls a man to authentic existence in the world. Fitting God into the earlier Heidegger, Bultmann avoided thinking of him as an object who confronts man like other objects in the world, but in the later Heidegger, God is not totally unlike the beings which confront man, for he is the source of their being. Consequently, both the later Heidegger and Ott are rejected by the Bultmannians.

Robinson himself cannot follow Ott because, remaining loyal to Bultmann's unbridgeable gulf between knowledge of objective things in this world and knowledge of authentic living brought to pass in encounter, he finds Ott deficient in his failure to recognize that "lectures and publications are not a witness in which a theologian presents himself as a believer, but are more nearly an 'unbelieving' thought-process of an objectifying kind" (48). "It would," concludes Robinson, "be regressing into metaphysical thinking to theologize about Heidegger's ontological difference between being and beings" (76).

II. The New Quest in the Barthian Tradition

The threat that Christianity could be termed nothing more than a myth was also felt by at least one adherent to the Barthian tradition. In the past Hermann Diem has affirmed Barth's hermeneutical circle in which one must interpret the

Bible only from the vantage point of the proclamation of the Word. Even down to the most recent edition of the second volume of his theology, Diem has continued to stress this hermeneutic. Here he declared that the historico-critical method was to be carried on only as the Scriptures are acknowledged to be a reflection of the history of Jesus Christ's own self-proclamation.[24] Consequently, if an historian comes to the text without acknowledging this starting point, "there remains nothing else for him to do but once again to become side-tracked in the pursuit of the historical Jesus, whose figure lies concealed behind Gospel proclamation" (142).

But since 1955, when he wrote these words, he has undergone a change of thinking which came to expression on the occasion of his inauguration as professor of theology at Tübingen in 1957.[25] At that time Diem declared that there must be recourse to the historical method in order to avoid a negative answer to the question of the continuity between the earthly Jesus and the Christ proclaimed after Easter. "With a negative reply to the historical question of truth—that is, with a historical proof of the discontinuity in the kerygmatic history—the theological question would already be negatively prejudiced, since it would then at least be doubtful whether the Christ who encounters us in the kerygmatic history is the earthly Jesus or only a myth" (205).

To preclude this negative answer, Diem appealed to H. E. Tödt's Heidelberg dissertation, *Der Menschensohn in der synoptischen Tradition* (1959). Todt argued that the tradition in which Jesus promised that those who confessed him before men, the Son of Man would confess before the angels of God (Luke 12:8-9), was a pure tradition from Jesus himself. The evidence of its purity is that it does not exclude all ambiguity over the question of whether Jesus called himself the Son of Man. Diem asserted that if this ambiguity were not present, and if Jesus here, as in other passages, had called

[24] H. Diem, *Dogmatics*, p. 146f.
[25] H. Diem, "The Earthly Jesus and the Christ of Faith," *Kerygma and History*, pp. 197-211.

himself the Son of Man, then this, like the other sayings, would simply be charged off to the Easter faith of the church, "which expressed this connection between the blessing of salvation and the Bringer of salvation by putting into the mouth of the earthly Jesus the self-designation Son of Man" (208). If the Easter faith of the early church had fully exercised itself in handling the tradition of Luke 12:8-9, then it would have effected an identification between Jesus and the Son of Man in this passage. Since it does not, this tradition stems back to Jesus himself.

Nevertheless, even though Jesus does not clearly identify himself as the Son of Man in this passage, yet his statement does carry with it an unmistakable claim to exaltedness, for Jesus asserted that confessing him before men was the condition upon which the Son of Man would confess one before God. While the Easter faith of the church did not change this statement as fully as it might, yet it passed it on as a part of the tradition of faith because it did express the greatness of Jesus that faith acknowledged. The conviction that salvation stemmed from the person of Jesus himself came from the event of the resurrection, in which there was "God's own witness to Jesus by his raising Jesus from the dead" (209).

This is the manner, then, in which Diem used the historical method to show that it opened up the possibility of a connection between the earthly Jesus and the Christ of faith, for the exalted way in which the earthly Jesus spoke of himself parallels the exaltation of the Christ of faith. Therefore the Christ of faith does not have to be charged with being a myth. However, remaining true to the essential concept of Dialectical Theology that revelation, while occurring in history, finds no support from it, Diem declared that it was not possible on the basis of historical research to say definitely that there is continuity between the earthly Jesus and the Christ of faith.

> Not even the most positive results of historical research concerning that continuity could guarantee to us that [Jesus] really will or actually must encounter us here [in the realm of his-

torical research]. . . . This encounter can only come about when the church simply dares to preach the Christ of the Scriptures in order that he may demonstrate himself to be the living and present Christ (211).

Because of his adherence to the Barthian tradition, which, in distinction from Bultmann, lays emphasis upon the person of Christ and his resurrection, Diem finds the parallel between the earthly Jesus and the Christ of faith in the exaltedness of the person of Jesus. This is quite a contrast to Robinson and Fuchs, who found the parallel to exist between the faith Jesus had and the faith the church had. Käsemann and Bornkamm stand somewhere between these two emphases, for while neither pointed explicitly to the exaltedness of the person of Jesus, both implied this by speaking of the unequalled authority implicit in Jesus' teaching (Käsemann) and in the "immediate present" of his whole manner of life (Bornkamm). But to the extent that the new quest of the historical Jesus focuses attention upon the thinking of Jesus rather than upon the uniqueness of his person, this new quest is confronted with the problem of how the early church came to preach not the thinking but the person of Jesus as the center of its message. This difficulty is in no wise lessened by the implication, noticeable particularly in Fuchs and Robinson, that Easter faith arose from the impact upon the disciples of Jesus' purpose to live for God at all costs, even death. If this was the epitome of the impression Jesus made on them, why did they not proclaim him as an example instead of a Saviour? The best answer the Bultmannian tradition can give is that of Bultmann himself, who declares that the decision Jesus demanded men to make concerning himself as the bearer of the Word of God implied a Christology which his followers made explicit after Easter.[26] But this is approaching the point of saying that the historical Jesus was one who considered himself as having supreme authority. Diem goes all the way and asserts that the historical Jesus had an exalted view of his own person and

[26] R. Bultmann, *Das Verhältnis der urchristlichen Christusbotschaft zum historischen Jesus*, p. 16.

that herein lies the parallel that must exist between the Christ of faith and the historical Jesus in order for Easter faith to be delivered from the threat of being a myth. Consistent with his emphasis upon the exaltedness of the person of Jesus both in history and in faith, Diem does not hesitate to assert that God raised Jesus from the dead. Thus, of the five proponents of the new quest who have been considered, Diem is the most consistent, for he sees the historical Jesus as unique and as risen.

But Diem is still confronted with one problem. He has done nothing more than show that Christianity does not have to be a myth. On the basis of his system, it could still be one. The only way he could avoid this possibility would be to verify the resurrection historically. But this is impossible, for a Barthian cannot consider this event as accessible to historical verification. Thus it is the question of whether Jesus rose from the dead or not that determines whether he really is a living Saviour or whether Christianity is just wishful thinking.

The new quest, however, does not concentrate its attention upon the resurrection. Instead, regarding the resurrection as a matter that can only be known by faith, it seeks to find elements in the Gospel tradition that have not been fully assimilated by this faith. To the extent that they are not assimilated by faith, they point to Jesus as he really was. But these elements must not be irrelevant or contrary to Easter faith, for the whole purpose of the new quest, in distinction from the old, is to demonstrate a parallel between the Jesus of history and Easter faith, so that it cannot be said that faith must be a myth.

Thus the new quest must limit itself to elements of tradition that play the dual role of being both continuous and discontinuous with faith. Robinson and Fuchs manage this by distinguishing between a tradition's style, which is discontinuous with faith, and the content of it, which is continuous. Käsemann finds a parallel in Jesus' unequalled claim to authority, but argues for its discontinuity in that it could derogate John the Baptist and be unlike both Hellenism and Judaism.

Diem found continuity in the exalted regard Jesus had for himself, but discontinuity in that he did not go so far as to identify himself with the Son of Man. Bornkamm cited Jesus' quality of "immediate present" as that which was germane to Easter faith, but was so unique that it could not have been the product of Easter faith. But to the extent that such elements of the tradition are discontinuous with Easter faith, they dodge the central issue of Christianity, which, as Form Criticism has shown, is Easter faith. Consequently, the new quest does not bridge Lessing's ugly ditch, for Easter faith must stand without any support in history.

Furthermore, since in the new quest faith exists independently of historical knowledge and is the motive for carrying out the new quest, it constitutes the norm for determining whether historical findings are useful or unimportant. The Bultmannian tradition singles out the faith and thinking of the historical Jesus, while Diem, with his Barthian predispositions, singles out a tradition which stresses Jesus' exaltedness. The results of this quest accord so well with the varieties of Easter faith of the "new questers" that there is more of a display of their faith than there is of what was ultimately important about Jesus.

III. Barth's and Bultmann's Attitudes toward the New Quest

Barth has bluntly refused to have anything to do with the new quest: "To my amazement," he declared, "the New Testament men have armed themselves with swords and staves and once again undertaken the search for the 'historical Jesus' —a search in which I now as before prefer not to participate."[27] Thus Barth has remained steadfast in his conviction that the only Jesus who could be known in the Gospels is the resurrected Jesus and, since the resurrection is not accessible by historical research, the new quest is completely futile.

[27] K. Barth, "How My Mind Has Changed," *The Christian Century*, 77 (1960), 75.

Rudolf Bultmann has also remained unmoved by the new quest, although he has taken the pains to give an account of his reasons,[28] presumably because his followers have been so prominent in it. Bultmann acknowledges that a number of things about the historical Jesus can be known: that he was confident that he was commissioned by God as a prophet to preach the will of God and invite men to ready themselves for the kingdom of God, that he fellowshipped with men and women of lowly estate, and that he was an exorcist. However, the *kerygma* was not interested in such matters. It proclaimed Jesus Christ as crucified and risen. Such proclamation was also the purpose of the Gospels, and when they set forth certain details regarding the historical Jesus, they did so only because they wanted to emphasize the fact (the *Dass*) of Jesus, without which there could have been no proclamation of Jesus as crucified and risen. But it is impossible to go beyond this *Dass* and determine from the Gospels any *Was* concerning Jesus that is relevant for the *kerygma*. It is impossible to discover from the Gospels why Jesus went to the cross. The Gospels' representation of Jesus as predicting his own death and going to Jerusalem for that purpose are *vaticinia ex eventu* (prophecies after the event), and thus express only the church's Easter faith. "Everything is guesswork" (12) when it comes to understanding why Jesus went to the cross. To try to find any historical support for the preaching of the cross in the historical Jesus is impossible.

Robinson, it will be remembered, had declared that it was absolutely necessary to uncover the deep intentions of Jesus and show that these were parallel to the *kerygma*, or else the *kerygma* would be a myth. Concerning the preaching of the cross he said that "it would none the less be a purely mythological *kerygma*—i.e., a *kerygma* speaking of a selfhood which never existed—if Jesus' death were looked upon only as . . . accidental or involuntary, i.e., as completely distinct from his existential selfhood."[29] But in replying to Bultmann's claim

[28] Bultmann, *Das Verhältnis der urchristlichen Christusbotschaft zum historischen Jesus.*

[29] Robinson, *A New Quest of the Historical Jesus*, p. 89.

that the Gospels are so interwoven with Easter faith that it is impossible to determine whether Jesus' deep intentions led him to the cross, Robinson seems to have weakened his stand somewhat. In the above quotation he had excluded the possibility that Jesus' death was "completely distinct" from his deep intentions. But now he stops short of saying that the cross was a result of these intentions:

> It is not a matter of how Jesus did or did not interpret what was going on in his final twenty-four hours; it is not a matter of his psychological processes, his stream of consciousness, at any given time. It is a matter of the emergence from Jesus of Nazareth of an understanding of existence consisting in the renunciation of the present evil aeon. . . .[30]

However, Robinson still does not go as far as Bultmann and say that, in addition to knowing nothing about the psychological processes of Jesus in the last twenty-four hours before the cross, we know nothing about his deep intentions throughout his entire ministry. Robinson believes that the basic motive of Jesus—to renounce all the support of this present evil world and live only for God—is historically verified. And while Robinson cannot say that it was this purpose that led him to die on the cross, he insists that because his whole life was one of dying daily to the world and bearing his cross, the preaching of the cross, while it has no historical parallel in the actual death of Jesus, has one in his life.

Two things should be noted from Robinson's interpretation. The New Testament insists that Jesus' death on the cross and not his "dying daily" is the most important thing about Jesus. This is borne out both by the fact that the Gospels themselves devote such a disproportionately large space to the events of the last week, and that the epistles, in speaking of Jesus, stress his death (as well as his resurrection, of course) to the almost complete exclusion of his life. Is not, therefore, Robinson's reinterpretation of the New Testament so radical as to lay himself open to the charge that his interpretation is a myth,

[30] J. Robinson, "The Recent Debate on the 'New Quest,'" *The Journal of Bible and Religion*, 30 (1962), 202.

not because he cannot find any basis for it in history, but because it breaks so radically from the primitive faith that one wonders whether it should be considered a continuation of it? Secondly, can he be so sure that the basis which he finds for authentic living in the Jesus of history is really there in the Gospels as something which cannot be explained by the Easter faith of the church? Bultmann declares that Easter faith so pervades the Gospels that it is impossible to see Jesus as distinct enough from it so that any parallel between him and Easter faith can be demonstrated.

Hence it becomes clear that only two alternatives remain open: either acknowledge that history offers no check against saying that Easter faith is a myth, or turn the searchlight of historical investigation on the center of Easter faith, on the resurrection of Jesus itself, and see if there is any possibility of verifying it historically. If the resurrection of Jesus could be established, then the church's Easter faith would be no vain thing. Furthermore, the earthly Jesus that this faith portrayed when it wrote the Gospels would find confirmation in the resurrection, for his Messianic consciousness, his miracles, his sinlessness, and his prediction that he would die and rise again would all be analogous to it. One could then accept the Gospel accounts of why Jesus went to the cross, and thus the preaching of the cross would not be a myth. Whatever discontinuities might exist between Easter faith and the Gospels would present no difficulty, for these would merely show that the Jesus pictured by the Gospels was not simply projected from the fact that he rose but did indeed derive from the apostles' memory of him.

Thus, whereas the new quest is hard to put to explain the Easter faith of the Gospels, the resurrection, if verified, would not only establish Easter faith but also make possible the acceptance of the Gospels as proper sources for the knowledge of the historical Jesus. The remaining chapters will therefore concern themselves with the historicity of the resurrection of Jesus, to see if there is any possibility of its being historically verified.

CHAPTER SIX

The Resurrection and Historical Reasoning

IF THE OUTCOME OF THE NEW QUEST OF THE HISTORICAL JESUS makes it imperative to face squarely the question of whether the resurrection can be verified historically, does contemporary thinking regarding the resurrection offer any possibility of doing this? A survey of the treatment of the resurrection of Jesus in recent years reveals some who by no means deny the historicity of the resurrection, but are so concerned with its theological aspect that they have very little to say about how the resurrection can be known as an historical event. Books which fall into this category are Floyd Filson, *Jesus Christ the Risen Lord* (1956), G. D. Yarnold, *Risen Indeed* (1959), Karl H. Rengstorf, *Die Auferstehung Jesu* (1960), and H. A. Williams, *Jesus and the Resurrection* (1961). A consideration of such books would not be germane to the purpose of this chapter. Neither will any help in solving the question of whether the resurrection of Jesus can be historically verified come from one like Paul Tillich, who clearly declares that Jesus himself did not rise from the dead. In a way reminiscent of the thinking of Schleiermacher and Hegel in the last century and Bultmann in the present century, Tillich asserts that the resurrection is nothing more than the awakening in the minds of the disciples after Jesus' death of the "New Being" that they had seen with such transparency in Jesus before his death. "[The negativity which is overcome in the resurrection of Jesus] is not," insists Tillich, "the death of an individual man. . . . Therefore the revival of an individual man or his reappearance as a spirit cannot be the event of the resurrection."[1]

The concern of this chapter is to consider those who say that Jesus did rise from the dead and make some attempt to relate their knowledge of this historical event to the question of verification by the historical method. A survey of the way in which this subject is handled on the contemporary scene reveals that knowledge of the resurrection can relate itself to the historical method in one of three ways. There are those who say that such knowledge is to be gained only by faith and does not depend in any way upon knowledge gained by the historical method. Others affirm that one aspect of their knowledge of the resurrection depends upon historical reasoning, while another aspect is known simply by faith itself apart from such reasoning. Then there is the new theological movement, headed by a young German theologian named Wolfhart Pannenberg, which declares that faith in the resurrection is only possible through a knowledge that is gained wholly by the historical method. Naturally, Pannenberg's thinking will be of the utmost interest, because the history of the debate that has continued since the Enlightenment regarding the historical foundations of Christianity seems to indicate that the charge that Christianity is a myth cannot be excluded unless the resurrection can receive historical verification. However, it is also instructive to see how successful those who represent the other two alternatives are in making faith either wholly or partially independent of historical knowledge.

I. Attempts to Sustain Knowledge of the Resurrection Apart from Historical Reasoning

While the representatives of this group deny that knowledge of the resurrection gained by the historical method can provide any positive basis for faith, yet each must make some judgment regarding the New Testament's resurrection nar-

[1] P. Tillich, *Systematic Theology*, II, 156.

ratives and show how an historical consideration of these narratives relates to one's faith.

A. Karl Barth

Chapter IV summarized the thinking of Karl Barth on the matter of Easter faith and history up through the publication of IV/1 of the *Church Dogmatics* in 1952. But since 1952, and especially with the publication of IV/2 in 1955, Barth has paid special attention to the question of the historicity of Jesus and the resurrection. Otto Weber, who has rendered great service to the church by his synopses of the *Church Dogmatics*, has remarked, "In no volume of the *Church Dogmatics* is the subject of history so often and forcefully presented as in IV/2."[2]

Barth's purpose in IV/2 was to expound the doctrine of reconciliation. Jesus has reconciled man both by his humiliation and his exaltation. In Christ's humiliation there was the dethronement of man's pride, for Jesus, in his death upon the cross, suffered God's punishment for man's presumption to exalt himself. In his exaltation, Jesus lifted man up from the degradation of his sins so that man might stand as reconciled before God. Knowledge of this reconciliation is imparted whenever Christ reveals himself, but it is in the historical incarnation of Jesus that this reconciliation was actually effected. In particular, it was during the forty days between his resurrection and ascension that the revelation of man as reconciled in Christ became fully manifest, for this was the time when Jesus, who had died for men, nevertheless rose again and appeared to them and thus made it evident that God was indeed gracious to them and that they were reconciled. Hence for Barth, the forty days when the risen Jesus revealed himself to his disciples is the center of revelation upon which the whole Christian message rests.

Barth does not hesitate to stress the historicity of these appearances. The resurrection

[2] O. Weber, *Karl Barths kirchliche Dogmatik*, p. 243.

is an event within the world, in time and space. It, too, takes place in the body. . . . It is an event which involves a definite seeing with the eyes and hearing with the ears and handling with the hands. . . . The event is not perhaps "historical" [*historisch*] in the modern sense but it is fixed and characterized as something that actually happened among men like other events and was experienced and later attested by them (IV/2, 143).

The way in which this event falls short of being *historisch* (that is, its knowledge being attainable by the historical method) is that one cannot argue back from the apostles' attestation of the resurrection appearances to the fact of them and thus to the reconciliation of God to men in Jesus Christ. Since the men who witnessed the resurrection were enabled to do so by a special electing work of God, "there can be no demonstration of the event that has apologetic value, and no such demonstration is attempted [in the recounting of the appearances] in I Cor. 15" (IV/2, 143). Any attempt to know the incidental facts of the resurrection that lie behind the New Testament texts—the empty tomb, the dead Jesus becoming alive, and the details of the appearances—"can only mean the leading away into a Babylonian captivity in which there is no attestation of this event [of the resurrection as reconciliation] and that can have nothing to do with the knowledge of this event" (IV/2, 149f.).

Knowledge of the resurrection does not come by way of the historical method, but rather by a special work of God. "Because the event [of revelation centering in the resurrection] takes place in the majesty of the will and act of God, the knowledge of it cannot derive from the knowing man, but only from the one who is revealed in it" (IV/2, 149). The only way in which a study of the New Testament resurrection accounts can be carried on profitably is when the resurrection event, to which the New Testament texts give witness, is an actual reality to the interpreter. He must himself have come to understand God's grace and love in Christ. "If painstaking investigation is to be meaningful as an introduction, the 'historical' element [*das 'Historische'*] to which investigation addresses itself will have to be the attestation of this event [*stattfindende Bezeugung dieses Ereignisses sein müssen*— lit., will have to be the presently occurring attestation of this event] . . ." (IV/2, 149). It is this presently enjoyed knowledge of Christ that thus causes the New Testament accounts of the resurrection to come to life and to fulfill their function of witnessing to the resurrection event in all of its revelational fullness. It is this immediate revelation of Christ, therefore, that provides the real depth of meaning and understanding for the New Testament witness of the resurrection. Historical investigation of the text is to be carried out, but it is only helpful when it is carried out under the knowledge of God's reconciling love and grace in Christ. Hence by itself historical investigation provides no basis for faith.

The question then arises, What is the purpose of the apostolic witness? Barth replies, "Because the resurrection 'is an event that took place for the apostles in their encounter with the living Christ, the knowledge of it will necessarily be ordered by their witness and continually oriented by it" (IV/2, 149). But if our investigation of the New Testament witness is to be undertaken only after we have a knowledge of Christ as the risen reconciler, how can this witness exercise any independent control of our knowledge of the resurrection? For this witness to control our knowledge of Christ, it must stand by itself over against one's immediate knowledge of Christ. This apostolic witness would then have to be an intermediate source of knowledge of the resurrection. Such knowledge would come, like that of other historical events, through a witness and could only be known by the historical method. The historical method, then, would not only control our knowledge of the apostolic witness but would control our immediate knowledge of the risen Christ, for according to Barth, this is what the apostolic witness should do. Thus his statement about the control the apostolic witness should exercise clashes with his assertion that knowledge of the resurrected Christ comes *only* from Christ himself.

Therefore it seems that Barth runs into difficulty in trying to derive knowledge of the resurrection as an historical event only from an immediate work of Jesus Christ. The apostolic witness is a fact of history, and faith must ever render respect to it. So long as the resurrection appearances led to the historical event of the apostolic witness to this fact, it is impossible to ignore this intermediate witness and declare that knowledge of the resurrection comes only from an immediate revelation of Christ himself. Thus in connection with the question of the apostolic witness, Barth finds it necessary to make a statement that opens the door to knowledge of the resurrection gained by the historical method. Hence there remains in Barth an unreconciled tension between faith and the historical method.

B. Hans Grass

In 1956 Hans Grass, professor of systematic theology at the University of Marburg, published a 300-page book on the resurrection, *Ostergeschehen und Osterberichte*,[3] in which he, like Barth, declares that historical reason gives precisely no aid to faith. But unlike Barth, Grass asserts that the manner in which Jesus appeared to his disciples was anything but palpable and tangible, and that therefore faith finds no support for its conviction regarding the resurrection by reasoning back from the apostolic witness to the resurrection itself. On the contrary, faith arises as Jesus makes himself immediately known to us today.

Though Grass regards the historical method as of no help for Easter faith, yet he has made an historical investigation of the resurrection. In the foreword he declares,

> Theology and, in particular, dogmatics cannot be carried out, in my opinion, without a continued taking into account of the findings and problems of historical investigation. The dualism between faith and knowledge, which has not only occurred inadvertently but is often justified theologically by an enthusiasm for faith, is very objectionable.

[3] Subsequent page references refer to the second edition, published in 1962. See Bibliography.

Thus Grass wants to give historical knowledge about the resurrection a full rein. However, as it turns out, faith still exists without any support whatsoever from this knowledge, because, in Grass' system of thought, the means by which the resurrected Jesus revealed himself both to the apostles and to us today is something so apart from the empirical world that it can be known only by faith and not by the historical method.

Consequently, he seeks to show that the New Testament references to the corporeality of Jesus' resurrection body are unhistorical. He argues that the Gospel accounts of the empty tomb are "legendary" (93), because as one compares the earlier with the later accounts one notes the growing tendency to try to give an apologetic for the reality of the resurrection appearances by showing them to be in ever closer connection with the empty tomb (86f.). The New Testament insistence upon the corporeality of Jesus' resurrection body can be explained as being borrowed from the Jewish concept of a resurrection of the flesh (266). Furthermore, the reference to Jesus' having risen on the "third day" came not because the tomb was found to be empty on that day but because "the early church, from the very first, must have been interested in determining when the resurrection had occurred after the death of Jesus" (128). Since Rabbinic exegesis understood the words of Hosea 6:2, "The third day he will raise us up," to mean that three days after the end of the world the resurrection of the dead would occur, it was easy for the church to understand that, three days after Jesus' death, his resurrection occurred (137).

But while Grass denies the historicity of all references to the corporeality of the resurrected Jesus, he still finds a kernel of historical truth in the record of the appearances of the risen Jesus. There is good historical evidence for at least the first two appearances—to Peter and to the twelve—which Paul mentions in I Corinthians 15:3-8. Grass argues that Paul must have received this tradition from the church in Damascus immediately after his conversion, and thus with this resurrection witness of Paul, "we come very near to the resurrection events themselves" (96). Grass reasons that these appearances must have taken place in Galilee rather than in Jerusalem, for there is every indication that the disciples fled home to Galilee with their hopes destroyed after the events of Good Friday (118). In the Galilean appearances Jesus established the apostles' faith once again and commissioned them to return to Jerusalem and preach. While the church was being built there, Jesus appeared to the 500 brethren and later to James, as Paul mentions in I Corinthians 15:6-7. Finally, he appeared to Paul on the Damascus road. Thus for Grass, all the history surrounding Easter hinges on the resurrection appearances. He declares, "A purely historical investigation of the New Testament traditions makes it evident, in my opinion, that the impulse that set the Easter history in motion was not the empty tomb, but the appearances" (119).

With Paul, however, these resurrection appearances came to an end. "Only the original witnesses shared in them" (279). Grass therefore affirms a period immediately following the resurrection when Jesus manifested himself to his disciples in a way that thereafter was never duplicated. During this period, however, Jesus did not have a "quasi-earthly existence" (229) which terminated at the ascension. Jesus' ascension and exaltation took place at the resurrection (230). The disciples did not witness the resurrection and exaltation, but came to "infer" (279) them from the spiritual appearances by which Jesus manifested himself to them. This inference was not made by anything palpable, such as touching his body and beholding the empty tomb. So impalpable were the resurrection appearances of Jesus that a "film camera" (229) could not have recorded them. The new body Jesus received at his resurrection was so spiritual and unlike the physical body he had during his earthly ministry that the remains of that body could still be in the tomb while Jesus manifested himself to his disciples in his new, "spiritual body"[4] (232). He did not manifest himself by means of a "corporeality coming into ap-

---

[4] *Sôma pneumatikón.* Cf. I Cor. 15:44.

pearance in this world" (32). Nevertheless, the appearance of Jesus to the disciples was so real and objective that they came to know with full certainty "the identity of the exalted Lord with the earthly and crucified person" (232). The apostles saw Jesus "face to face" (231).

But this period of such manifestations to men ended and has never recurred. Since then, Jesus Christ, the living and exalted Lord, has indeed manifested himself to men, but in a different way. Men have known him by way of personal encounter. There is a sense in which such encounters are appearances, but they are quite different from the appearances the apostles witnessed. Present-day "appearances" come on the occasion of the proclamation of the message of Christ, which traces back to the message of the apostles and to the unique manifestations of Christ that they witnessed. "Jesus himself reveals himself in the witness [of the church] as the Lord, by gaining power over the hearts of men through the word of his witnesses" (276). Though such a revelation does not involve seeing Jesus "face to face" so that one becomes, like the apostles, confronted with Jesus in his spiritual body, yet believers today infer the resurrection and exaltation of Jesus from these encounters. "The event of the resurrection, as the presupposition of the living presence of the Lord, can only be inferred. . . . The certainty of the Lord as living carries with it the certainty of his having become alive and of the divine origin of the reality" (279).

Only those who have experienced an "appearance" of Jesus can infer his resurrection. One cannot, for example, simply observe the remarkable change in the disciples from their despair on Good Friday to their boldness at Pentecost and infer that the risen Jesus must have appeared to them. One must have encountered Christ and thus be in a position to make a "theological consideration" of this remarkable change before one can see that only the resurrection appearances can explain it.

A theological consideration will satisfactorily demonstrate the shortcomings of all psychological and historical attempts to explain the appearances of the risen Jesus. It will show that between the condition of the apostles before Easter and their Easter faith there is a gap, which cannot be filled by any attempts to explain it that are immanental [*innerweltlichen*] . . . . The attempt to facilitate belief in the resurrection cannot be made by a reasoning that works along purportedly historical lines and appeals to psychology and logic (242).

According to Grass, faith finds its support solely in the risen Christ, whose manifestation to men in this world is not made via anything which pertains to this world. Historical investigation of the resurrection accounts should be carried on as far as they deal with matters that pertain to this world, for faith must never give the impression that it has no concern for historical knowledge. But historical investigation can never become the basis for a knowledge of the resurrection of Christ, for this would mean that the resurrection could be known by means of something within this world. Therefore, the power of the argument for the resurrection that comes from the radical change in the apostles between Good Friday and Pentecost is only felt by those who consider the argument from the vantage point of a "theological consideration." Powerful though this argument may be, it does not make it any easier for people to believe, for faith can only be effected by the person of Jesus himself through the witness of the church.

Indeed, the consideration of the apostles' change of behavior would not make it easier to believe in the resurrection if some immanental explanation for this change could be advanced. Not even a "theological consideration" would help one to believe the resurrection if the apostles' Easter faith could be accounted for immanentally, for how could a theological consideration claim that the apostles' faith was due to the resurrection if the evidence pointed to something in the world as its cause? But if no immanental explanation for the apostles' change can be adduced, then surely this is going to make faith in the resurrection easier than would be the case if there were some immanental explanation. If, indeed, this change can find no adequate explanation apart from the appearances of the resurrected Jesus, this fact is then patent, whether there is a "theological consideration" of it or not. If the facts do not warrant such a conclusion, then a theological consideration cannot make the facts lead to such a conclusion, and if the facts do warrant it, then at best a theological consideration will simply help a person to become willing to own up to the facts.

Since Grass asserts that the change in the apostles' behavior is impossible to explain immanentally, it follows that Easter faith can only be helped by this historical argument. If, as Grass affirms, Jesus appeared to certain men so that this knowledge of Jesus as risen reversed the course of their lives and, in turn, the course of history, then it is difficult to see why faith is not facilitated by looking at this momentous reversal and the fact that it could not be explained by anything immanental. Grass has tried very hard to remove all palpability from that which gives knowledge of the resurrection so that it might exist in a realm where it would be known only by faith and not by the historical method and reason. But in this he has been unsuccessful, for even though the resurrection made itself known by nothing palpable, yet the effects it produced were highly palpable. Historical reason is always working backwards from known effects to causes that can be inferred from these effects, and therefore, so long as the resurrection of Jesus produced palpable effects in history, the resurrection can be known by history, and Easter faith cannot avoid finding a support in historical reasoning.

Note. Grass acknowledges that his view of the resurrection is very similar to that of Emil Brunner.[5] While Brunner asserts the resurrection as a fact, he discredits anything in the Gospel records that would make it a "worldly-fact," such as the empty tomb (368). He stresses that Jesus appeared only to those who already had faith, so that there was nothing tangible in this world that produced faith in the resurrection. (He seems to overlook the fact, however, that Paul was not a believer when the risen Jesus appeared to him.) Consequently, our faith today that Jesus is risen is not dependent upon the

[5] E. Brunner, *The Christian Doctrine of Creation and Redemption: Dogmatics*, II, 366-372.

historical validity of the apostolic witness, for this would make our faith dependent upon a "worldly-fact." "Our faith is not based upon the record of [the apostles'] experiences of the resurrection. . . . Indeed, we might say: we would believe in him as the risen Lord, even if there were no narratives of the resurrection at all" (371). But like Grass, Brunner cannot, as a Christian theologian, cut himself completely adrift from the apostolic witness, and so he adds that resurrection narratives do indeed exist and that these, along with all the other Scriptures, are a witness to the person of Jesus Christ. We come to know Jesus through the occasion of this Scriptural witness: "Through [the Scriptural witness] Jesus authenticates himself to us as the Living and Present Lord" (371). But the question to be posed for Brunner, as well as for Grass and Barth, is that, if the apostolic witness is an historical fact which comes as a result of the resurrection appearances of Jesus, must it not provide some support for our knowledge of Jesus and be something more than just the occasion for this knowledge?

John Knox of Union Theological Seminary, New York City, occupies a position very like that of Grass.[6] He regards the statements in the Gospels concerning the empty tomb as the church's inference from the resurrection appearances (76). He also declares that the appearances did occur, but not in the sense of being observable (69). Even though he affirms that there could have been no church had there been no resurrection (60), yet he declares that this historical argument is meaningless to the world and useless to the church (66). For him it is faith that gives knowledge of the resurrection. Since the church has faith, it does not need any arguments to bolster its faith, and since the world does not have faith, historical arguments will be of no avail.

But unlike Grass, Knox does not differentiate between the appearances to the apostles and the manifestations that Jesus has made of himself to all subsequent Christians. One might conclude, therefore, that Christians have no need of the apostolic witness, since they have had a confrontation with Christ that is just as immediate as that of the apostles. But like Brunner, Knox finds it difficult to ignore the apostolic witness, and so he affirms that the church's memory of Jesus, which originated with the apostles, is indispensable. Yet why should this witness be indispensable if the essential knowledge of Christianity can be known immediately from Christ?

[6] J. Knox, *The Church and the Reality of Christ.*

The Resurrection and Historical Reasoning

C. Hans F. von Campenhausen

Campenhausen, a professor of ancient church history at Heidelberg, has made historical knowledge a bit more important for faith than did Grass, without making it any kind of support for faith. He begins his treatise on the Easter events[7] by declaring that his purpose is to get back to the historical kernel behind the Easter narrative, for such a result, "even for the theological understanding of the message of the resurrection, will not be altogether a matter of indifference" (8). He concludes his investigation by saying that he has shown that "there is no reason for a far-reaching skepticism regarding the relationship of the basic Easter events, when they are judged by an historical criterion" (54). In short, his position is that historical considerations, far from making faith impossible, open the door to faith, but he stops short of saying that they exert any pressure to go through this door.

His argument commences with a review of the historical evidence for the validity of the resurrection appearances in I Corinthians 15:5-8. He regards not only the appearances to Peter and to the apostolic band as having taken place in Galilee, but also those to the 500 brethren and to James. Unlike Grass, he believes that the Gospel of Mark gives an essentially historical picture in its report regarding the empty tomb.

Mark concludes with the statement of 16:8 in which it is declared that the women left the empty tomb without obeying the angel's command to tell the disciples to meet Jesus in Galilee. What was the author's reason for concluding his book with such a remarkable and unlikely statement? Campenhausen finds this in Matthew 28:11-15, which indicates that the Jews, during the rise of the early church, charged that the disciples had stolen Jesus' body in order to support their claim that he had risen. Mark 16:8 was written as an apologetical device to answer this charge. Mark 15:47 shows that only

[7] H. von Campenhausen, *Der Ablauf der Osterereignisse und das leere Grab.*

157

Mary Magdalene and Mary the mother of Jesus, and not the disciples, saw where Jesus was buried. Mark 16:8 climaxes this theme by asserting that it was only these women who knew about the empty tomb and that they did not inform the disciples of this fact. Thus these last verses in Mark reply to the Jewish charge in that they relieve the disciples of all suspicion by showing that they had no knowledge of the empty tomb, and at the same time affirm that the tomb was empty.

Indeed, there are some things about Mark 15:47—16:8 which argue against its historicity. In addition to this apologetical motif, there is the inclusion of the purely legendary idea of the angel's presence at the tomb. However, there are greater evidences for its basic historicity: the women are specifically named, the report is brief and factual, and the author even goes so far as to base his case upon the report of women, who in that culture were regarded as unfit witnesses (41). Furthermore, there are certain considerations which lead to the conclusion that the tomb where Jesus was laid was indeed empty. The most satisfactory explanation for the New Testament emphasis upon "the third day" is not the citation of an obscure passage in Hosea 6:2, but rather that Jesus' tomb was really found to be empty on that day. Then, too, it is impossible to suppose that the church was not interested in the tomb of Jesus when it believed and preached that he was risen. The apologetical attempt of Matthew to refute unworthy explanations for its emptiness demonstrates this concern. Therefore Campenhausen argues that an investigation of the tomb of Jesus was made from the very first. Concerning the results of such an interpretation, Campenhausen concludes,

> In all probability, the tomb showed itself to be empty, and if we do not want to explain everything in terms of the contemporary Jewish assertions of fraud and humbug, there is no reason why the discovery of this tomb did not take place through the persons and at the time given to us by [Mark]. All other [hypotheses for explaining the empty tomb] are uncontrollable (42).

It should be observed that Campenhausen, in making this

assertion, is not going so far as to say that the empty tomb, discovered on the third day, could only be explained supernaturally by the resurrection of Christ. He is simply saying that a purely historical consideration of the facts leads to the conclusion that the women discovered that Jesus' tomb was empty on the third day. Other explanations of Mark's report of an empty tomb may be advanced, but the difficulty with these is that they are "uncontrollable." By this Campenhausen means that the historical data do not force one to say that the disciples stole the body of Jesus or that the grave was changed between Good Friday and Easter Sunday so that the women went to the wrong tomb. Those propounding such theories do so largely because they *want* to deny the resurrection in some way. If there were good historical arguments for these ways of denying the reality of the empty tomb, it would mean that one would be forced to admit that history argued against faith. However, history simply shows that the tomb was empty on Easter morning. Hence one can believe that the explanation for this is that Jesus rose from the dead, but one does not have to accept this explanation any more than one has to accept the decision of unbelief that the report of the empty tomb in the Gospels is ultimately a deception or a delusion.

Having thus established that the tomb in which Jesus was laid had become empty, Campenhausen is then able to commence his reconstruction of the Easter events. There are several reasons why he believes that the women did (contrary to Mark 16:8) report their discovery to the disciples. Since 16:8 was written for an apologetical purpose, its historicity is called in question. Then, too, it is unlikely that the women would remain silent about their discovery. Thus, unlike Grass, who declared that the appearances in Galilee were responsible for the subsequent events in the post-Easter history, Campenhausen asserts, "The decisive impulse, which set the subsequent course of events in motion, was the discovery of the empty tomb" (50).

But in order to make this discovery so basic to the subsequent events, Campenhausen must explain why the apostles would remain in Jerusalem after Good Friday and not flee to

Galilee as Grass and many others have supposed. Campenhausen declares that the theory of the immediate flight to
Galilee is a "legend of modern criticism" (44) that is to be
discarded because all the Gospels teach that the disciples
remained in Jerusalem, and because there are good psychological reasons for their remaining there. Contrary to the time-
worn assumption that the disciples, after the death of Jesus,
were sunk in despair, Campenhausen asserts that even as early
as the Last Supper they had begun to become reconciled to
the fact that Jesus was going to die, because they saw that he
was willing it upon himself (46). Furthermore, the tears
Peter shed after his denial of Jesus were not those of agoniz-
ing remorse, because the look Jesus gave him was not one of
condemnation but of compassion. Then Campenhausen reasons that after Jesus' death the disciples, under Peter's leadership and deriving strength from the encouragement Peter
had received, had cheered each other up as they had talked
things over (46ff.). Therefore, by the time they had received
the women's report of the empty tomb, they were already so
reconciled to what had transpired that this report was all that
was needed to bring them to the decision to make an orderly
and deliberate journey back to Galilee, where they had walked
with Jesus.

The reason Campenhausen thus replaces the dark outlines
in which the disciples' state of mind is usually described is
that he wants to avoid allowing such evidences of the resurrection as the empty tomb and the appearances to produce
a radical change in the disciples' outlook and behavior:

> This somber picture of their disillusionment provides the
> welcome foil for a sudden, miraculous, and liberating turn [in
> the disciples' outlook], which could only be caused through an
> encounter with the risen Lord himself, an event that was com-
> pletely unexplainable [in terms of ordinary causes], and which,
> though completely unexpected from a psychological standpoint,
> had nevertheless entered into their experience (45).

Campenhausen avoids such a reconstruction because its explanation would necessitate a supernatural intervention. He

cannot have the disciples making a panicky flight to Galilee, for then there would be no trend in their psychological state that could account for the appearances. Consequently, the appearances could only be explained supernaturally, and thus history would support a knowledge of the resurrection. In order to keep faith based on an immediate working of God and yet compatible with history, Campenhausen explains the course of events between the Last Supper and the preaching of the disciples at Jerusalem as being motivated by gradual encouragements which could be explained either naturally or supernaturally. There is the reconciliation at the Last Supper to the fact that Jesus must die, Jesus' look of love at Peter, who had denied him, mutual encouragement as they talk with one another after Jesus' death, the women's report of an empty tomb, and then the trip to Galilee, which helps shake off the sorrow of Jerusalem and brings them back to their accustomed environs. Then come the appearances in Galilee, which, building on a level of encouragement that was now much higher than at the time of Jesus' death, provide just that increment of courage to motivate the disciples to return to Jerusalem to preach (50f.).

It is through faith and an immediate working of God rather than through historical reasoning that Campenhausen himself believes in the resurrection appearances and the empty tomb as being the result of the resurrection of Jesus.

> The dry historical data, which we can ascertain, are by no means a sufficient reproduction of the fullness of the resurrection message of primitive Christianity. This message cannot be understood without auxiliary and illuminating interpretation of the events and without an unfolding of that power that makes a claim upon one and imparts to the historical events their full meaning. . . . The credibility of the Easter message does not rest upon strictly historical proofs, but rather . . . upon the existential verification of the Spirit. . . (52f.).

In order to keep his faith based solely upon a present and immediate working of God, Campenhausen has so reconstructed the course of Easter history that it would be equally possible whether the resurrection occurred as he believed or whether the empty tomb and the appearances actually came about through some ordinary cause. He concludes his booklet by saying, "The course of the Easter events, which we have reconstructed, are neither absolutely miraculous nor absolutely beyond the possibility of human experience. This reconstruction is very capable of being explained in a purely 'natural' way. . ." (54). The empty tomb could be explained by someone's shifting the body of Jesus to another tomb or by the disciples' stealing the body (52). The appearances could be understood "very well as simply 'visions' in the sense of hallucinations" (54, note). Hence history demands neither the supernatural nor the natural explanation. History, for Campenhausen, opens the door to faith, but it exerts no pressure towards the door. Thus, with his scheme for reconstructing Easter history, he has avoided the difficulty of Grass's position, in which there is a radical changeabout in the behavior of the disciples that ordinary explanations cannot account for, but that, nevertheless, does not facilitate faith. Campenhausen's system does not facilitate faith because there are no radical changeabouts. But it does show that history does not make faith impossible.

But it is this very strategy of Campenhausen's system which constitutes one of its chief difficulties. The normal procedure in carrying out the historical method would be to consider not only the fact of the empty tomb, but also, as much as the data will permit, the reason that it was empty. But Campenhausen does not want to go into the question of why the tomb was empty. Thus he declares that all the rationalistic attempts to explain the empty tomb were "uncontrollable"(42). By this he means, as we have seen, that the theory that the disciples stole the body or that the grave site was changed between Good Friday and Easter morning is not demanded by historical data. But why does he not demonstrate the inadequacy of these classical rationalistic explanations for the Gospels' account of the empty tomb? Why, in a book with so much to say about the empty tomb, does he not show how impossible it is to follow the theory of Reimarus that the disciples had stolen the body of Jesus, because there would then be no explanation of why the disciples were willing to persevere in the preaching of the Gospel despite untold suffering and death?[8] Another rationalistic explanation for the empty tomb is that the body of Jesus had been secretly removed from the tomb between Good Friday and Easter, so that when the women came to the tomb they found it empty and supposed that Jesus had risen. Guillame Baldensperger has written one of the best developments of this hypothesis.[9] But Campenhausen simply mentions this book and argues against one detail of it without refuting Baldensperger's whole reconstruction (27, note).

> *Note.* Baldensperger depends heavily upon John 19:31, which declares that the Jews, who were anxious not to defile the land by the body of one who had been crucified (cf. Deut. 21:23), pressed for a speedy disposal of the bodies of those who had been crucified on that day. The Gospel records declare that Jesus was therefore buried in the tomb of Joseph of Arimathea, but Baldensperger argues that there must have been a burial prior to this. The Jews would not have wanted Jesus buried in the garden tomb of a prominent man, where it would all too easily have become a shrine. The usual place for burying criminals was at the site of execution, and to fulfill the Jews' demand to have the bodies buried before sundown when the Sabbath would begin, it was only natural for the body of Jesus to be thrown into one of the numerous tombs surrounding Golgotha. Furthermore, such a burying place would be thoroughly unsuitable for a shrine and its location difficult to remember, since there were so many tombs there and all of them unmarked. Thus the disciples did not believe the women's report of the empty tomb; they thought it would be impossible to identify his tomb among so many. Had they known, on the other hand, that he had been buried in the garden tomb of Joseph of Arimathea, they could very easily have checked the women's report.
> However, unbeknown to the disciples or the women, Joseph of Arimathea had asked Pilate for permission to remove the body of Jesus and place it in his own grave. Permission was granted, and Baldensperger argues that Joseph removed the

---

[8] *See* Chapter 2, pp. 33.
[9] G. Baldensperger, *Le tombeau vide.*

body at night so that no one knew about it except his servants
who helped him. Joseph embalmed the body of Jesus when he
buried him (John 19:39). Had the women known about this
burial and embalming, they would not have come to the tomb
bearing spices, which they were obviously going to use to
embalm Jesus. According to Baldensperger, Joseph kept his
deed a secret until his death. It was only many years later,
when the Jews began to ask taunting questions about details
concerning Jesus' burial, that the church became interested in
this subject itself. In order to refute the Jews' attacks, the
church began to teach the physical resurrection of Jesus. Prior
to that time Christians had been mystics, concerned only with
their inner religious life and indifferent to thoughts of such an
objective nature as the continued existence of Jesus. But
under the Jewish polemic they began to develop a theological
dogma about such matters. At about this time, Joseph of
Arimathea died, and his servants, no longer feeling bound to
keep their master's secret, told it to the church. The church
utilized this report for their apologetic against the Jews, but
they combined it with the long-ignored report of the women
that the tomb (which was now called the tomb of Joseph of
Arimathea) was empty.

The great difficulty with Baldensperger's historical reconstruction is that the New Testament always regards the Jewish opposition to the church as arising from the preaching of
the resurrection (e.g., Acts 4:1-2), and not, as Baldensperger
would have it, the cause for the church's development of this
doctrine. If the preaching of the resurrection was not the cause
of the Jewish opposition, then this preaching is difficult to
explain on Baldensperger's premise that the early Christians
were mystics. Perhaps he would say that the early Christians
had reduplicated the spirit of Jesus in their lives so that the
Jews hated them as they had hated Jesus for his purity of life.
But if the Jews had opposed them simply because of their
ethical lives, then it is not clear why the Jews would taunt the
church about details regarding the burial of Jesus. Furthermore, if the early Christians were not concerned about external things, they would not have found the report of the deed
of Joseph of Arimathea useful for maintaining their cause,
and they certainly would not have developed the story of the
burial and resurrection of Jesus that appears in the four Gospels.

But if, as the New Testament declares, Jewish opposition
arose because of the preaching of the resurrection, this opposition must have come very soon after the church began to

preach. If the Jews could have pointed to the occupied tomb of Jesus, or even have raised the objection that it could not be located, then the Christian message would have been effectively suppressed. But the Christian church continued because its report could not be refuted. The tradition of Joseph of Arimathea is so central to all the four Gospels that it must have been used to answer the Jewish polemic. But if, in the early days of the church, it was claimed that Jesus had been buried there, it would have been a simple matter to make a check. Baldensperger, however, has to postulate that neither the Jewish opposition nor the knowledge concerning Joseph came for many years—enough years so that it would have been impossible to check the tomb. Hence Baldensperger's reconstruction raises some very serious difficulties.

Why is it that Campenhausen does not take the trouble to show the inadequacy of Baldensperger's approach from the standpoint of historical reason? The answer is simply that he wants to maintain an Easter history that is ambiguous and that can be explained either naturally or supernaturally. He does not want to close the door to a rationalistic explanation for the empty tomb any more than he wants to close it to a supernatural explanation. If, on the other hand, he were to say that the rationalistic explanations for the empty tomb were impossible, then he would leave open only the supernatural alternative, and thus his reconstruction of Easter history would become a support for faith.

Campenhausen's reconstruction of Easter history is in many ways the most interesting of all the contemporary works on the resurrection, for it sets forth the only possible way to make Easter faith independent of history. Only by having an Easter history that can, with equal ease, be either natural or supernatural, is it possible to have an Easter faith which is neither hindered nor helped by history. But if he were to leave this middle ground and seek to explain why the tomb was empty and why the disciples thought they saw Jesus, the result would be a natural or supernatural explanation and faith would then be either supported or countered by history. But because Campenhausen does not follow the usual historical procedure and seek after the causes for these facts, it seems that his reconstruction is not so much history as theology. Therefore it appears that history, if it were allowed to speak freely, would have something to say for or against faith. Thus Campenhausen, despite his attempt to construct a history that is impartial to faith, succeeds actually in showing, like Barth and Grass, that faith cannot have a knowledge of the resurrection which can remain unaffected by the apostolic witness and the historical method.

II. Attempts to Sustain Knowledge of the Resurrection Partially from Historical Reasoning

The thesis that historical knowledge provides partial but not full support for faith seems rather popular today. Michael Ramsey, Archbishop of Canterbury, summarizes his position as follows: "Decisive proof [of the resurrection] can never be provided. Belief in the resurrection, involving as it does the most strict historical considerations, involves also belief in Jesus Christ."[10] Likewise, Merrill C. Tenney, Dean of the Graduate School of Wheaton College, Illinois, says, "Although true faith is essentially a voluntary affirmation independent of proof, the Scriptures nowhere demand committal without some reasonable basis."[11] But with such statements both of these men involve themselves in a logical difficulty. How can one depend and yet not depend upon the evidences?

There are two other men who have taken the position that faith is partially dependent upon historical reason and partially free from it, but who have not, like Ramsey and Tenney, become entangled in a contradiction. These men have avoided this pitfall by allowing historical reason to support faith's knowledge of a certain aspect of the resurrection, while faith's knowledge of the remaining aspect is not based upon objective evidences.

[10] M. Ramsey, *The Resurrection of Christ*, p. 36.
[11] M. Tenney, *The Reality of the Resurrection*, p. 105.

The Resurrection and Historical Reasoning

A. Gerhard Koch

In a way reminiscent of Bultmann's handling of the historical Jesus, Gerhard Koch of Berlin divides the resurrection into a "that" (*Dass*), the knowledge of which is available through the historical method, and into the fullness of its existential meaning, the knowledge of which comes only through an immediate encounter with the risen Jesus. In order to give this first aspect of the resurrection its due, Koch devotes a considerable portion of his 300-page book[12] to such crucial historical questions as the empty tomb, the return to Galilee, the appearances, and the apostles' witness at Jerusalem. He is convinced that the tomb was empty on Easter morning. The Marcan account of the empty tomb contains none of the apologetical tendencies found in the reports of the Gospels that were written later (30). Likewise the best explanation for the theme of the "third day" in the resurrection passages of the New Testament is that the grave was actually discovered to be empty on that day (33). This whole matter of the empty tomb cannot be sidestepped, declares Koch, without running the risk of making the resurrection appearances "a pious supposition" (157). Koch is also convinced that "the death of Jesus had driven the disciples into confusion and dispersement" (41). The only thing left for them to do, therefore, was to return to Galilee and the work they had left when they followed Jesus (44). It was not in Jerusalem but in Galilee that Jesus first appeared to the disciples. These appearances were something that really happened to them. "The New Testament reports make it explicit that the sorrow of the disciples was overcome not by inner experiences nor by the current apocalyptical hopes. God himself had intervened" (53).

But having said all this, Koch emphasizes that one must not suppose that he achieves a full knowledge of the resurrection by inferring it from the fact of the empty tomb. Neither does one achieve a full knowledge of the resurrection

[12] G. Koch, *Die Auferstehung Jesu Christi.*

"through considering the flight of the disciples back to Galilee
and the radical change in their disposition that followed"
(43). To seek for full knowledge in this way involves one in
an "objective" knowledge of the resurrection, which is highly
undesirable:

> For centuries thinking has been carried on on the assumption
> that objects could only be known through their objectivity. But
> today it is apparent that such thinking is not only inadequate
> but misleading. It removes one from his historical situation and
> makes one think of himself as a subject who can make decisions
> about objects without becoming involved or concerned about
> them (159).

Thus in the matter of the resurrection one must not think of
himself as the subject who masters the knowledge of the resurrection but as one who is instead mastered by it.

In order for the knowledge of the resurrection to master
one, it must be capable of carrying out two functions. First,
this knowledge must confront and stand over against one so
that it does not become simply an idea that is thought. But in
standing over against one, it must not be something that can
be subsumed under a general category or idea and thus
thought of with detachment like other objects in this world.

The delicate balance Koch must maintain becomes clear in
his consideration of the corporeality of the body in which
Jesus appeared to the disciples. On the one hand he asserts,
"The word 'corporeality' must not be discarded, because it
is the guardian angel that sees to it that the resurrection
event is *historically* interpreted and not allowed to be lost in
the fog of a world of pious thought" (240). But, on the other
hand, the New Testament record of the corporeality of Jesus'
resurrection body must not be pressed so literally that we
think of it as an object that can be subject to man's thought.
"We must renounce the assumption that the disciples saw
Jesus before themselves in the same way that one can see an
object" (232). Instead, we must realize that when the apostles
sought to give witness to the meaning of this resurrection
event, which was so unusual that there were no analogies in

168

their experience to describe it, they had no other choice than to use mythical language. By "mythical" language, Koch means the same thing as Bultmann: language expressing the other world in terms of this world. The other-worldly meaning that the disciples sought to convey when they spoke of the corporeality of the body in which Jesus manifested himself was that in Jesus God had really come to be with them. They also used mythical language when they said that Jesus had ascended into heaven. The otherworldly idea that the ascension was intended to convey was that Jesus was really God, who belonged in heaven, so that in his appearances Jesus had actually mediated a knowledge of God to the apostles. "The departure to heaven had become their comfort that in Jesus Christ heaven is the near and open heaven" (280). Thus it must not be inferred that, because the New Testament speaks of these appearances being terminated after forty days by the ascension, it is no longer possible to have an encounter with the living Christ. Rather, the ascension means that heaven and earth, God and men, have been brought together so that in continued encounters with Jesus Christ men can have the knowledge of God mediated to them. The great message of the New Testament is that "what happened to the disciples and apostles will happen exactly and in no other wise to all those who, open to Jesus and living in his vicinity, come after them" (280).

Thus the corporeality of the resurrection body of Jesus must be demythologized and reinterpreted so that it conveys the idea that God himself is really with us in Christ. But this demythologizing must not be carried so far that the idea of God being with us in Christ becomes simply a timeless idea devoid of all historicity. Instead, the resurrection, along with the corporeality, must remain a bare historical fact that can stand over against a man and encounter him so that he becomes mastered by it. The following quotation summarizes Koch's delicate balancing act:

> Historical criticism has indeed shown how the revelation of the New Testament is set forth in terms of the world of that

day. This revelation can make no direct claim on men today. Simply to hang on to the history of that time would not be the solution to the questions that confront us today. On the other hand, a "that" [*Dass*] must be found in this New Testament history, or else there is no possibility of having men addressed by a claim that will change their whole existence. . . . Thus there remains only the narrow path in which one divests revelation of every worldly form so that he can turn his gaze upon the punctual *Dass* that is to be found in history (286).

It is the historical method that maintains this *Dass* by showing that the apostles' faith can only be accounted for through the resurrection, but it is the actual encounters with Christ that one has today that cause one to know the reality of the resurrection in the fullness of its existential meaning. It is through an encounter that comes as one places himself in the context of the church that one is able to understand what the apostles were trying to say by means of the mythical language they used to witness to the resurrection.

Has Koch been successful in allowing the historical method to go only as far as establishing the *Dass* of the resurrection but not as far as establishing its *Was*, that is, its nature and meaning? According to Koch, the risen Jesus has appeared to him in exactly the same way as he appeared to the original apostles. And like the apostles, he has sought to render a witness to this most meaningful of all possible events. But Koch acknowledges that the terms by which he witnesses to the resurrection differ considerably from the terms by which the apostles witnessed to it. Koch asserts the continuation of the appearances while the New Testament stresses their termination. Luke limits them to forty days (Acts 1:3), and Paul declares that he was the very last one to receive them (I Cor. 15:8). The writer of John also implies the same when he speaks of future believers "not seeing but believing" (John 20:29). Koch refuses to use any worldly analogy for Jesus' resurrection body. But the New Testament, while asserting that Jesus' resurrection body was different from the body he had before his death, nevertheless emphasizes that Jesus could eat, speak, walk, and be touched in his resurrection state.

Koch tries to explain the difference between his witness and that of the original disciples by saying that the apostolic witness can be explained as a borrowing from the thought-forms and concepts of that culture. But it should be observed that the thought-forms of Koch's culture are the obvious explanation for the way in which he lays down his witness to the resurrection. No one can read Koch very long without realizing how much he has been influenced by existentialism and Bultmann. The thought-forms of New Testament times, however, cannot account for all aspects of the apostolic witness to the resurrection. For example, while Paul himself does not speak directly about Jesus' resurrection body, yet his references to a *sôma pneumatikón* in I Corinthians 15:44ff. are not a borrowing from either the Greek idea of a disembodied spirit or the Jewish concept of the resurrection of the flesh.[13] The only remaining explanation is that Paul got this idea of the "spiritual body" from the tradition by which he learned of the appearances of Jesus to the apostles. The resurrection appearances in the Gospels, which also derive from this tradition, fit this concept very well.

There are certain other features about the apostolic witness that are surprising. According to the Gospels, Jesus performed many miracles before his death, but none occur in the accounts of his appearances. It has also been observed that the emphasis upon seeing Jesus in the apostolic witness to the resurrection appearances is singular in comparison with the Biblical tendency as a whole, in which the chief emphasis is on hearing in order to receive revelation.[14] Finally, in all other instances of a resurrection in the Bible, the subject retains mortality, but the apostolic witness is that Jesus will die no more. Thus there are certain ways in which the apostles' witness diverges from the thought structure of their contemporary world, and the question becomes very pertinent as to where the apostles got these ideas if not from their involvement with the resurrected Lord. But if these ideas could only be ex-

[13] O. Cullmann, *Christology of the New Testament,* p. 33; K. Rengstorf, *Die Auferstehung Jesu,* pp. 81ff.
[14] Rengstorf, *op. cit.,* pp. 117-127.

plained from the resurrection itself, then historical reasoning not only tells us of the fact of the resurrection but something about its nature.

However, Koch declares that he, along with the apostles, is a witness to the resurrection of Jesus. He feels that his witness is superior, because he is able to talk about it in an existential language that does not, like the apostolic language, run the danger of leading people into the pitfall of thinking of the resurrection in objective terms. But the language by which he witnesses to the resurrection is obviously borrowed from the thinking of existentialism, particularly that of Bultmann and the early Heidegger. Thus there is no difficulty in explaining Koch's witness historically; it is simply the product of existentialism.

Which, then, can justify the claim to a better witness to the resurrection? If the apostolic witness could be explained from the culture of that day, but Koch's could not, then the apostles are the ones who should be demythologized in favor of Koch, but when the reverse is the case, Koch should be demythologized in favor of the apostles.

Thus it becomes clear that if the resurrection did occur, it left certain impressions upon its witnesses that cannot be explained by any other factor in their environment. These impressions are indications not only of the fact but also of the nature and meaning of the resurrection. Therefore, it seems that one must go farther than Koch and use historical reasoning to find the meaning of the resurrection as well as the fact of it.

B. Richard R. Niebuhr

Niebuhr, professor of divinity at the Harvard Divinity School, also views the resurrection as having two aspects, one of which is supported by historical reason and one of which is known in a purely immediate way.[15] These two aspects of

---

[15] The references that follow pertain to Niebuhr's book *Resurrection and Historical Reason. See* Bibliography.

the resurrection correspond to an antinomy between the regular and the accidental that inheres in nature, history, and
even in faith. Historical reason supports faith's knowledge of
the resurrection so far as it partakes of regularity, but it offers
no help in knowing the accidental and spontaneous aspect
of the resurrection of Jesus.

Niebuhr distinguishes his treatment of the resurrection from
others considered thus far because he views it as wholly a
part of history and the world, instead of something wholly
other that somehow touches or even breaks into this world.
In fact, the resurrection is so much a part of this world that he
considers it the supreme expression and the very essence of
the world. History and nature are characterized both by a
spontaneity and a necessity that originated in creation. There
is a necessary aspect to phenomena, because the world came
into being as the direct result of God's act of creation. But
God created not out of necessity but out of freedom and grace,
and therefore all phenomena have a spontaneous as well
as a necessary aspect. It is this spontaneous or contingent
aspect of phenomena that is the more predominant, because
it stems from the freedom and grace of God, which is his
most central characteristic.

> Creation *ex nihilo* asserts both cause and effect, and yet insists
> that the relationship between them is not necessary. Christian
> metaphysics affirms the contingency of creation, and, by the
> same logic, a similar contingency has to be affirmed of every
> moment in that creation, that is to say, in the whole course of
> history. Contingency is here the abstract metaphysical term for
> what Christian faith calls divine love (168).

While history is essentially contingency, there remains within
it the opposite characteristic of causality, though this is always
subordinate.

The knowledge that events do come about by necessity and
that there are analogies between them provides only a super-
ficial understanding of history. For example, the phenomenon
of death "profoundly qualifies" (127) much that takes place
in history. But it is a mistake to think of death as the decisive

category for nature and history, for the chief characteristic of history is actually its contingency, and "in the resurrection of Christ the spontaneity, particularity, and independence of historical events rise to the surface in a single eruption" (177). Thus the resurrection is not to be considered a miracle that belongs to a class of phenomena characterized by their negative relationship to nature. Instead, it "epitomizes the original creativity that informs all history and underlies every conception of nature" (177).

But the resurrection, like the history it so perfectly represents, also partakes of the subordinate, cause-effect continuum of reality. Thus Jesus appeared to his disciples not only in a way that was "totally unfamiliar" to them but that was also "familiar" (162). "The weight of the [resurrection] accounts falls on the signs by which Jesus' identity is disclosed. In each instance these are historical signs from the past life of Jesus, familiar to the witnesses by virtue of their memory" (173f.). Hence the resurrected Jesus bore some analogy to himself as he was before he died. Without this identity, it would have been impossible for the disciples to have had faith in Jesus.

Nevertheless, the apostles' faith was not simply an acknowledgment of this identity. There was also a great difference between Jesus' resurrection body and his body before death. In the resurrection appearances the disciples were confronted by the "totally unfamiliar," so that it was only by "their faith that these men were able to assimilate the startling synthesis of the known and the strange presented to them in the risen Christ and see more deeply into the reality of God's providence . . ." (162). Thus the disciples' faith came, in part, as the result of the signs by which Jesus manifested his identity to them, but this was only the subordinate aspect of their faith. Its primary quality was the spontaneity by which they were able, despite the totally unfamiliar aspects of Jesus' appearances, to see that he was risen and to understand that this was a loving work of God's providence and grace. Thus the Apostolate came to be formed primarily by a faith which corresponded to the spontaneity inhering in history and in the resurrection itself.

The subsequent forming of the church also came about in a way which combines the accidental and the necessary, with the emphasis falling upon the accidental. "Accidental though the relationship between the Apostolate and church may be," asserts Niebuhr, "we do not gain the right to declare ourselves free of the apostolic witness; the relationship, for all its contingency, is still unalterable" (29). Likewise, it is impossible for us of the later church to gain a proof of the resurrection from the appearances, for "the very quality of historical independence, which must characterize the resurrection appearances if they are historical at all, prevents us from talking about any 'proof' of Jesus' appearance to his disciples" (175f.). Our faith in the resurrection arises primarily because of a spontaneity which is the essence of history. However, we cannot ignore the historical foundations of this faith; we remain bound to the apostolic witness and the cause-effect relationship that links it with the resurrection appearances. "Apart from the resurrection of Jesus . . . the Apostolate . . . appears as a spoke of a wheel without a hub" (160). While our faith is, like all history, primarily spontaneous, there is also the subordinate cause-effect aspect that corresponds to the historical argument that the Apostolate and the early church could not have arisen except through the appearances of the risen Jesus.

Thus in Niebuhr one sees a stream of history beginning with creation and continuing with the resurrection, the forming of the Apostolate, and the rise of the church. Where, then, will history end? Niebuhr has nothing to say about the future resurrection of the dead as following necessarily from the resurrection of Jesus, for this would remove the all-important element of spontaneity from future history and tie it to a cause-effect law. The most that Niebuhr can say concerning the Christian hope is that the resurrection "raises in our hearts a correspondingly greater sense of the future" (177). Jesus, by his resurrection, did release us from the fear of death, for by faith in the resurrection we know that the decisive category for history is not death nor the second law of thermodynamics but something that corresponds to the freedom, love, and grace of God.

Niebuhr sees a continuum of spontaneity in history that makes Easter faith correspond to the resurrection of Jesus. But the correspondence between faith and the resurrection is not such that one can argue back, by inference, from the faith of the apostles to the fact of the resurrection. The apostles' faith, like the resurrection, is primarily spontaneous, and this being the case, it is impossible to seek the cause of Easter faith in anything but this faith. Niebuhr, then, makes Easter faith primarily independent of historical reason, but like Koch, he does not cut himself completely adrift from the apostolic witness, for there is a secondary aspect of faith that ties it to the apostolic witness and to the resurrection by historical reasoning. Thus he avoids the difficulty of Barth, Grass, and Campenhausen, for whom the apostolic witness can be only the occasion and not at all the cause for faith.

But is Niebuhr really able to let historical reason have only a partial and secondary function for faith? As one examines the Easter faith of the early church, it is difficult to find anything in it that is not simply a reflex of the appearances of the risen Jesus. According to Paul, Easter faith is wholly the result of the resurrection of Christ, for "if Christ be not raised from the dead, your faith is in vain" (I Cor. 15:14). In Chapter I we saw how the salient themes of the New Testament found their source and meaning in the resurrection. How then can it be asserted that there is a spontaneity in Easter faith that causes it to be something that does not stem primarily from the fact that Jesus rose? If spontaneity were really the primary quality of both Easter faith and the resurrection, then we would expect a very great difference and only a small correspondence between the resurrection and faith. But the apostolic faith recorded in the New Testament is everything one would expect if Jesus really rose and appeared to the apostles as they assert.

Consequently, it appears that the cause-effect relationship which Niebuhr declares exists between the resurrection and faith is not something secondary but all-embracing. If historical reason can find a cause adequate to explain an effect, it looks no farther, and therefore it seems that Niebuhr, having granted some basis for faith in historical reason, must go all the way and make it the entire basis.

> *Note.* Thomas Kepler has taken a position very similar to that of Niebuhr. He declares, "The unusual (such as the resurrection of Jesus) does happen, and when it occurs it is not contrary to the laws of nature, but above the known laws of nature; that is, not understood, since man does not know all that there is to be known about the laws of this mysterious universe."[16]

III. Pannenberg's Attempt to Sustain Knowledge of the Resurrection Wholly by Historical Reason

We have seen the embarrassment of those who allow historical reasoning no power in supporting faith in the resurrection. They are confronted with the apostolic witness to the resurrection, which as an historical record must be handled according to historical methodology. But their refusal to allow historical reason to have any function for faith leads them to make the apostolic witness to the resurrection really of no import for Easter faith. We have also seen how those who make faith partially dependent on the apostolic witness controlled by historical reason have an inconsistency that can only be removed if they make faith entirely dependent upon that apostolic witness. Therefore it is with interest that we examine the attempt of a new generation of German theologians, headed up by Wolfhart Pannenberg, to make faith wholly dependent upon historical reason.

With the publication in 1961 of *Offenbarung als Geschichte*,[17] it has become evident that a new theological movement is gaining momentum among some of the younger theologians of Germany. Each of the four scholars contributing to this

[16] T. Kepler, *The Meaning and Mystery of the Resurrection*, p. 171.
[17] Henceforth cited as *OaG*.

booklet supports, from the vantage point of his particular specialty, the thesis that revelation is mediated only through historical events: Wolfhart Pannenberg as a systematic theologian (Mainz), Rolf Rendtorff as an Old Testament exegete (Heidelberg), Ulrich Wilckens as a New Testament scholar (Kirchliche Hochschule, Berlin), and Trutz Rendtorff as a church historian. Since 1951 these and others who were then doctoral students at Heidelberg have been meeting regularly to formulate the basic ideology found in this booklet. Others sympathetic with this movement are Klaus Koch of Hamburg, Dieter Rössler of Göttingen, and Martin Elze of Tübingen. Pannenberg has become the chief spokesman for this movement, not because he was originally responsible for the basic approach to revelation as history,[18] but because as one whose specialty is systematics, he provides the over-all synthesis for the historical and exegetical work of the others.

Pannenberg characterizes this movement as a reaction against the "Theology of the Word" (*OaG* 132), which in recent decades has been expressed most pointedly by Karl Barth, who has insisted that revelation be controlled by what comes immediately from Jesus Christ, and by Rudolf Bultmann, who has removed revelation from history to the *kerygma*. To Pannenberg such attempts are basically a "flight into a harbor that is safe from the flood of the historico-critical method."[19] Pannenberg and his associates are convinced that a careful and critical understanding of the Biblical text makes it clear that God's revelation does not come to man immediately but always mediately via the events of history. The history in which revelation takes place is not a special redemptive history known only through faith, but is regular history that can be known through the historical method.

[18] In *OaG* 132, note, Pannenberg credits Rolf Rendtorff with providing the basis seed thought that the Old Testament always views revelation as mediated to man through historical events. Rendtorff, in turn, was stimulated in this direction by the writings of W. Zimmerli.

[19] W. Pannenberg, "Heilsgeschehen und Geschichte," *Kerygma und Dogma*, 5 (1959), 218. This article is henceforth cited as *HuG*.

The theologian Paul Althaus[20] regards Pannenberg's approach as a swing of the pendulum to an opposite extreme from that of Bultmann. According to Althaus, whereas Bultmann has oversimplified matters by dissolving history into a faith that arises from hearing the *kerygma,* Pannenberg has gone to the opposite extreme and oversimplified matters by making faith to consist in a mere knowledge of what has happened in history. Althaus believes, as is indicated by the title of his article on Pannenberg, "Revelation as History and Faith," that the correct center is to see revelation as coming both mediately through history and immediately through faith.

In understanding history as the medium for revelation, Pannenberg does not start with any particular part or strand of history, but with history as a whole. "Only from the vantage point of universal history is it possible to find the complete meaning of any single event" (*HuG* 280). But in order to see history as a whole, it is necessary to determine the unifying element of history and thus have some idea of what the future holds. There is a regularity in history and a connectedness between its events, but there is also such irregularity that it is impossible to see any unifying theme in it. History chafes at any attempt, such as Toynbee's, to subsume it under certain forms or patterns. Hence, the unity of history should be sought neither in its regularity nor in its irregularity and contingency. Rather, "the unity of history can . . . only be understood in a way in which its connection and contingency have a common root" (*HuG* 284). This common root can only be the transcendent God. "The God, who through his transcendent freedom, is the origin of the contingency that is found in the world, also establishes the unity of the contingent events in such a way that the contingency of the connected events is not excluded" (*HuG* 284f.).

But Pannenberg is convinced that such an understanding of history has been hindered by the custom of trying to fit all of it into the Procrustean bed of what is analogous to our

[20] P. Althaus, "Offenbarung als Geschichte und Glaube," *Theologische Literaturzeitung,* 87 (1962), col. 323.

everyday experience. He deplores what Ernst Troeltsch called the "all-prevailing power of analogy,"[21] because it allows one to know only those things as having happened that are already familiar to the historian. Thus man's experience is set up as the norm for an understanding of history, and the possibility of history confronting one with new things is, a priori, excluded. Pannenberg is not at all impressed with the argument so often advanced by historians that to admit the possibility of overly-pronounced deviations in history is to make all historical knowledge impossible.[22] To him the principle of analogy should not impose a limit on what can be known. Instead, the historian should be open to the possibility that over pronounced deviations do occur, and the principle of analogy should be used for knowing these events as well as ordinary happenings. The following statement shows how this can be done (*HuG* 266f., note):

> If analogies are applied with an acknowledgment of the limitation of their validity, then they will certainly not function as a criterion for the reality of what a tradition declares has happened, as Troeltsch . . . has decreed. Just because a reported event breaks with the analogy of what is otherwise customary or usually reported is no reason, in itself, for disputing its occurrence. But it is an entirely different matter, when there are analogies that would explain that the report of the unusual is conveyed in the literary form of a myth or a legend, or that the reporter could well be subject to hallucinations. Thus when there is evidence that the report stems from certain imaginative states of mind—and not simply when something unusual is reported—historical reason is led to a negative conclusion by the principle of analogy.

Thus Pannenberg wants to use the principle of analogy to decide whether an historical report is simply the product of someone's imagination or is, rather, caused by something that did happen in reality. From his own experience he knows the difference between imagining something to have happened and

[21] E. Troeltsch, "Ueber historische und dogmatische Methode in der Theologie," *Gesammelte Schriften*, II, 732.

[22] Cf. Marc Bloch's use of this argument, Chapter 1, pp. 23.

witnessing its happening. He wants to apply this experience as an analogy for deciding the truth or falsity of all reports, for it would be a contradiction in terms to say that something happened that was imagined, or that something was imagined that happened. But Pannenberg is unwilling to say that something reported to him is imaginary just because it never happened to him. He will evaluate this report on the basis of how imaginative reports can be distinguished from factual ones. Consequently, Pannenberg uses the principle of analogy to know the unanalogous as well as the analogous.

When the historian thus becomes free to acknowledge both the contingency and the continuity of history and to see its unifying element in the transcendent God, he then becomes free to let history speak to him. The very fact that such a position gives him a full openness to history means that he has made peace with what history as a whole is trying to say. In that history finds its unity in the God who maintains continuity and yet works toward a goal by constantly doing new things, history therefore becomes understood as essentially apocalyptic. An historian with the apocalyptic view of history will be drawn toward the Biblical history and its central event of the resurrection of Christ because here God is thought of as doing new things and working toward a goal. Such an historian will not regard, a priori, the report of Jesus' rising from the dead as impossible. But neither will he accept it uncritically. "It is the close examination of the reports of the resurrection that determine its historicity, and not the prior judgment that all events in history must be more or less the same" (*HuG* 266f., note). If the study of these reports can be explained as arising from the imagination, they are to be discredited; if not, then the resurrection is to be believed.

Pannenberg is assured that the resurrection of Jesus did occur. While on a tour of the United States in the spring of 1963, he delivered a lecture at Fuller Theological Seminary entitled, "Did *Jesus* Really Rise from the Dead?" During the course of this lecture Pannenberg affirmed that while there is much in the resurrection reports that is mythical, yet it is impossible to explain them wholly as the work of the apostles' imagination. The apostles were too discouraged after the death of Jesus to have talked themselves into believing that Jesus was risen. The only satisfactory explanation for their sudden faith was that Jesus appeared to them. Furthermore, the early Christian community could not have survived if the tomb of Jesus had not been empty. An occupied tomb would not only have destroyed their faith, but it would have given the Jewish polemic against the church an invincible weapon. Hence it is impossible to charge off the Biblical reports of the resurrection wholly to the imagination, and, consequently, Pannenberg arrives at an historical verification of the resurrection.

True to his thesis that history is the exclusive medium for revelation, Pannenberg asserts that this historical knowledge provides the sole basis for faith. "It is not at all necessary for one first to have faith in order to find the revelation of God in the history of Israel and Jesus Christ. Rather, true faith is first awakened through an impartial observation of these events" (*OaG* 100f.). Faith is not only based thus upon the fact of the resurrection of Jesus but also upon the historically verifiable meaning of the resurrection. History, according to Pannenberg, is both the happenings of the past themselves and the report of these occurrences, which is always conveyed by human beings. Human beings are anything but neutral, robot-like repeaters of what happened, for they pass on their reports in terms of their peculiar outlook and culture. This outlook is based on past traditions and future aspirations and so is both a product of history and a part of history itself. Thus the apostles reported the fact of the resurrection of Jesus and interpreted it as a guarantee that the people of God would rise from the dead because these apostles were a part of the Jewish culture in which the apocalyptic view of history prevailed. They did not distort history by interpreting the resurrection of Jesus in this way. The resurrection took place within an historical context that would naturally render such an interpretation, and, consequently, the apocalyptic interpretation of the resurrection is as much a part of its history as the event itself. Revelation, therefore, is mediated solely by history because "the events of history speak their own language, the language of the events, [and] this language can only be heard in the world of ideas of the people in which these events occurred" (*OaG* 112). The faith that acknowledges the resurrection to have happened has no trouble accepting this apocalyptic interpretation as true, for this faith only became open to the possibility of the occurrence of the resurrection through regarding, a priori, the apocalyptic interpretation of history as its true meaning.

Hence Pannenberg in his reply to the critique of Althaus[23] is insistent that both the meaning and fact of the resurrection come from history itself and are based on historical reasoning:

> An historical faith is not limited in that it cannot get through to the meaning of events, but can only see them as brute facts. . . . Rather, events always bring along their original meaning out of the context in which they are reported as happening. . . . That the God of Israel is revealed as God in the Christ event is a conviction that, admittedly, only allows itself to be justified with reference to the universal connection of all happenings. . . .[24]

Althaus objected that Pannenberg had broken down the Biblical antithesis between faith and sight (II Cor. 5:7) in that he had made faith a virtual knowledge. But while Pannenberg declares that faith is knowledge of what is true about history, yet this knowledge does not actually show us that we will participate in the future resurrection of the dead, but only promises it. Thus while faith is the knowledge of Christ as risen and of history as apocalyptic, yet there is an element of trust in faith because it looks toward a future fulfillment of the promise found in the resurrection (*OaG* 101).

For Pannenberg, then, faith finds its basis fully in a history that is known through historical reasoning. Martin Kähler, it will be remembered,[25] shrank from this position because it

---

[23] Althaus, *op. cit.*

[24] W. Pannenberg, "Einsicht und Glaube," *Theologische Literaturzeitung*, 88 (1963), cols. 86, 88.

[25] See Chapter 3, pp. 71.

carried with it the corollary that ordinary people are not capable of believing on their own but only as they submit themselves to the authority of the learned historian. But Pannenberg is quite willing to accept this corollary. He concedes that one may believe without first proving that his faith is justified so long as he has the prospect that "the ground of his faith will prove to be sound."[26] Not the simple believer but theology has the special task of establishing the trustworthiness of the knowledge on which faith rests. But in recent centuries theology has failed in this task. Thus "the atmosphere of confidence in what the minister proclaims . . . must be formed anew, and one hopes that theology, in completely critical openness, will dedicate all its energies to this task."[27]

Pannenberg, with his firm purpose to keep faith based on history at all costs, has surely striven valiantly to bridge Lessing's ugly ditch. It would seem that so far as he is concerned, he has been successful in this task, for knowledge both of the event as well as of the meaning of the resurrection of Jesus is derived from historical reasoning. There are, however, certain difficulties in Pannenberg's system that make it problematical whether he has really bridged the ditch. Aside from the difficulty that only those can have an immediate knowledge of revelation who are trained historians, there is the difficulty that Pannenberg regards revelation as being mediated through all of history and not through just one part.

It will be remembered that Pannenberg starts with history as a whole, and determining its unifying characteristic to be the transcendent God, he then turns to Biblical history and the resurrection of Jesus as the best representation of history as a whole. This Biblical history cannot be grasped and accepted as true until one has first seen the basic structure of the whole of history. Thus Pannenberg repeatedly inveighs against the idea that revelation is confined to a particular segment of history that in theological language is often called *Heilsgeschichte*, or "redemptive history." "Redemptive history is not a

---

[26] Pannenberg, "Einsicht und Glaube," cols. 84f.
[27] *Ibid.*, col. 85.

super-history; instead, it gathers all events into itself because of its universal purpose" (*HuG* 230). Pannenberg is against Barth's concept of a redemptive history that occurs in a sort of "ghetto" that is distinct from all the rest of history (*HuG* 261).

Since revelation, therefore, is derived from history as a whole instead of just one strand of it, one need not wait to receive revelation until he experiences a bit of special history or a report concerning it. The early Israelites (or their Semitic ancestors) began to think of history in essentially apocalyptic terms, not through some special work that was performed in their midst, but simply through observing history as it is. "Israel is not to be artificially isolated from its early environment through the assertion of a supernatural revelation that took place at some particular time" (*OaG* 97). God worked in a no more special way in the milieu of Israel's history than in that of any other people. Presumably, then, Israel came to learn of God through a history that was no different from that of other peoples.

But the question that must be asked of Pannenberg is, Why did Israel, in distinction from the other nations, come to the conclusion that history was apocalyptic? Did God give this nation a special insight into the true nature of history? Althaus[28] charged Pannenberg with failing to give any place to the Holy Spirit in opening one's eyes to accept revelation. In his reply Pannenberg declared that men did, indeed, need to have an "enlightenment"[29] of the Holy Spirit to overcome their prejudices, which would otherwise blind them to the knowledge of God mediated by history. But in keeping with his thesis that history is revelation, Pannenberg is unwilling to understand this enlightenment of the Holy Spirit as anything supernatural or special, that is, as anything that occurs apart from forces already existent in history. Rather, the enlightenment of the Holy Spirit is something contained in history itself so that history carries with it a "fully convincing power"

[28] Althaus, *op. cit., passim.*
[29] Pannenberg, "Einsicht und Glaube," col. 89.

(*OaG* 100) to reveal God as transcendent and the Biblical history as the representation of this fact. Thus Pannenberg could say that "no man comes to a knowledge of God out of his own reason and ability" (*OaG* 100). History is so fully the revelation of the triune God that history itself performs the task of illuminating a man so that he overcomes his prejudices and sees God revealed therein.

But this means that Pannenberg is faced with the problem of a history that, on the one hand, in its totality reveals God, and yet, on the other hand, reveals him only to certain select people like Israel and the Christian church. Why is it that when Paul preached the resurrection in Athens, some believed while others mocked? (Acts 17:32-34). In the person of Paul the very essence of what history is was confronting these people, because here was Paul preaching the resurrection and interpreting it apocalyptically. Here, if anywhere, there should have been a "fully convincing power" of the Holy Spirit to overcome the prejudice of the Greek mind against an apocalyptic view of history. But this was true only for some of those who heard Paul.

The obvious solution to why only Israel and some on Mars Hill believed is that God does not work only in the whole of history but also in a special way at particular times and places within it. However, to say this involves one in a supernaturalism, or to use Pannenberg's phrase, in a "two-story"[30] view of history. Pannenberg declares that he cannot accept supernaturalism because it would destroy all possibility of gaining historical knowledge. "There should be no talk of supernaturalism, which is unacceptable for the critically oriented reason of the historian, because it arbitrarily cuts off historical investigation of immanental causes and analogies through the assertion of a transcendental intervention [*Eingriff*]" (*HuG* 286).

But the events that occur in Pannenberg's one-story history are no less difficult for the historical method to handle than events occurring in a two-story history. Pannenberg speaks of God as "transcendental" and the contingent action of the res-

[30] Contained in a letter to the author.

urrection as a "breaking out" [*Aufbruch*] (*HuG* 237) in history. Pannenberg, by his reapplication of the principle of analogy, can know of such analogy-contradicting events as a resurrection from the dead, and therefore there is no reason why his method could not control the knowledge of supernatural events. A supernaturalism would break into the normal cause-effect sequence of events just as much as contingent events do in Pannenberg's thought. But just as these contingent events do not arbitrarily set aside the study of causes and effects in Pannenberg's historiography, so they would not have to do so in a supernatural world view.

Thus, if one can think of God as intervening supernaturally in history, then there is no difficulty in understanding how only the nation of Israel came to its peculiar view of history: God simply intervened in her, milieu and not in any other. Then, too, there is no difficulty in understanding why some do not believe the revelation mediated by history: God simply does not work supernaturally in the heart of everyone who hears the Gospel in order to overcome their prejudices so that they might own up to the truth of what is to be known in history. To understand the Holy Spirit as intervening specially in the behalf of certain people so that they acknowledge the truth mediated by history is not to deny that revelation is mediated solely through history. The work of the Holy Spirit would be conceived of as enabling a man to own up to what was already to be seen in history, rather than supplementing it in any way.

Thus, indeed, Pannenberg has provided some insights into how it is possible for historical reason to bridge Lessing's ugly ditch and therefore find a complete basis for faith in history. However, certain difficulties, such as his demand that ordinary people depend upon the theologian-historian to provide their basis for faith, and his inability to account satisfactorily for unbelief, cause us to continue our search for a more adequate solution to the problem of faith and history.

CHAPTER SEVEN

An Early Christian Approach

S INCE MODERN SOLUTIONS TO THE PROBLEM OF EASTER FAITH
and history are not entirely satisfying, it is reasonable to turn
from the modern scene, and its development from the time of
the Enlightenment, and focus our attention on the thinking of
the New Testament. In the writings of Luke (his Gospel
and Acts) one finds an approach to the problem of Easter
faith and history that is remarkably pertinent to the question
as it is being discussed today.

I. The Prologue to Luke's Gospel

[1]Inasmuch as many have undertaken to compile a narrative
of the things which have been fulfilled among us, [2]just as they
were delivered to us by those who from the beginning were eyewitnesses and ministers of the word, [3]it seemed good to me also,
having followed all things closely from the beginning, to write
an orderly account for you, most excellent Theophilus, [4]that you
may know the certainty concerning the things in which you
have been instructed (Luke 1:1-4).[1]

In this way Luke began his Gospel. A.D. 55-60 was the very
earliest that this Gospel could have been written, and thus
almost three decades had passed since the events recorded in
the Gospel had transpired. Therefore, in this Prologue Luke

---

[1] The author's translation.

188

frankly acknowledges that he was not an eyewitness of these events. But he is nonetheless justified in composing a Gospel, for others who were not eyewitnesses were also writing up the oral tradition given by the apostles, who had witnessed the events of Jesus' life. Furthermore, Luke had done some research on his own, for he had traced all things accurately from the first.

Having shown his justification for writing such an account, Luke then proceeds to tell his purpose in writing. He has set things down "in an orderly manner" so that his reader, Theophilus, might have a "certainty" regarding the oral instruction that he had received. The RSV translates *tèn aspháleian* not as "certainty" but as "truth," and this is, to be sure, a possible meaning. It has this meaning in Acts 21:34; 22:30; and 25:26, where it is used to denote the attempt of the Romans to understand why the Jews wanted to kill Paul. However, the word can also have the meaning of "certainty" in Greek usage. This meaning appears in the New Testament in Acts 2:36, where the word is used as an adverb: "Let all the house of Israel therefore know assuredly (*asphalôs*) that God has made him both Lord and Christ, this Jesus whom you crucified." The word has the sense of "truth" or "clarification" when it is a question of overcoming an obscurity regarding certain matters, but it comes to mean "certainty" when it is a question of substantiating the truth of an assertion whose meaning is, in itself, already clear.

Luke addressed his Gospel to one man, a "most excellent Theophilus," but he had, in all probability, a larger audience in mind, for it was the custom in his time to dedicate a literary work to a prominent individual who then would acknowledge the honor by using his influence to see that the work gained wider circulation. Theophilus was a man who had been instructed in Christian things, and it does not appear that it was Luke's purpose to remedy or clarify any obscurity in the instruction that either he or the wider reading public had received. Had Luke's purpose been to overcome a heresy or to clarify a misconception that his readers had acquired

189

from their Christian instruction, Luke-Acts would reveal a stress on some aspect of Christian truth, as Paul stressed justification in writing Galatians or as James stressed a consistent ethical life in his epistle. But in Luke-Acts there is no such stress upon any particulars of Christian teaching, and therefore *aspháleian* does not have to mean "truth" in the sense of clarification. But there is, as we shall see, reason for understanding *tēn aspháleian* as certainty that would provide verification for the perfectly good instruction the readers had already received.

From the way Luke speaks in verses 1 and 2, it appears that he regarded himself as being related to the basic events of Christianity in two different ways. According to verse 2, the report of these events had been transmitted to him by eyewitnesses, but in verse 1 he declares that these events have led to a fulfillment of which he is a contemporary. Hence he has access to the knowledge of these events both by the reports of the eyewitnesses and by the fulfillment that has come as their result. These events, which are the ministry, death, resurrection, and ascension of Jesus Christ, comprise the subject material of Luke and the other Gospels. But because Luke was not only interested in these events by themselves but also in their fulfillment, he has carried his narrative on beyond the ascension of Christ, and in the Acts of the Apostles he has told what transpired as a result of the Christ event. In the latter half of Acts there appear the famous "we" passages,[2] in which the writer expressly indicates that he has participated in the events recorded there.

The correspondence between verses 1-2 and verse 4 should be observed. In verses 1-2 there is both the Christ event and its fulfillment; in verse 4 there is both Christian instruction and *tēn aspháleian*. Both Luke and Theophilus had received Christian instruction regarding the Christ event; both had received knowledge that stemmed ultimately from the eyewitnesses. But Luke had also participated in a fulfillment of this event. If it could be shown that this event in which Luke

[2] Acts 16:10-17; 20:5–21:8; 27:1–28:16.

participated was a fulfillment in the sense that it could not have happened without the Christ event as its cause, then this fulfillment would provide certainty for the Christian instruction regarding the Christ event that Theophilus and other Christians had received.

Some find it difficult, however, to regard the prologue to Luke's Gospel as applying to Acts as well, for in our Bibles these books are separated by the Gospel of John. But there are examples from the literature of that time of work of more than one section having, like Luke-Acts, a major prologue at the beginning and a minor prologue introducing a new section, with the prologue at the beginning setting the theme for the whole. For example, Josephus, at the beginning of the first book of *Against Apion*, states that his purpose was to write a refutation of those Greek claims that the Jewish race was not of great antiquity. In II. 1 he reviews, in a manner similar to Acts 1:1, the contents of the former book. Then he proceeds to tell how he will refute the charges that a certain Greek named Apion has made against the Jews. Hence, though passing to a new book so distinct from the preceding book that it merits a new introduction, Josephus, like Luke, is continuing the same theme. Concerning Acts 1:1 Cadbury has remarked,

> The impression made on the English reader by Acts 1:1, that the author is making a new start or at least preparing a kind of sequel to his gospel, would not occur to an early reader. The book of Acts is no afterthought. The word "treatise" [in the Authorized Version] implies a more complete work than does [the Greek] *lógos*. The reference to the preceding book, and the renewed address to the patron, are typical of these secondary prefaces in Greek and Latin literature, and are intended to recall the original preface to the reader. Luke 1:1-4, therefore, is not merely of indirect value to the student of Acts as an introduction to another work written by the same author and addressed to the same patron. It is the real preface to Acts as well as to the Gospel, written by the author when he contemplated not merely one but both volumes.[3]

[3] H. Cadbury, "Commentary on the Preface of Luke," *The Beginnings of Christianity*, II, 491f.

Thus Acts is the continuation of the Gospel of Luke, and since it records events in which Luke participates, Acts could be the fulfillment mentioned in Luke 1:1. But before seeing whether this is possible, and whether such a fulfillment could give certainty regarding the Christ event of the Gospel of Luke, it is necessary to consider two introductory questions regarding the book of Acts.

II. Two Introductory Questions

If the events of the second half of Acts, where the "we" passages occur, are really the "fulfillment among us" of the Christ event, then it must be possible for the writer of Acts to have been a companion of Paul. However, there are some scholars today who find it difficult to believe that the writer of this book could have known Paul personally. Ernest Haenchen, professor at Münster and author of the latest commentary on Acts in the famous Meyer's series, cannot regard the writer as Paul's companion because he feels that the difference between the thinking of Acts and that of Paul's epistles is too great.[4] As Haenchen sees it, in Acts Paul clashed with the Jews because of his preaching of the resurrection, whereas the epistles reveal that the clash came because of Paul's declaration that Gentiles need not be circumcised. Furthermore, Acts regards Paul as performing more miracles and as being a more eloquent speaker than his epistles would allow. Finally, Luke regards only the twelve as bona fide apostles, whereas the Pauline epistles speak of Paul as equal with the twelve. Therefore, argues Haenchen, the writer of Acts could not have been the traveling companion of Paul, as the "we" passages imply.

How then does Haenchen account for the "we" passages? He argues that their purpose is simply to make the reader feel at one with the story or to increase its vividness. But if this is their explanation, why were the "we" passages not placed at more crucial places in the narrative, such as the

[4] E. Haenchen, *Die Apostelgeschichte*, pp. 99-103.

Jerusalem Conference of chapter 15 or at the climactic triumph of the Gospel in the heathen world at chapter 19, where it would be best for the reader to feel that he really enters into the happenings? In a subsequent article[5] Haenchen has attempted to show that the "we" passages do indeed occur at such crucial points. But his argument is not convincing enough to enable Hans Conzelmann, a close associate, to understand the "we" passages simply as literary devices to make crucial points vivid and bring the reader into the story. Nor can Conzelmann understand these passages as being taken from the diary of one of Paul's associates. But neither is Conzelmann able to solve the problem of the "we" passages by saying that they indicate the times when the author of the book was with Paul, for like Haenchen he finds the thinking of Acts and Paul too diverse. Thus his only alternative is to declare, "The riddle of the 'we' passages remains, as ever, unsolved."[6]

But some great names in the history of interpretation have been able to regard the author of Acts as the companion of Paul. Martin Dibelius, who in the 20s opened up new avenues of studying Acts with his "style criticism" and whose findings have been of help to Haenchen and Conzelmann, declares that the only plausible explanation for the "we" passages is that they indicate when the author was actually with Paul. "My whole view," declared Dibelius,

> is completely opposed to the one which was known to the generation of our teachers (with the exception of Harnack) as the "critical" view. They do not tire of telling us that the Acts of the Apostles could not have been written by Luke, Paul's companion, because it contained more errors than could have been made by one who was so close to Paul. This theory somewhat exaggerates the proximity to Paul and the number of errors.[7]

Harnack went even farther than Dibelius in seeing the essential agreement between Paul and Luke. According to Harnack,

[5] E. Haenchen, "Das 'Wir' in der Apostelgeschichte und das Itinerar," *Zeitschrift für Theologie und Kirche,* 58 (1961), 329-366.

[6] H. Conzelmann, *Die Apostelgeschichte,* p. 6.

[7] M. Dibelius, *Studies in the Acts of the Apostles,* p. 136.

the one who wrote Acts 13:38-39, which speaks of justification by faith apart from the works of the law, "was a near disciple of St. Paul."[8]

In addition to answering the great objection against the Lucan authorship, Harnack gave the following positive argument that Luke, the beloved physician and companion of Paul spoken of in the epistles, was the author of Luke.[9] Since the last "we" passage brings the author with Paul to Rome, it is likely that the author would be one of those whom Paul mentions in Colossians and Philemon as being with him in Rome. Aristarchus, whom Acts 27:2 records as accompanying Paul from Rome, is one of the six persons who are with Paul (Phm. 24); the other five are Mark, Jesus Justus, Epaphras, Demas, and Luke (Col. 4:10, 12; Phm. 24). Of these five, church tradition has singled out Luke as the author of Acts. But since he was such an obscure person, it is unlikely that it would have singled him out without good historical basis for so doing. Furthermore, the person speaking of himself as one of the "we" was not just a fellow traveler with Paul but was also a preacher of the Gospel, for he declares in Acts 16:10, "We sought to go forth into Macedonia, concluding that God had called us to preach the Gospel unto them." According to Philemon 24, Luke is termed one of Paul's "fellow workers."

Consequently, the evidence points to Luke as the author of the book and the one whom the "we" passages regard as participating in some of the events of the latter half of Acts. Thus there is reason to believe that the author of Luke-Acts did participate in an event that he regarded as the fulfillment of the Christ event recorded in his Gospel.

As for the date of Acts, Harnack changed from the position he held in 1906 that the book was written somewhere between A.D. 78–93[10] to the position held in his 1908 and 1911 books that Acts was written in the early 60s, before the death of Paul

---

[8] A. Harnack, *Luke the Physician*, p. 19, note.
[9] *Ibid.*, pp. 12-24.
[10] *Ibid.*, p. 24.

and the destruction of Jerusalem.[11] Harnack argued that, had there been a long period of time between the imprisonment recorded in Acts 28 and the writing of the book, the writer would surely have added more material. Then, too, Acts pictures the Jews as anything but defeated, and this is a point of view one would hardly expect if the book had been written after the destruction of Jerusalem in A.D. 70. Finally, there is no evidence that the writer of Acts depended upon the Pauline epistles for his material—a fact that is easier to explain if this book was written in the 60s than in the 80s, when Paul's letters were widely distributed in the churches. To the objection that this would mean that Luke, in his record of the Olivet discourse, could know of the destruction of Jerusalem before it happened, Harnack replied that even if this discourse were written after the destruction of Jerusalem, it still speaks of many things that were not fulfilled at that time, e.g., the coming of the Son of man and the shaking of the heavens. Therefore, since there are some events in this Olivet discourse that had not yet happened at the time of writing, whatever its date of composition, there is no reason why it could not have been written before the destruction of Jerusalem in A.D. 70.

Thus Luke, the beloved physician and companion of Paul, was the author of Luke-Acts. He wrote Acts at a time when it was still possible to speak of events in which he had participated as a recent fulfillment of the Christ event. But if Acts records the fulfillment of the Christ event that will lead to the certainty of that event, then this fact must be fully established by letting the book of Acts itself reveal that it was written for this purpose. The way a book begins and ends is often helpful in determining its purpose, but the beginning and ending of Acts are not without their problems. Hence it is necessary to consider these problems before using the beginning and ending of Acts as evidence of the purpose of the book.

[11] Harnack, *The Acts of the Apostles* and *The Date of Acts and of the Synoptic Gospels.*

There have been a number of interpreters[12] who have argued that the ending of Luke (24:50-53) and the beginning of Acts (1:1-5) were an interpolation added later, when the canon was becoming fixed and Luke-Acts was artificially broken into two parts so that the Gospel would have the same scope as the other Gospels. They reason that there is a clumsiness about these verses that indicates the work of a redactor instead of the usually flawless style of Luke. Crediting these verses to Luke would make him responsible for telling of the ascension three times: Luke 24:52; Acts 1:2; and Acts 1:9. After speaking of the ascension in Acts 1:2, the narrative then shifts to a time prior to the ascension and the events leading up to it. Then, too, Acts 1:6, with its question regarding Israel's future, seems to connect better with the section ending at Luke 24:49, in which Jesus speaks of the Gospel's spread to the Gentiles, than it would with Acts 1:5's mention of the forthcoming enduement of the Holy Spirit. Finally, it is argued that, had Luke begun Acts with a summary of the Gospel, he would surely have gone on after 1:2 with a summary of what lay ahead in the second treatise. Instead, verse 3 connects itself with verse 2 by means of a relative clause in which the narrative of Acts is awkwardly begun.

But the basic objection to the argument that Luke 24:50– Acts 1:5 is an interpolation is that it is harder to conceive of these difficulties as arising from a redactor, whose aim is to smooth things up, than from Luke himself, whose purpose in these verses, when once discerned, can adequately account for them. First of all, it should be noted that the function of Acts 1:1-2 is to summarize Luke's Gospel. Verse 1 summarizes the whole Gospel of Luke as an account of what Jesus "began to do and teach," and then verse 2 summarizes the last few verses of Luke 24. Verse 2 recalls the commands the risen

[12] P. Menoud, "Remarques sur les textes de l'ascension dans Luc/ Actes," *Neutestamentliche Studien für R. Bultmann*, pp. 148-156; E. Meyer, *Ursprung und Anfänge des Christentums*, I, 34-35; H. Sahlin, *Der Messias und das Gottesvolk*, pp. 11-18; and E. Trocmé, *Le "Livre des Actes" et l'histoire*, pp. 30-34.

Jesus gave to his disciples (Luke 24:44-49) and his ascension (Luke 24:50-53).

It would seem that, following the summary of his Gospel in Acts 1:1-2, Luke should have gone on and introduced a summary of the book that is to follow. However, Acts 1:3 simply commences the narrative of Acts without giving any preview of what is to come. But this presents no insuperable difficulty, for there are examples in ancient literature where a later section of a work is introduced simply by a summary of the preceding section.[13] Neither should it be argued that the *mèn* with which Acts 1:1 begins demands a following and corresponding *dé*, for the *mèn* can exist alone for the purpose of giving emphasis to what it introduces.[14] In introducing Acts 1:1-2 with a *mèn* without a following *dé*, it was Luke's purpose simply to reiterate the contents of the preceding Gospel so that they would remain fixed in the reader's mind as he continued with the second treatise. It could also be that Luke gave no summary of what is to come in Acts because this was already done in the prologue to Luke with its reference to the fulfillment of the Christ event which came later.

But why does Luke begin the narrative of Acts at a point of time prior to the ascension and the end of Luke, and thus give another account of the ascension in Acts 1:9-11? It may well be, as Barrett and van Stempvoort propose,[15] that Luke reiterated the account of the ascension at Acts 1:9-11 because it plays a different role in Acts than in Luke. In Luke 24 the resurrection appearances and the ascension are linked together as though they all occurred on one day. This was the way Luke effected his purpose of showing the resurrection appearances and the ascension as the climax of the Christ event. To have mentioned in Luke 24 that forty days transpired

[13] E.g., Josephus, *Antiquities*. Books VIII and XIII begin with summaries of what has preceded, but these summaries are not followed by a summary of what lies ahead.

[14] B. Reicke, "Zum sprachlichen Verständnis von Kol. 2:23," *Theologica Studia*, 6 (1953), 43.

[15] C. Barrett, *Luke the Historian in Recent Study*, pp. 55-57; P. van · Stempvoort, "The Interpretation of the Ascension in Luke and Acts," *New Testament Studies*, 5 (1958), 35-36, 39.

between the resurrection and the ascension would have detracted from showing the ascension as the great climax to the resurrection. In Acts 1, on the other hand, the resurrection appearances and the ascension function not as a climax but as the basis for the forthcoming narrative of Acts. It suits the purpose of showing that the resurrection appearances are the basis for what follows to declare that they occurred during forty days, for this allows sufficient time for the apostles to grasp the fact and meaning of Jesus' resurrection through the instruction he gave during the appearances of this period. In this way, then, the resurrection becomes the basis for all that follows. The reiteration of the ascension emphasizes the foundational function of the resurrection appearances for the narrative that follows by terminating them and thus setting them off from that narrative.

Thus the three accounts of the ascension in Luke 24:50–Acts 1:9 are not the result of clumsy editing, for each has its distinctive function. Luke 24:51 provides the climax to the Gospel of Luke. Acts 1:2 reiterates this climax so that the reader will not forget the point of the Gospel while proceeding with Acts. Acts 1:9-11 sets forth the ascension as terminating the resurrection appearances so they can function as the basis for what follows.

In answer to the objection that Acts 1:6 cannot be relevant to 1:5, it need only be observed, as Reicke has pointed out,[16] that verses 6-8, in which the apostles are directed toward the evangelization of the world, come as a necessary checkmate to the Jewish tendency, which the apostles shared, to be interested chiefly in Israel. This interest could have been encouraged by the command of verses 4-5 to remain in Jerusalem for the baptism of the Spirit. Furthermore, to try to connect Acts 1:6 immediately with Luke 24:49 involves one in the embarrassment, as Kümmel has indicated,[17] of having the apostles returning in Acts 1:12 from somewhere without

[16] B. Reicke, *Glaube und Leben der Urgemeinde*, p. 16.
[17] W. Kümmel, "Das Urchristentum," *Theologische Rundschau*, N.F. 22 (1954), 195f.

ever having left the building where they were still assembled in Luke 24:49. Hence it is concluded that the easiest explanation for the present beginning of Acts is that it stemmed from Luke himself, and therefore it can provide data for understanding Luke's purpose in writing this book.

But did Luke intend the book to end where it now does? Theodor Zahn declared that "a more awkward conclusion of the work could scarcely be imagined."[18] He felt that, since the reader's anticipation of the triumph that would be reached at Rome had been whetted at a number of points ever since Acts 19:21, he could only be sadly disappointed by the fact that nothing decisive happens in chapter 28. However, Zahn admitted that the book's present ending did bring it to a "significant point" in the history of Christianity, so that any further information in Luke's mind would have been placed in a new book, the third in a series commencing with the Gospel and Acts.

It should also be noted that the present ending of Acts, undramatic though it may be, bears every indication of being a reasonably conceived termination. It cannot be understood as stemming from something accidental, like the author's sudden death or the mutilation of the text. Therefore, even if Luke intended a third treatise to Theophilus (which is unlikely), it would be quite legitimate to investigate the purpose of Acts itself with its present ending. Consequently, the present ending of the book, as well as its beginning, represent what the author intended, and thus one is justified in working with them to detect the author's purpose.

III. The Purpose of Acts

The task of understanding this book's purpose would be much simpler if Luke had spelled it out explicitly and in full detail. Many feel that Acts 1:8 is the key to the book's purpose. This verse tells how the Gospel was to be preached at Jerusalem and then expand outward until it reached the

[18] T. Zahn, *Introduction to the New Testament*, III, 57.

uttermost parts of the earth. And indeed, everything up through chapter 19 of Acts follows this pattern, for the Gospel begins in Jerusalem (chs. 1-7), goes to Samaria (ch. 8), and then onward to such remote places as Ephesus (ch. 19), where the preaching of it is accompanied by such power that the citadels of paganism are shaken to the ground.

Furthermore, the theme of this verse harmonizes well with the foregleam of Acts' context that is implied by the summary of the Gospel given in Acts 1:1 in the words, "all that Jesus began both to do and teach." The word "began" occupies an emphatic position in the Greek text, and this fact, coupled with the stress in Acts on the work that Jesus continued to do through the outpoured Holy Spirit and the church, implies that the basic emphasis of Luke-Acts concerns what Jesus has done: the Gospel relates the earlier phase of his work done upon the earth, whereas Acts shows what Jesus continued to do from heaven. Some interpreters, however, have regarded the "began" as a carry-over into the Greek of a Semitic auxiliary verb.[19] But even if this were the case, the inference of a continuation of the work of Jesus from the Gospel into Acts could hardly be missed because of the fact that Acts begins by summarizing the preceding treatise as an account of what Jesus did and taught. Thus Eduard Meyer, who believed that the "began" should not receive the stress but was simply an auxiliary for "do and teach," nevertheless declared that if Luke had followed Acts 1:1-2 with a summary of this second treatise, it would have read, "The second book, however, will consist of the completion of Jesus' work through the fulfillment of his promise and the extension of his teaching."[20]

But the great difficulty with understanding Acts simply as the working of the heavenly Jesus to bring the Gospel to the far reaches of earth lies in its last eight chapters, in which Paul, instead of preaching the Gospel to new areas, returns to the starting point, Jerusalem, and there becomes and remains a prisoner of Rome until the end of the book. No climax

[19] E.g., Haenchen, *Die Apostelgeschichte*, p. 106, note.
[20] E. Meyer, *Ursprung und Anfänge des Christentums*, I, 34, note.

in terms of Acts 1:8 can be found in the fact that at the end of the book Paul preaches at Rome (28:30-31), for a church already exists there (28:15), and Paul's preaching produces no unusual results. Hence the book's purpose, if it has one, must certainly include the theme of 1:8 and 1:1, but must also show why chapters 20-28 are important and how the abrupt conclusion of Acts is a fitting climax.

There are other themes in Acts besides that of Jesus' work in spreading the Gospel to the world that should also be taken into consideration in determining the purpose of the book. There is the stress on Christianity's continuity with Judaism and the Old Testament, which appears in all the sermons preached to the Jews and in Paul's defense before the Romans. There is the stress on Judaism's hatred of Christianity, which begins at 4:1 and continues to the end. There is also the stress on the favor that Christianity receives from those who are generally neutral, e.g., the common people at Jerusalem (2:47; 5:13), and from the Roman officials (13:8-12; 18:12-17; etc.).

Finally, there is the unmistakable stress on Paul. "It is plain that Paul is Luke's hero," remarks F. F. Bruce,[21] "and the main object of some passages in Acts seems to be to show how Paul stands head and shoulders above other men." Peter, the chief apostle, is named only 55 times, while Paul (or Saul) is named 140 times. A possible explanation for this emphasis on Paul is Luke's close association with him; however, it is well to hold open the possibility that Luke, in his acquaintance with Paul, grasped a concept which centered around him. To set forth this concept, it was necessary to give Paul the prominent role he has in Acts.

Thus the five great themes of Acts are (1) the spread of the Gospel, (2) the continuity between Christianity and the Old Testament, (3) the Jewish persecution of Christians, (4) Christianity's favor with the neutrals, and (5) the pre-eminence of Paul. Among the recent expositions of Acts there are four rather distinct and singular theories regarding Luke's purpose

[21] F. F. Bruce, *The Acts of the Apostles,* p. 32.

in writing this book, and each of these finds its basis in some of these themes as the center around which the whole of the book is to be understood. Each of these theories should be evaluated on the basis of how well it can see these emphases and the other peculiarities of Acts as part of a coherent whole.

A. Four Contemporary Theories

The first theory to be considered states that one of Luke's major purposes in writing Acts was to show a Roman official, such as Theophilus, that Christianity was the perfect expression of Judaism, so that he would feel inclined to grant Christianity Judaism's status of being a *religio licita* ("legal religion") in the Roman empire.

> *Note.* Julius Caesar, as an exception to his order that all *collegia*, or "secret societies," be disbanded (Suetonius, *The Deified Julius*, XLII. 3), had granted the Jews a special dispensation whereby the worship in their synagogues might be continued (Josephus, *Antiquities*, XIV. 10. 2, 8). This special dispensation was renewed by Augustus (*Antiquities*, XVI. 6. 1-6). But during the reign of Claudius it was decreed that the Jews should leave Rome (Acts 18:1-2). There is some question, however, whether all Jews were forced to leave. Acts 16:20-21 indicates that there was a tension between the Jews and the Roman rulers because the Jews sought to make converts of the Romans. Perhaps the expulsion under Claudius involved only the chief offenders, because Suetonius (*The Deified Claudius*, XXV. 4) seems to indicate that only those Jews who had created a disturbance were forced to leave. Likewise Dio, in his *Roman History*, LX. 6. 6, asserts that, owing to their great numbers, not all Jews were ejected. In any event, during the reign of Nero the Jews were again treated with favor. Nero's wife was a Jewess and quite religious (Josephus, *Antiquities*, XX. 8. 11; *The Life*, 16). During the reign of Trajan, Caesar's rule prohibiting the *collegia* was revived and applied against the Christians (Pliny, *Letters*, X. 33, 34), so that Christianity was treated as a *religio illicita*. The Jews, however, continued to enjoy their status as a *religio licita*. Writing at the end of the second century, Tertullian (*Apology*, 21) stated that Judaism was a *religio licita* and, therefore, since Christianity also found

An Early Christian Approach

its support in the Jewish writings (though it did not adhere to the Jewish customs regarding food, the Sabbath, and circumcision), it should be accorded the same privilege. He further argued (*Apology*, 39) that Christianity should not be counted as a *collegium* that should be condemned, since it in no way posed a threat to the Roman empire.

B. S. Easton's treatise on "The Purpose of Acts,"[22] written in 1935, is a classical attempt to understand this as the primary purpose for which Acts was written. Of the five great emphases of Acts, Easton finds the themes of continuity with Judaism and the favor that neutrals accorded Christianity as most helpful. He also goes to great lengths to argue that the polity of the Christian church in Acts was modelled after that of the Jewish synagogue.

But there are two difficulties in understanding Acts in this way. Acts, in stressing the continuity that Christianity has with the Old Testament, presupposes that its readers have such a knowledge of the Old Testament and its theology that the book would hardly be what a pagan Roman official would grasp. On the contrary, every evidence indicates that the readers the writer of Acts had in view were people who, like Theophilus and the Christians of that day, were well versed in the Old Testament. Thus Meyer declares that

Luke had in mind only readers who were Christians or very close to becoming such. Acts is a book for the Christian church, not for the pagan world. . . . Throughout Luke presupposes an acquaintance with the Holy Scriptures and Jewish points of view and institutions.[23]

The second difficulty with Easton's theory is that it clashes with the theme of Jewish opposition. Surely a pagan official would not be encouraged to regard Christianity as a virtual Judaism when it was brought to his attention that Christianity tended to rouse Jewish hostility.

[22] B. Easton, *Early Christianity. The Purpose of Acts and Other Papers*, pp. 33-118.
[23] Meyer, *op. cit.*, p. 9.

It should also be pointed out that Easton's theory does not account for Luke's emphasis on the spread of the Gospel outwards from Jerusalem. But Easton feels that this theme is very basic to Acts and so he declares that Luke had a second purpose, namely, to comfort Christians who were suffering persecution by describing the powerful way in which Christianity had been able to overcome every obstacle. Indeed, it is possible that Luke did have two purposes for this book, but this approach must not be adopted until it has been ascertained that a single purpose cannot be perceived which accounts for all the data.

A second theory seeks to understand the purpose of Acts by starting with Luke's stress on Paul. According to Étienne Trocmé,[24] there were two great branches of the church around A.D. 80-85. There was an anti-Pauline, Judaizing element that was rooted particularly in the churches of Alexandria. These churches claimed superiority over the Pauline churches of Asia Minor, Macedonia, and Achaia because the Alexandrian churches could trace their origin back to the twelve apostles and the Jerusalem church. The Pauline churches could not do this, for Paul was not one of the twelve. The Pauline churches, therefore, needed an interpretation of their origin that would show not only their superiority over the Alexandrian churches but would also show them to be a continuation of Judaism and thus worthy of being counted as a *religio licita* (52).

According to Trocmé, Luke-Acts was composed to counter the claim of the Alexandrian churches by stressing the unity of God's working from the Old Testament through the life of Jesus to the bringing of the Gospel to the Gentiles (59). Paul in particular symbolized this unity with the past and with Israel, for he had his co-worker circumcised (Acts 16:3) and he was deferential to the High Priest, though standing accused before him (Acts 23:2-5). But it is Paul who is chiefly responsible for bringing the Gospel to the Gentiles. "It seems," declares Trocmé, "that the author of Luke-Acts, in order to

[24] E. Trocmé, *Le "Livre des Actes" et l'historie*. Subsequent page references refer to this book.

defend Paul against the attacks of the Jewish Christians, presents him as the only one who perpetuated the work of the twelve apostles" (67). Thus while Paul was not an official apostle like one of the twelve, yet he and Barnabas were commissioned by them to carry the decision of the Jerusalem conference back to Antioch (Acts 15:30). In fact, they had already been called "apostles" (Acts 14:4, 14) in the broader sense, for they were the official representatives of the twelve.

But Luke wanted to show Paul as "the only perpetuator" of the work of the twelve apostles, and so he described how Barnabas broke away from Paul (Acts 15:37ff.). Thus from Luke-Acts the Pauline churches could see that their founder was the one whom God had uniquely ordained to bridge the gap between God's working in the Old Testament and the Jerusalem church to his working among the Gentiles. Far from feeling inferior to the Alexandrian churches, the Pauline churches had the right to feel superior.

Indeed, Trocmé's theory provides an explanation for the emphases in Acts on Paul, the continuity with the Old Testament, and the expansion of Christianity. But it clashes with the other emphases. If the Pauline churches needed to show continuity with Judaism in order to be considered a *religio licita*, why did Luke stress the clash between Christianity and Judaism? Furthermore, if this was really Luke's purpose and if (as Trocmé assumes) the writer of Acts felt considerable freedom to shape his narrative so it would answer to the specific problem he was trying to solve, would it not have been far better to make Paul every bit the equal of the twelve apostles, as Paul himself did in his epistles? Likewise, would not Luke have made Paul's ministry to the Gentiles something that was directly decreed by the Jerusalem apostles so as to establish definitely that he was "the only perpetuator" of their work?

Trocmé also has difficulty making sense out of the ending of Acts. According to him, Acts was written some 25 years after Paul's imprisonment at Rome. However, nothing beyond 28:31 is mentioned, Trocmé declares, because this was a decisive and climactic moment in the history of salvation. Here the Jews reject the offer of salvation and as a result the Gospel is given to the Gentiles with finality (50, 55). Thus the book climaxes by showing that the final rejection by the Jews completes the bridge over which the Gospel is to be brought henceforth only to the Gentiles. But why was not the bridge completed earlier when Paul also spoke of turning from the Jews to the Gentiles (Acts 13:46-47; 18:6)? If it was not completed earlier by such statements, why was it completed at this time?

A third theory is that of J. C. O'Neill,[25] who argues that Luke's primary aim in writing Acts was to "preach the Gospel to unbelievers" (173). It was "the unprecedented growth of Christianity from the smallest beginnings, a growth which depended utterly on God's initiative," which, "despite all the set-backs [Christianity] encountered, was used to support its claim to be the only true religion" (170). Acts also has the secondary aim of showing how the church discovered that its true destiny was that of being entirely independent of Judaism. This discovery came when at Rome Paul turned with finality from the Jews to the Gentiles.

> Right up to the last journey to Jerusalem Paul had regarded the church as still essentially part of the Jewish nation. . . . Yet still the Jews try to kill him and refuse to accept the Gospel, so that, with a note of finality, he is at length forced to declare, "Let it be known to you that this, the salvation of God, has been sent to the Gentiles. They will hear" (70).

To be sure, O'Neill's theory does provide an explanation for Luke's emphasis on Christianity's growth and his emphasis on Paul, for he is the one who finally understands that Christianity's destiny is to be separate from the Jews and to minister to the Gentiles. Such an understanding of Acts also accords well with the theme of the miraculous spread of the Gospel, the favor that Christianity receives from the Romans, and the hostility it engenders among the Jews. But this theory does not make peace with the great emphasis appearing throughout

[25] J. C. O'Neill, *The Theology of Acts.*

the book that Christianity is nothing more than what truly orthodox Judaism should be, so that the Gospel is always being extended to the Jews. Paul always acted in accordance with this principle, and his action at the end of the book is no departure from it.

A fourth theory is that of Floyd Filson.[26] He tries to construct a theory that not only includes the strong points of the other theories considered but that also attempts to overcome their objections. He declares that Luke's primary purpose in writing Luke-Acts was to win converts to Christianity in the Roman world by showing that Christianity must be true because of its miraculous spread despite all opposition. But to achieve this purpose, Filson argues that it would be helpful for Christianity to enjoy Judaism's status as a *religio licita*, and therefore there is the emphasis in Acts that Christianity is the continuation of Judaism and that it enjoys favor with the Roman officials. Luke also emphasized Paul and set him forth as a great hero in order to overcome the unpopularity he had engendered among the Gentiles for his preaching against polytheism and moral laxity, and the hatred that he had incurred from the Jews for what they thought was disloyalty to the Mosaic law.

But how can Filson account for the theme of Jewish opposition to the Gospel? Such a theme should not be stressed when one's purpose is to give Christianity the status Judaism enjoys. Filson seeks to answer this problem by claiming that the theme of Jewish hostility to the church functions to show that the Jews had forfeited their right to be God's people and that the Christians had now inherited this privilege. However, it is feared that this argument would be quite difficult for readers to grasp who were not familiar enough with the Old Testament to see how Christians were the continuation of the heritage the Jews had rejected. Furthermore, it has already been shown that the presupposition of the author of Acts that his readers have a knowledge of the Old Testament argues strongly against the supposition that it was written to win

[26] F. Filson, *Three Crucial Decades,* pp. 16f.

converts from the pagan world. Filson has struggled admirably to make all the themes of Acts harmonize to the effecting of one purpose, but the difficulty of his position indicates that another approach to the question should be sought.

B. *Another Approach*

The starting point for the theory now to be advanced is the observation that in Acts the expansion of Christianity to the Gentile world is of crucial importance. The theme of the book implied by Acts 1:1 as well as the program for world evangelization outlined in 1:8 make it impossible to avoid seeing this theme as very basic to the purpose of Acts. "The central factor in the narrative of Acts is the word preached by the apostles and their successors. The process described in the book is the constitution and expansion of the church. . . ."[27]

However, it should be observed that this theme achieves its climax, not in chapter 28, when Paul preached at Rome, but in his ministry at Ephesus (ch. 19), which is the climax of the Gentile mission. A comparison between chapters 19 and 28 makes this obvious. In chapter 28 Paul simply preached where a church already existed, and with no outstanding success, but in chapter 19 not only was a new church founded, but there was a grand fulfillment of the theme that Jesus would powerfully work to spread the Gospel to the world, for Paul performed "special powers"—the sick were healed through his handkerchiefs, demons were cast out, and men gave up their practice of witchcraft. "All the residents of Asia heard the word of the Lord" (19:10), and so mightily did the word of the Lord grow and prevail that the idol manufacturers were threatened with extinction.

The work done by the risen Jesus in bringing these triumphs to pass was in keeping with the *grace of God* that characterized this Gentile mission. The message that was presented was summarized as the "word of grace" (14:3;

[27] B. Reicke, "The Risen Lord and His Church," *Interpretation*, 13 (1959), 165f.

20:24), and the hearers were enjoined to adhere to the grace of God (13:43; 20:32). This involved simply repentance toward God and faith in Christ (13:38-39; 16:31; 20:21). It was through God's sovereign election and effectual working that the Gentiles came to believe (13:48; 16:14), and thus Luke characterized the converts as "those who through grace had believed" (18:27). In the words of Peter at the Jerusalem Council, the Gentiles were saved through grace (15:11).

At the conclusion of his ministry at Ephesus, Paul felt constrained to return to Jerusalem (19:21; 20:16, 22; 21:13). The reason for going there given in Romans and II Corinthians, namely, to bring the Gentile churches' offering, is mentioned only in a very incidental way by Luke (24:17). For Luke, Paul's primary purpose in returning was to "testify to the Gospel of the grace of God" (20:22-24; cf. 23:11). Thus upon arrival at Jerusalem Paul reported to James and the elders how God had worked through his ministry to bring the Gospel to the Gentiles (21:19-20a). They glorified God for this news but then made it clear that Judaism in general would not share their joy over the success of the Gentile mission, for even among Jewish believers the notion was prevalent that Paul's teaching of the grace of God meant not merely that the Gentiles did not need to adhere to the Jewish distinctives of circumcision and diet, but that the Jews themselves should give up these distinctives (20:20b-25). Hence they recommended that Paul submit to a Jewish vow for seven days in order to demonstrate his loyalty to Judaism. This Paul was willing to do in order to show that for a Jew to acknowledge that salvation was by grace did not mean that he must renounce his distinctively Jewish practices.

But Paul had also brought with him from Ephesus a Gentile convert named Trophimus. Certain Jews from Ephesus had recognized them at Jerusalem, and as these Jews saw Paul remaining in the temple in fulfillment of his vow, the jealousy that such Jews had felt as they had seen the Gospel going to the Gentiles (Acts 13:45; 17:5) without requiring them to be circumcised led them to the false conclusion that Paul had committed the supreme sacrilege of bringing a Gentile into the temple precincts. Thus the result of Paul's presence at Jerusalem for the purpose of testifying to the grace of God was the arousing of such antagonism that a riot resulted that threatened his life and brought the entire city into an uproar.

Luke's narrative stresses how difficult it was for the Romans to ascertain the cause of this riot. To the understanding ear its ultimate cause became manifest as Paul spoke to the multitudes from the steps leading into the fortress (22:1ff.). He declared that it was the appearance of the risen Jesus to him on the Damascus road that had led ultimately to his ministry to the Gentiles. But when the multitudes heard of Paul's ministry to the Gentiles, they shouted, "Away with such a fellow from the earth! For he ought not to live" (22:22). However, even if the Romans could have understood the Aramaic language in which Paul spoke, they could not have grasped how such apparently unrelated issues as the resurrection of Christ and the Jewish sense of superiority over the Gentiles could have brought the whole city of Jerusalem into an uproar. Therefore they brought Paul before the Sanhedrin "to know the real reason why the Jews accused him" (22:30). As in his previous speech, so here Paul declared that the resurrection was the basic reason for the riot. But here Paul did not speak of the resurrection of Jesus but of the future resurrection of the dead: "With respect to the hope and the resurrection of the dead I am on trial" (23:6).

One should not assume that Paul made this statement simply as a clever move to bring his accusers (the Pharisees, who believed in the resurrection, and the Sadducees, who did not) into conflict so that they would be distracted from doing violence to him. This was, to be sure, part of his motive, for had Paul not been able to do this, the Jews could have made the Romans believe their false charges against him. But this statement, while very effective in producing the riot, was also a declaration of the basic reason for the clash that had arisen between the Jews and Paul. It was given not only to help the

Romans understand the issues at stake but also to establish a common ground with the Pharisees.

It was the Pharisees who were the champions of Jewish orthodoxy. Unlike the Sadducees, they believed in the future resurrection and in angels and spiritual beings (Acts 23:8). While the priests and ruling class were, for the most part, Sadducees, yet it was the Pharisees who controlled the thinking of the common man. Josephus declared, "When [the Sadducees] become magistrates . . . they addict themselves to the notions of the Pharisees, because the multitude would not otherwise bear them" (*Antiquities*, XVIII. 1. 4). He also said, "[The Pharisees] have so great power over the multitude, that when they say anything against the king or against the highpriest, they are presently believed" (*Antiquities*, XIII. 10. 5). Consequently, Paul's declaration that he was being accused for believing the resurrection of the dead was an attempt to show that, far from being at odds with the Pharisees, he was at one with them and was therefore a representative of the orthodoxy to which the Jewish masses adhered. Thus in commenting on Paul's statement Haenchen asserts, "Paul was not saying that he *had been* a Pharisee, but that he was *one at the time*, and for this reason he was being accused."[28] Hence Paul declared that he had "hope in God, which these also accept, that there will be a resurrection both of the just and the unjust" (Acts 24:15).

But while Paul's belief in the resurrection classed him with the Pharisees and with orthodox Judaism, yet his particular understanding of the resurrection set him at odds with them. The Jews looked forward to the future resurrection as the time when they would enjoy the fulfillment of the promises God had made in the Old Testament. According to Acts 26:6f., they worshipped God night and day in the hope of attaining to the resurrection and the enjoyment of the promised blessings. Paul, however, believed that the fulfillment of these promises was no longer simply a future event but one that had already occurred in the resurrection of Jesus. To the

[28] Haenchen, *Die Apostelgeschichte*, p. 566.

Jews in Antioch in Pisidia Paul proclaimed, "We bring you the good news that what God promised to the fathers, this he has fulfilled to us their children by raising Jesus" (Acts 13: 32f.). Thus Paul differentiated himself from the Pharisees, not by denying that the fulfillment of the promises was dependent upon the resurrection, but by declaring that this fulfillment had already occurred. For the Pharisees the middle point of history lay in the future; for Paul and New Testament thinking in general it lay in the past, in the event of the resurrection of Jesus.[29] For the Jews the blessings of the Messianic age would be enjoyed in the future, but for Christian thinking the resurrection of Jesus had already made the firstfruits of these blessings available and had assured their full enjoyment (including the resurrection of the body) at the second coming of Jesus. The Jews objected strongly to such teaching, not only because it asserted their guilt in having crucified the Messiah (cf. 4:1-2; 5:28), but also because upon it was based the message of grace that Paul preached to the Gentiles and that made the Jewish distinctives of no ultimate value. But Paul claimed that in ministering to the Gentiles he was anything but a desecrator of Judaism who had defiled the temple, for the Gentile mission he led stemmed from the resurrection of Jesus, which answered to the hope that beat in the breast of every orthodox Jew.

Of course the Romans were unable to grasp all this from one statement. However, in the letter accompanying Paul to Caesarea (where he was taken for his safety), it appears that they had come to realize that he was guilty of no criminal offense worthy of death and that the problem between him and the Jews was of a theological nature (23:29). But, since the peace had been disturbed and the Jews were still plotting against Paul's life, it was therefore necessary for the Romans to continue their investigation of the matter. At the hearing held a week later before the procurator Felix at Caesarea, the Jews were given the chance to state their charges against Paul. They realized that if they admitted that the riot over

[29] O. Cullmann, *Christ and Time*, pp. 81ff.

Paul had arisen from a theological dispute within Judaism, the Romans would condemn them for letting their religious differences disturb the peace. Therefore they sought to cite charges that would show Paul to be opposed in such a way to Judaism and the peace of the Roman empire that he should be given the death penalty.

According to Acts 24:5-6, they brought three charges against Paul. First they claimed that he had agitated the Jews. Such a charge could well have reminded Felix of the Egyptian whom some had confused with Paul at the time of his arrest (21:38). This Egyptian was stopped only after Felix had sent troops against him and his 4,000 followers, who had encamped on the Mount of Olives waiting to invade Jerusalem after its walls had fallen down (Josephus, *Antiquities,* XX. 8. 6). The Jews also charged that Paul headed up a sinister and heretical sect. The Jews had received special permission from Rome to assemble and carry out their religious worship (Josephus, *Antiquities,* XIV. 10. 2, 8.), but if they could prove that Paul headed up a sect which was contrary to Judaism, then he would be guilty of transgressing the law, in effect since the reign of Julius Caesar, which banned all *collegia* or "special societies" (Suetonius, *The Deified Julius,* XLII. 3). The third charge the Jews brought against Paul was that he had profaned the temple. The Romans had given the Jews the right to execute even a Roman citizen if he defiled the temple by bringing a Gentile beyond the Court of the Gentiles (Josephus, *Jewish Wars,* VI. 126). If the Jews could prove any of these charges, then they would be rid of Paul.

Paul denied the charges one by one and declared that the Jews could offer no proof of any of them. He insisted that, far from being the leader of any new religion, he had taught nothing more than the resurrection of the dead, which the Jews themselves believed. Paul's whole conduct in Jerusalem had shown his loyalty to Judaism, for he had returned to bring alms and offerings to the Jewish nation, and when arrested was fulfilling a vow of purification in the temple. Because the procurator Felix understood about Christianity, he was convinced of Paul's innocence, but because he did not want to displease the Jews by releasing Paul, he made it appear that he wished to investigate further (Acts 24:22). However, nothing more was done during the remainder of Felix' procuratorship, and Paul remained in prison in Caesarea.

Two years later, when Festus had become the procurator of Judea, the Jews again tried to bring Paul to Jerusalem for judgment. But the hearing was held at Caesarea, and again the Jews failed to prove their charges (25:7). To placate the Jews, Festus offered to try Paul at Jerusalem, but to avoid this Paul made appeal to be heard by Nero at Rome, and this was accepted. By now it had become evident to Festus, both through his own investigation and through the records left from Felix' procuratorship, that there was no basis to the Jews' political charges against Paul and that, instead, the matter between Paul and the Jews concerned "certain points of dispute with him about their own superstition and about one Jesus, who was dead but whom Paul asserted to be alive" (25:19). At last Rome was at the heart of the problem. Festus could not avoid investigating these religious questions, because he had agreed that Paul should be sent to Rome, and this meant that certain charges had to be sent along with him (25:26-27). According to Roman law, "after the appeal has been filed, letters should be sent by the official from whom the appeal is taken, to him who is to hear it, whether this be the emperor or someone else. . . ."[30]

Festus was at a loss to know what to say and so he sought for help from the king, Agrippa II. It was arranged that Agrippa should hear Paul and decide what should be included in the letter that was to accompany him to Rome. Luke cites both Festus and Paul as acknowledging that Agrippa was unusually capable in handling questions dealing with the

[30] *Digest of Justinian,* XLIX. 6. 1. Of course this codification of Roman law was made at the behest of the Emperor Justinian five centuries after the time of Paul, but there is a good probability that the law cited here had been in effect for many centuries.

Jewish religion (Acts 25:26; 26:3), and this is corroborated by what can be learned about him from Josephus.

Note. As a lad growing up in Rome in close relationship to the Emperor Claudius, Agrippa II persuaded him to let the Jews keep control of the high priest's vestments (*Antiquities,* XX. 1. 1-2). When the emperor passed on this decision to the Jews, he described the young Agrippa as a man of "very great piety." Bernice, Agrippa II's sister, took a vow in the temple in hopes that she might be cured of some disease (*Jewish Wars,* II. 310). Though her behaviour was morally odious, two of her husbands were persuaded by Agrippa II to submit to circumcision, and a third who would have married her refused on this account (*Antiquities,* XX. 7. 1-3). Agrippa had, at great expense, brought timbers from Lebanon to raise the foundation of the sinking temple (*Jewish Wars,* V. 36). When the procurator Florus treated the Jerusalem populace with great cruelty, Bernice, at the risk of her own life (Agrippa II was away in Alexandria), pleaded with Florus to be lenient (*Jewish Wars,* II. 310). Agrippa II had the power to appoint the Jewish high priest (*Antiquities,* XX. 9. 11).

Thus, as Paul stood before Agrippa, all was in readiness for Rome to ascertain whether Paul was a bona fide Jew or whether he was to be condemned for propagating a *religio illicita.* Rome had to investigate, and in the person of Agrippa it was capable of discerning how far Paul might have deviated from Judaism so that something definite could be written to Rome.

In his defense before Agrippa (Acts 26:1-32), Paul's point was that there was nothing about his leadership of the Gentile mission that made him any less than the most orthodox Pharisee. Orthodox Judaism believed in the resurrection of the dead, and Paul spearheaded the Gentile mission because the risen Jesus had commissioned him to carry it out. So long as Paul could show that his work was the result of his belief in the resurrection, he could not be charged with a departure from Judaism, for the hope of the resurrection was of the very essence of Judaism. Thus, after certain complimentary remarks concerning Agrippa, Paul began his defense by asserting that the Jews knew that he had always been most orthodox, and when of age, had become a Pharisee, which was the epitome of orthodoxy (vv. 4-5). How ridiculous, therefore, declared Paul, that he should now be accused by the Jews of cherishing the hope of the resurrection, which formed the very focal point of Jewish yearnings and strivings! (vv. 6-7) But Paul realized, as did Agrippa (who was well informed about Christianity—v. 23), that the point of contention between Paul and the Jews was that he believed that the promise of the resurrection had already been fulfilled in the resurrection of Jesus Christ. Thus, turning from Agrippa, Paul apostrophized the Jewish nation and said, "Why is it thought incredible by any of you that God raises the dead?" (v. 8) By this he meant, Why do you think it is impossible that God should have accomplished and assured the future resurrection of the dead in the resurrection of Jesus?

But Paul himself knew full well how easy it had been for him as an orthodox Jew to deny that God raised Jesus from the dead. Paul had vigorously and mercilessly persecuted the Christian Jews (vv. 9-11). As he traveled toward Damascus to carry out this persecution, he was smitten to the ground by the bright light of one who rebuked Paul for persecuting him. Furthermore, this one claimed absolute authority over him, for he declared that it was impossible for Paul now to kick against the ox-goads.[31] Upon inquiring who his adversary was, Paul learned that it was Jesus. The natural thing to expect was condemnation and punishment from the one whom Paul had so vigorously and mercilessly persecuted; however, the strong adversative (*allà*) at the beginning of verse 16 indicates that Jesus reacted in quite an unexpected fashion.

---

[31] The phrase "It is hard for you to kick against the ox-goads" was a common proverb in that day. A goad was a sharp-pointed stick used to drive animals to expend greater efforts. The phrase was hence often used by the Greeks to point out the futility of striving against fate or against the gods. Thus in Paul's case, this statement meant, "It is now as futile for you to work any longer against me as it is for an ox to kick against the goad." This statement, therefore, does not point up the difficulty Paul was having in overcoming the pangs of conscience while persecuting the Christians, but, rather, the impossibility of continuing this persecution. See K. Lake and H. Cadbury, *The Acts of the Apostles*, p. 318.

Instead of condemning Paul, he commissioned him to preach (vv. 16-18):

> I have appeared to you for this purpose, to appoint you to serve and bear witness to the things in which you have seen me and to those in which I will appear to you, delivering you from the people and from the Gentiles—to whom I send you to open their eyes, that they may turn from darkness to light and from the power of Satan to God, that they may receive forgiveness of sins and a place among those who are sanctified by faith in me.

Almost every word of this charter denotes some aspect of the grace of God that characterized Paul's conversion and the forthcoming Gentile mission. The Jews, despite their prerogatives, are classed along with Gentiles as needing to be turned from the power of Satan to God. Instead of being assured of the inheritance simply because they were Jews and obeyed the law, they, like the Gentiles, would receive it only by faith in Jesus Christ.

The resultative *Hóthen* ("wherefore"), which introduces the statement of how Paul preached to both Jews and Gentiles as equals (vv. 19-20), stresses how this consequent ministry found its cause wholly in the resurrection of Jesus, which became known to Paul on the Damascus road. It was because Paul counted the Jews as equals with the Gentiles that the Jews seized him in the temple and tried to kill him (v. 21). They should have realized that in seeking to kill Paul they were doing just what Paul himself had once done. But Paul had changed without giving up in the slightest the essential Jewish conviction that God raises the dead. The Jews should have known that the very change that had occurred in Paul was proof that the risen Jesus had indeed appeared to him. Even their Scriptures proved that the Messiah, after suffering and rising again, should give life both to the Jews and to the Gentiles (vv. 22-23). Consequently, in leading the Gentile mission Paul was acting in full consistency with Judaism.

Upon hearing this defense, Agrippa regarded Paul as innocent and acknowledged that he could have been set at liberty if he had not appealed to Caesar (26:32). But now

Paul had to be sent to Rome with a letter explaining the circumstances. Luke does not record what Agrippa and Festus wrote to Caesar. However, Cadbury concludes, "We are led to suppose that the memorandum Festus sent, after consultation with Agrippa, was quite favorable."[32] The great evidence for this is the treatment accorded Paul in Rome. According to the last two verses of Acts,

> Paul abode two whole years in his own hired dwelling, and received all that went in unto him, preaching the kingdom of God and teaching the things concerning the Lord Jesus Christ with all boldness (*parrēsías*), none forbidding (*akōlútōs*) him. (ASV).

The adverb *akōlútōs* carries with it the unmistakable connotation that Rome gave Paul explicit permission to preach.[33] It was because of this permission that he was able to speak with *parrēsías*, that is, openly and freely. If, as the Roman Jews declared, Christianity was a sect that was spoken against everywhere (28:22), such freedom would come only if the Roman officials were assured that Paul and his teaching were essentially Jewish and that, therefore, Paul was promoting a *religio licita*. The only way the officials in Rome would know this would be through the letter sent by Agrippa and Festus.

What is the meaning of this action and why does Paul's freedom to preach at Rome form a fitting climax to Acts? During Paul's trial before the Romans, the two possible explanations of why Paul had led the Gentile mission had been advanced. Since Judaism itself would never produce such a mission,[34] the only possible explanations for it were that (1) Paul led it as a renegade Jew, or that (2) somehow Paul's understanding of Judaism became modified to the extent that he felt com-

---

[32] H. Cadbury, "Roman Law and the Trial of Paul," *The Beginnings of Christianity*, V, 320.

[33] J. Moulton and G. Milligan, *The Vocabulary of the Greek New Testament*, p. 20, point out that this word is "of constant occurrence in legal documents," and that its connotation "is legal to the last."

[34] The Jews did seek to make converts among the Gentiles. Jesus spoke of the Pharisees compassing land and sea to make one proselyte (Matt. 23:15). But a Gentile could only become a full-fledged Jew to the extent that he was willing to submit to all the Jewish distinctives.

pelled to carry out this mission while remaining loyal in every other way to the tenets of Judaism. The Romans became convinced of the falsity of the first possibility, for the letter that Agrippa II sent to Rome must have declared that Paul was a bona fide Jew who, even while he remained a prisoner, had every right to practice and propagate his religion. This fact having been established, the only other possibility was that Paul's orthodox Judaism had become modified so that he felt impelled to head up the Gentile mission. In rejecting the first possibility, the Romans, without realizing it, provided support for Paul's claim that he had led the mission because of a command received from the risen Christ. Somehow it must be understood how Paul, who remained completely loyal to the basic tenets of orthodox Judaism, could nevertheless cease to glory in the Jewish distinctives. No motivation residing in Paul nor deriving from his background as a Pharisee can account for his doing this in heading up the Gentile mission, for his pride in these distinctives had been so great that he had been as zealous to persecute the Church as the Jews were now zealous to persecute him. The explanation for the Gentile mission must, therefore, derive from something apart from Paul and his background. It must derive from something outside the natural sphere. Paul's explanation is that the risen Jesus appeared to him, and since no explanation from the natural sphere is possible, and since the only proposal for an explanation deriving from the supernatural sphere is the resurrection of Jesus, therefore this is the explanation for the Gentile mission that is to be accepted.

The ending of Acts, therefore, brings the book to a climax. Almost everyone agrees that the theme of the book is, as Acts 1:1,8 indicate, the mighty works of the risen and ascended Jesus in enabling the Gospel to be carried to the uttermost parts of the earth. Paul's ministry at Ephesus, at the conclusion of the third and last missionary journey, is a climactic fulfillment of the promise of Acts 1:8 that the witnesses of Jesus would receive power to preach the Gospel in the uttermost parts of the earth. Here a great center of paganism crumbles before the power of the risen Jesus, which is manifest both in the words and works of Paul. The function of the remainder of Acts (chapters 20 to 28) is not to continue the theme of Acts 1:8 by showing still greater triumphs of the risen Jesus, but to bring the reader back to the reason for these triumphs by showing how the Gentile mission could only have resulted from the resurrection. The outcome of the clash between the Jews and Paul (the theme of 20 through 28) proves that the only explanation for Paul and his Gentile mission is that the risen Jesus appeared to him and commissioned him to preach. The ending of the book, with its indication that Paul was allowed to preach freely in Rome, can only be explained, as we have shown, by the fact that Jesus rose from the dead. Thus there is a return to the theme of the resurrection and ascension of Christ with which Acts commenced (1:2-11) and which was the foundation for the narrative in chapters 1:12–19:41 of the spread of the Gospel to the uttermost parts of the earth.

Consequently, the basic theme of all of Acts is the work that Jesus continued to do as the risen and ascended Christ. The works that he did, even though they occurred a generation after the resurrection itself, prove that he rose, because Paul and the Gentile mission that he led could not be explained in any other way than that it came through a commission received from the risen Christ. The Gentile mission, therefore, was a fulfillment of the resurrection and ascension, which were the climax of the Christ event as set forth in Luke's Gospel; and because the Gentile mission, as led by Paul, could only be accounted for as stemming from the work of the risen Christ, it therefore functions as the means whereby one may know the certainty of the Christ event. Luke had witnessed this fulfillment, for he had been Paul's companion during some parts of the missionary journeys. He had also been with Paul on the trip to Rome, where the proof that the risen Jesus had commissioned Paul was inadvertently given by the Romans in that they allowed Paul to preach freely while he awaited trial. Consequently, he could speak of the "fulfillment among us" of the Christ event and of how this fulfillment provided certainty regarding this event.

But the conversion of Paul on the Damascus road was not the sole cause of the Gentile mission. There was also the Jerusalem conference of Acts 15, which was called because the question had arisen as to whether Gentile converts needed to adhere to the Jewish distinctives of circumcision and dietary regulations in order to be saved (Acts 15:1-2). Had the Jerusalem conference (Acts 15:7-29) not given the answer that Gentile converts need not keep these distinctives, it is doubtful that the Gospel would have found much root in the Gentile world. But the decisive event that led the apostles at the Jerusalem conference to give such an answer was the unmistakable way in which God had worked to show Peter, in the house of Cornelius, that the Gospel was meant for the Gentiles as well as for the Jews (Acts 10:34-48; cf. 15:7-9, 14). This event, however, would not have taught the apostles this lesson apart from the way Jesus Christ had appeared to them during the forty days between Easter and the ascension.

The unmistakable evidence at Cornelius' house that the Gentiles were to receive the salvation of Christ by grace alone was the fact that the Holy Spirit fell upon the Gentiles assembled there just after Peter had finished declaring that the forgiveness of sins was granted to everyone who believed in the name of Jesus. Peter and the believing Jews who were with him saw the parallel between these circumstances and those in which they had first come to receive the Holy Spirit, and thus Peter was forced to conclude, when reporting the incident at Jerusalem, "If then God gave the same gift to them [the Gentiles] as he gave to us when we believed in the Lord Jesus Christ, who was I that I could withstand God [and not admit them to equal fellowship]?" (11:17)

After Jesus had been crucified the disciples were in despair. They did not believe the report of the women that the tomb was empty (Luke 24:11). The appearances of the risen Jesus did not immediately dispel their unbelieving thoughts (Luke 24:41), for their joy was so great at seeing Jesus that their minds could not comprehend all that it meant until Jesus "opened their understanding that they might understand the

Scriptures" (Luke 24:45). But as soon as they came to belief, Jesus promised that they would receive the Holy Spirit (Luke 24:49; cf. Acts 1:3 with 1:4-8), and in a few days this promise was fulfilled (Acts 2:1ff.).

The belief or knowledge that Jesus was risen, with the consequent blessing of receiving the Holy Spirit, came to the apostles, as well as to the Jews who believed at Pentecost, purely by grace. The apostles had not shown much willingness to stand for their master as Jesus was led off to be crucified. Just as the Jewish populace had stood helplessly by while their leaders and the Gentiles concurred in putting Jesus to death, so the apostles were conspicuously absent at the trial and crucifixion of Jesus. Peter, indeed, had tried to do something but had only managed to deny Jesus three times. And someone other than the apostles had buried Jesus.

Nevertheless, Jesus appeared to the apostles, brought them to believe in him, and poured out the Holy Spirit on them and on other Jews as they came to believe the apostles' message. These blessings were not given to these Jews because of their adherence to circumcision and their virtuous living, but rather in spite of their sin.

What was true for the apostles and Jews in general was true in a special way for Peter, for he had gone so far as to deny Christ. Consequently, he was most able to perceive the parallel between what happened at Cornelius' house and what had happened to him. God had given the blessings of the Holy Spirit to the Gentiles in the same gracious way that he had given the Holy Spirit to the apostles and other believing Jews. Peter summed up the whole argument very cogently at the conference. After citing the incident at Cornelius' house, where God had given the Holy Spirit to the Gentiles just as he had done to the Jews, he concluded, "But we believe that we shall be saved by the grace of the Lord Jesus, just as they will" (Acts 15:11). This argument was what led the council to decide that Gentiles did not have to adhere to the Jewish distinctives in order to be saved, and thus an obstacle that would have greatly hindered the Gentile mission was removed.

Apart from this grace of God that was evident in the resurrection appearances of Jesus, there was no force on earth that could have led a Jew to admit that an uncircumcised Gentile who ate unclean food was equally the partaker of the blessings promised in the Old Testament. At the very thought of fellowshipping and even eating with Gentiles, Peter the Jew recoiled and said, "No, Lord; for I have never eaten anything that is common or unclean" (Acts 10:14). Likewise it is not difficult to understand how the demand that Gentile Christians be circumcised came from *believing* Pharisees (Acts 15:5). But the gracious way in which Jesus had appeared to the apostles had introduced the cause that had later led the Jewish apostles to surrender this most basic Jewish conviction and admit Gentiles to equal fellowship. Therefore, just as the Gentile mission depended in part on Paul's leadership, which in turn depended upon the resurrection appearance to him on the Damascus road, so also the Gentile mission depended in part on the Jerusalem Council, whose decision can only find its ultimate explanation in the gracious appearances of Jesus to the apostles during the forty days. Hence the Gentile mission can only be explained, according to Acts, on the basis of the resurrection of Christ.

Luke's purpose in writing Acts was therefore to show that the Gentile mission was the fulfillment of the Christ event as brought to a climax in the resurrection and the ascension. Since this mission could be explained in no other way, it provided the certainty for the Christ event. Hence readers like Theophilus, who were removed from the Christ event by a generation, could find verification of it through the Gentile mission.

From the Gentile mission Theophilus received verification of more than just the "brute fact" that Jesus arose from the dead and appeared to his disciples. For one thing, he could know that this was a work that God had accomplished. A resurrection from the dead constitutes a work whose magnitude is tantamount to that involved in the original creation. Both in creation and in the resurrection, life comes to exist at a point where it had not existed. Such a work would be possible only for God, who, by definition, would have power sufficient for such a task. Thus Acts 26:8 quotes Paul as saying, "Why should it be thought incredible by any of you that God should raise the dead?" Since Theophilus could know from the Gentile mission that a resurrection from the dead had occurred, he could also know that the resurrection had been the work of God.

From the Gentile mission Theophilus also received verification that the God who raised Jesus from the dead had a loving purpose in mind in so doing. The Gentile mission was the result of the work of certain Jews who at one time had been so proud of their status symbols as Jews that they would not even consider relinquishing them and thus assuming an equal footing with the Gentiles. But something had happened to remove this pride and to give these men instead a love sufficient to motivate them to offer to the Gentiles the Jewish convenantal blessings without demanding, in return, any acknowledgment of Jewish superiority in the form of submitting to Jewish distinctives. The only possible cause for this change from pride to love was the appearances of the risen Jesus to the apostles. Since the resurrection of Jesus is the sole cause for the Gentile mission, and since this mission is a manifestation of love, therefore its cause, the God who raised Jesus from the dead, must also be loving. Thus from the Gentile mission, Theophilus could know that God was a loving God.

But one other fact Theophilus could know from the Gentile mission, which made it possible to credit the teaching of the apostles, was that the apostles had been entrusted with a teaching office whereby they became the inspired organs of divine revelation. It was not simply the appearances of the risen Jesus that constituted the cause that eventuated in the Gentile mission, but it was the fact that the risen Jesus spoke to the apostles during these appearances and instructed them regarding the meaning of his resurrection in connection with the redemptive purpose of God. Thus in Luke 24:45-49 the risen Jesus told the apostles that because of his resurrection, they were to preach repentance and the forgiveness of sins to all nations. Then in verse 48 he concludes, "Ye are witnesses of these things." The obvious inference is that they are to witness to the meaning as well as to the fact of Jesus' resurrection. Likewise Acts 1:3 declares that during the forty days of the appearances Jesus spoke to the apostles regarding the kingdom of God. Something of what he taught follows in verses 4-7, and then in Acts 1:8 Jesus declares that the apostles are to be his witnesses to the whole world. Again, the implication is that, as witnesses, they are to pass on what he has taught them. Similarly, from the references in Acts that describe what the apostles did as witnesses, it becomes clear that being a witness involved not only declaring the fact that Jesus had risen (Acts 2:32), but also the meaning of his resurrection (Acts 5:32).

According to Acts 22:15 Paul also became a witness both of the fact and meaning of Jesus' resurrection through his experience on the Damascus road, for Ananias declared to Paul, "You will be a witness for [Jesus] to all men of what you have seen and heard." Hence it becomes evident that the apostles were commissioned not only to report the fact of Jesus' resurrection, but also its meaning, which they had received from the risen Jesus. Thus Jesus had endowed them with a teaching office.

From Acts 26:16 it is apparent that Paul's position as a witness depended both upon what he had learned from Jesus' original appearance to him and also upon subsequent revelations: "I have appeared to you for this purpose, to appoint you to serve and bear witness to the things in which you have seen me and to those in which I will appear to you." Thus Paul was endowed with a teaching office in which he was an organ for transmitting divine revelation to men. According to Jesus, this teaching office was a primary requisite for carrying out the mission to the Gentiles, for after telling Paul he is to be a witness of these revelations, Jesus outlines the Gentile mission (vv. 17-18): "delivering you from the people and from the Gentiles—to whom I send you to open their eyes, that they may turn from darkness to light and from the power of Satan to God, that they may receive forgiveness of sins and a place among those who are sanctified by faith in me."

According to Paul's testimony, it was what Jesus said to him on the Damascus road that had led him to carry out the Gentile mission, for after quoting Jesus' words, Paul declared, "Wherefore I was not disobedient to the heavenly vision . . . but declared to the Gentiles that they should repent and turn to God and perform deeds worthy of repentance." But it seems that the future revelations mentioned in Acts 26:16 also aided him, for he affirmed in verse 22 that it was the constant help he had received from God that enabled him to persist so long and effectively in the mission to the Gentiles; and a part of this help was doubtless the teaching that he continued to receive from Christ. Because he was endowed with this teaching office, Paul knew that he was to carry out the Gentile mission, and through it he also came to receive the theological understanding by which he could see how such a mission fitted into God's total redemptive plan. The motivation that led Paul to carry out the Gentile mission can be fully explained only through his having received such an understanding. Paul must have been convinced that this understanding was from God and that he was especially ordained to mediate to men an interpretation of this event, or else he could not have subjected himself to the suffering and calumnies in which the Gentile mission involved him. We can be sure that this teaching office was from God for the same reason that Paul was sure, viz., that the change the receipt of this understanding brought about could not have originated from Paul as he was before the Damascus-road experience.

Since the mission to the Gentiles cannot be explained apart from the granting of this teaching ministry to Paul by the risen Jesus, and since the Gentile mission is an unquestioned fact of history, Paul's divinely given teaching ministry is therefore historically verifiable. Consequently, Theophilus could know that the teaching of the apostles and of Paul was from God, for they had been appointed by Christ to have a teaching office and to be his witnesses. Among other things, Theophilus could know the truth of Paul's declaration that because Jesus had risen from the dead, believers would also rise at the second coming of Christ.

Note. There are two very significant passages in the Pauline epistles that show how important Paul's consciousness of having received a teaching office from the risen Christ was for his carrying out the Gentile mission. In Ephesians 3:1-10 Paul tells how he has been commissioned to preach the Gospel to the Gentiles, and how his ability to fulfill this mission has resulted from receiving special revelation from Christ. In verses 2-6 he tells of the mystery made known to him through revelation, that the Gentiles were to be fellow heirs with the Jews of the blessings of God. Then in verses 7-10 Paul declares that, in receiving this revelation, he received the grace necessary to preach the Gospel to the Gentiles: "Of this gospel I was made a minister according to the gift of God's grace that was given me by the working of his power. To me . . . this grace was given, to preach to the Gentiles the unsearchable riches of Christ . . . ." It is clear that by "the grace given me to preach to the Gentiles," Paul also implies that he has been made an organ to receive the special revelation of God's mysteries. Consequently, Paul sees his ability to carry out the Gentile mission as dependent in part on the fact that he had been endowed with a teaching office from God.[35]

Paul made the same point in Galatians 1:11-17, but here he linked his being endowed with the teaching office more explicitly with his conversion on the road to Damascus. In verses 11-12 Paul declared that the Gospel that he preached did not come from a human source or agent but simply through the revelation of Jesus Christ. In other words, Paul was convinced that he was an organ of special revelation and that he had received a teaching office from Christ. Verses 13-14 cite as evidence for the proof of this assertion the fact that Paul, before his conversion, was so imbued with zeal for Judaism and for persecuting the church that it would have been psychologically impossible for him to be receptive to the

[35] Thus C. Masson, *L'épître de Saint Paul aux Éphésiens*, p. 174, declares, "The stewardship of God's grace which was given to Paul for the benefit of the Gentiles included both the revelation of the mystery which he mentions in v. 3a as well as the mission of making this mystery known to the Gentiles through the preaching of the Gospel (v. 7)."

teachings of Christianity.[36] Hence, the fact that Paul is now preaching the Gospel can only be explained by his experience on the Damascus road. He declared that it was there that "God . . . was pleased to reveal his son to me, in order that I might preach him among the Gentiles . . ." (vv. 15-16). Paul therefore cites the revelation of Christ and the Gospel to him as that which led him to preach to the Gentiles. Thus it becomes evident that this consciousness of being an organ of revelation was a very real factor in leading Paul to launch the Gentile mission. Since this mission, which is an established fact of history, cannot be explained apart from the motivation of Paul, which must include as a salient fact the consciousness of having received a teaching office from Christ, therefore Paul actually was given this teaching office by the risen Christ. Since this teaching office came in connection with a resurrection that is the work of a God who is loving, it therefore follows that what Paul taught is the message of the loving God who raised Jesus from the dead.

It should be noted in passing that such a line of argument makes it possible for one to arrive at the truth of Scripture from the resurrection of Christ without having to set up as an a priori that the Scriptures are inspired and true. From the Gentile mission comes the argument not only for the resurrection of Christ but also for the divine origin of the teaching office of the apostles, or in other words, their inspiration. Thus it follows that the apostolic writings of the New Testament are inspired. Other New Testament writings (Mark, Luke-Acts, Hebrews, and Jude) find their authority by virtue of the fact that their authors, who were close associates of the apostles, wrote in such a way that both their message and the spirit in which they spoke qualify them to speak alongside of the apostles. The Old Testament's inspiration, then, becomes certain because the New Testament apostles taught it (cf. II Tim. 3:16-17) and constantly implied it by their quotation of it as the Word of God.

Hence it becomes possible to verify the Bible's inspiration from the resurrection. If the resurrection can be established simply by the application of the historical method to the fact of the Gentile mission, then the Christian can arrive at a con-

---

[36] H. Schlier, *Der Brief an die Galater*, p. 52, sums up the point of verses 13-14 as follows: "Paul's pre-Christian past serves unmistakably as a guarantee that there can be no talk of any kind of reception (even an unconscious one!) of the Gospel (with its emphasis on grace) from the spokesmen of the Christian community. His inner bent of mind and his way of acting were wholly incompatible with the Christian message."

viction regarding the resurrection and the teaching office of
the apostles without any a prioris or arguments in a circle.
Through such a procedure a basis is laid not only for the
inspiration of Scripture but for a presuppositionless hermeneutic in interpreting Scripture, which is almost as important as
the doctrine of inspiration for finding a sure Word from God.
With no presuppositions but those the Bible itself sets forth,
and with the evidence that the Bible itself is the inspired Word
of God, many of the dangers of missing what God has said in
Scripture are thus avoided.

It is proposed that this understanding of the purpose of
Acts not only shows how the ending of Acts makes a fitting
climax to the book, but also accounts for its five emphases.
The fact that the Gospel, beginning at Jerusalem, went to the
world via the Gentile mission provides the basis whereby
Theophilus could know the certainty of the Christ event recorded in the Gospel. The emphasis on Paul is understandable
because he is the leader of the mission to the Gentiles. The
theme of Judaism's antipathy to Christianity is essential, for
it makes clear that one could not for a moment regard the
Gentile mission as an outgrowth of proud Judaism, and thus
it points to the resurrection as the only possible cause. But
neither could the mission be a result of a revolt against the
orthodox essentials of Judaism, because the resurrection, which
instigated the Gentile mission, was the essential tenet of
Jewish orthodoxy. The theme of the favor Christianity received from the Roman authorities likewise emphasizes that
essentially Christianity is the same as Judaism, for it, too, is
capable of existing peaceably under Roman government. The
fact that Acts does presume a knowledge of the Old Testament
on the part of its readers coheres with the evidence that Acts
was written to provide Christians, removed by a generation
from the Christ event, with a confirmation of this event.

IV. Luke's Doctrine of Faith

If the foregoing is the proper understanding of Luke's purpose in writing Acts, it becomes evident that he is dealing with
the question of Easter faith in a way that has considerable

relevancy to the contemporary discussion. In that Luke argued for the resurrection of Jesus by pointing to a subsequent historical event that could not be explained without it, he reminds one of Pannenberg, who also argues for the resurrection of Jesus by declaring that subsequent historical events could not be accounted for otherwise. But the difficulty with Pannenberg is his understanding of how faith in the resurrection comes to exist. Since for Pannenberg faith can only come through historical reasoning, he has to make the faith of the ordinary Christian dependent on the authority of the learned theologian-historian, and since history itself is the power of the Holy Spirit needed to engender faith, he also has the difficulty of explaining why it is that many who are confronted by history do not believe in the resurrection. The question to be asked, therefore, is how Luke, who uses an historical argument to assert the resurrection of Christ, understands faith in the resurrection to originate. There are three crucial places in Luke's thinking where faith in the resurrection arises: (1) when the apostles themselves come to believe, (2) when people like the reader, Theophilus, or King Agrippa are confronted with an historical argument that should lead them to a knowledge of the resurrection, and (3) when, as is usually the case, ordinary people are confronted with the simple preaching of the Gospel and come to believe.

A. The Faith of the Apostles

In Luke's recounting of the way the eleven apostles and Paul came to believe that Jesus was risen, it becomes evident that their faith is based on a certainty stemming from the empirical realm. In Acts 1:3 Luke summarizes the resurrection appearances to the eleven as a means whereby the resurrection of Jesus was made known "through many infallible proofs" (*en polloîs tekmēríois*). The word *tekmérion* ("infallible proof") does not occur elsewhere in the New Testament. When Aristotle used this word in a discussion regarding the nature of logic, it was distinguished from a mere *sēmeîon* ("sign" or "indication") in that it was a "demonstrable proof."[37]

[37] Cf. Aristotle, *Rhetoric*, I. 2. 16-18. Cf. *Prior Analytics*, II. 27.

According to Aristotle, a *sēmeîon* could be the basis for a probable argument to prove a conclusion, but a *tekmērion* was a necessary sign that could be made into a demonstrative syllogism that could not be refuted. In the medical vocabulary of the ancient physician Galen, it was used to denote demonstrable evidence as to the identity of a given disease.[38]

An examination of the twenty-fourth chapter of Luke's Gospel shows what Luke meant in Acts 1:3. There were many demonstrable proofs by which the apostles were led to the inescapable conclusion that Jesus had risen. In the first place there were certain identities between the risen Jesus and the Jesus they had known before death. As before, his body had flesh and bones, he was able to eat, and the wounds in his hands and feet were visible (Luke 24:39, 41-43).[39] It was the characteristic way in which the risen Jesus broke bread with his disciples that opened their eyes to see that he was the Jesus they had known before death (Luke 24:31; cf. Acts 10:41). Then, too, the resurrected Jesus reiterated the scriptural teaching he had given the disciples before death: "These are the words which I spoke to you while I was still with you. . ." (Luke 24:44).

Secondly, Luke records four separate appearances of Jesus to different people or groups of people assembled in different places. There was the appearance to the two disciples on the Emmaus road (24:11-31), the appearance to Peter alone (24:34), and the appearance to the eleven and the other disciples (24:36-43). Luke 24:44-51 was no doubt a separate appearance, too, for even though Luke's *modus operandi* in the last chapter of his Gospel is to run the resurrection appearances together so that they climax with the ascension,[40] there is nothing in the text of Luke 24 to forbid a harmonization be-

[38] W. Hobart, *The Medical Language of St. Luke*, p. 184.

[39] The textual evidence for Luke 24:40 and its close similarity to John 20:20 lead to the conclusion that it is a later interpolation designed to make Luke correspond more fully with John. However, the command in 24:39, "See my hands and my feet that it is I myself," can hardly be anything but a reference to the wounds that were inflicted upon Jesus when he died.

[40] Cf. Chapter 7, pp. 197f.

tween it and Luke's declaration of the appearances that occurred during the forty days (Acts 1:3).[41]

Finally, there is the evidence of the empty tomb, which, though not as decisive in Luke's thinking as the appearances for bringing the apostles to Easter faith, is nevertheless a *sine qua non* for their faith. It should be observed that the apostles' knowledge that Jesus is risen is not based simply on the risen Jesus but also on knowledge that is separate from him at any given appearance. His behavior known from his previous fellowship with them, the continuity between the resurrection body and the previous body, the knowledge that others in different places, times, and circumstances have come to identify him as the Jesus they had known, and the empty tomb—this knowledge that is apart from the risen Jesus himself is essential for showing the apostles that Jesus had really risen from the dead. Thus Luke 24 makes it evident that the apostles' knowledge of Jesus as risen was wholly the result of overwhelming empirical evidence.

C. H. Dodd, who dislikes the thought of faith being based on evidences, has wondered if Aristotle would not have preferred it if Luke had used the word *sēmeíon* rather than *tekmérion* in Acts 1:3.[42] However, since Luke often uses the term *sēmeíon* in Luke-Acts, Dodd concedes that he must have deliberately chosen this rare word in order to emphasize that the apostles came to knowledge of the resurrection through inescapable empirical evidence.

But while Luke stressed that the apostles' faith was based on empirical evidence, he still emphasized that the ability to own up to the conclusion that Jesus was risen was made possible wholly by the gracious and supernatural work of God. Jesus did not manifest himself to everyone, but only to those "who were chosen by God as witnesses" (Acts 10:41; cf. Acts 1:2-3). Thus even being confronted with the empirical evidence that Jesus was risen was a gracious work of God. But also the very ability to own up to the inescapable conclusions of the

[41] E. Klostermann, *Das Lukas Evangelium*, p. 240.
[42] C. Dodd, "The Appearances of the Risen Christ: An Essay in Form-Criticism of the Gospels," *Studies in the Gospels*, pp. 26f., note.

evidence was wholly a supernatural enablement, for the disciples on the road to Emmaus had to have their eyes opened in order to recognize Jesus when he broke the bread (Luke 24:31). Similar wording is used to describe the work of grace that had to occur in the apostles' hearts for them to understand the instruction that Jesus gave them from the Old Testament Scriptures. Though Jesus based his teaching on "Thus it is written. . ." (Luke 24:46), so that the data necessary for understanding what the Old Testament meant was there, yet it was necessary for him to open the minds of the apostles in order for the data to bring home their meaning to them.

The way such paradoxical thinking coheres in Luke's mind is indicated by some similar language that occurs in Paul's defense before Agrippa. In Acts 26:18 the risen Jesus is reported as sending Paul to the Gentiles "to open their eyes, that they may turn from darkness to light and from the power of Satan to God. . . ." Thus Luke believed that men, before they are the objects of the grace of God, are blinded by the supernatural power of Satan. Consequently, even though they may be confronted by the inescapable evidence that Jesus is risen, the Satanic power that holds them in darkness is so strong that they must be objects of the grace of God in order to own up to the truth. Man's inability to believe, due to sin and Satan, is not owing to the fact that he lacks the evidences necessary to believe the resurrection until he is illumined by the Holy Spirit, but to the fact that he does not want to own up to the inescapable evidences when confronted with them. When men have the evidences but refuse to own up to them because they do not want to, they are, in Luke's thinking, responsible to believe and culpable if they do not believe. The disciples on the Emmaus road, who had access to all the evidences necessary for knowing that Jesus was risen and that Old Testament Scripture was thus fulfilled, could not believe because they did not want to believe. Their eyes were closed. They were nevertheless responsible to believe, for Jesus chided them and said, "O foolish men, and slow of heart to believe all that the prophets have spoken!" (Luke 24:25) This foolishness, this disinclination to own up to the evidences, was removed when Jesus opened their eyes. On the basis of this understanding therefore, we can see how Luke can say that faith must find its basis in the strongest possible empirical evidence and yet can only exist through the supernatural work of God.

Paul also encountered demonstrable proof that Jesus was risen from the dead. There could be no question that the one who encountered him on the Damascus road was, as Paul addressed him, "Lord" (Acts 26:15), for surely he would have to have sovereign authority to produce a greater light than that of a midday desert sun and to speak to Paul from heaven. Likewise, only because he was Lord did he have authority to tell Paul he could no longer persecute the Christians, for Paul already had the highest authority of Israel to carry out this persecution. But since this Lord commanded him to stop persecuting Christians, this Lord must have been in sympathy with them. And since the Lord who had stopped him must be the opposite of the Lord he thought he was serving and on the side of the Christians, Paul asked him to identify himself. The answer, "I am Jesus whom thou persecutest," cohered with all that was indubitably known thus far about his antagonist. Therefore the Jesus whom the Christians worshipped, whom Paul thought was dead, was alive and had supreme power as the Lord. Although it is not made explicit in the accounts of Paul's conversion, it is apparent that, according to Luke's understanding, Paul before his conversion was blinded by Satanic power, the very power from which the unbelieving Jews who were now persecuting Paul (cf. Acts 26:17f.) needed to be delivered. When Jesus met Paul on the Damascus road, his eyes were opened to own up to the evidence that Jesus was the risen Lord.

Consequently, like Pannenberg, Luke sees that revelational knowledge is to come from the empirical stuff that confronts one and impinges itself upon one's senses. But unlike Pannenberg, Luke believes that the problem with men is so serious that they will never by themselves own up to the truth that is before them. Only those will believe "whose hearts are

234

opened to hear" (Acts 16:10), who are ordained to eternal life (Acts 13:48). Luke's explanation why some do not believe, therefore, is that God works on the basis of a particularism in which only some are elected to eternal life.

B. *The Faith of a Theophilus*

The certainty Theophilus required came through a process of reasoning backwards from the Gentile mission to the resurrection of Christ. Apparently Luke regards the certainty thus achieved as no less than the certainty the apostles received as they reasoned from the infallible proofs to the conclusion that it was the risen Jesus who was standing before them. In both cases, certainty came through an inferential reasoning from data that was confronting them.

Since Luke presupposes certainty for both Theophilus and the apostles, it would therefore be natural to expect that the faith of a Theophilus would come about in the same way as did the apostles' faith. This supposition finds confirmation in Acts 26, where Paul makes his defense before Agrippa II and Festus. The reasoning process by which Agrippa could have owned up to the truth of what Paul said is the same as that which is implied for Theophilus, for in Paul's defense he presents a summary statement of the argument of Acts. Consequently, the reaction of these men in verses 24-29 to Paul's defense gives more insight into Luke's understanding of the nature of faith and unbelief.

Agrippa and Festus had access to data from which they could become certain of the resurrection of Jesus Christ. Agrippa had knowledge of the things about which Paul spoke, for Agrippa could have checked Paul's claim that the Jews knew perfectly well that he had been a very orthodox Jew (cf. 26:4f.). What Paul had done in carrying out the Gentile mission was also a matter of open knowledge. Agrippa could determine whether Paul had become a renegade Jew or had remained loyal to orthodox Judaism. That Paul had always been and was still an orthodox Jew who had nevertheless led the Gentile mission was an enigma that could only be explained by the resurrection of Jesus.

In response to the defense he had heard, Festus cried out, "Paul, you are mad; your great learning is turning you mad" (26:24). What Paul had said seemed to Festus like madness, even though the reasoning to support it was cogent. But Festus, because of his enslavement to Satan and darkness, declared that what was reasonable was madness. His response was a confirmation of I Corinthians 2:14, "The natural man receives not [lit., does not welcome, *déchetai*] the things of the spirit of God, for they are foolishness to him." But Festus' statement that Paul was mad does not mean that he did not grasp Paul's argument for the resurrection. To the contrary, to be able to judge Paul mad Festus must have understood what he said. Haenchen remarks, "Festus must surely have had a surprisingly good understanding of what Paul had been saying, in order to have been able thus to deny the teaching of the resurrection."[43]

Agrippa was scarcely more receptive to Paul's argument, though he had a better understanding of Judaism than Festus. He knew the prophets (26:27) and he was well acquainted with Christianity, for none of its major events—the death of Christ, his resurrection, and the founding of the church—"had escaped his notice, for this was not done in a corner" (26:26). In short, Agrippa already had independent knowledge of the essential facts of Paul's argument for the resurrection.

This knowledge placed Agrippa in a difficult position. He did not want to acknowledge the truth of what Paul said and thus lose the favor of the Jews. But neither did he want to deny Paul's argument for the resurrection, for this would be tantamount to denying Judaism, which also regarded the resurrection of the dead as its central tenet. His way of escape was to say, "With but little additional pressure you

[43] Haenchen, *Die Apostelgeschichte,* p. 614.

would persuade me to play the part of a Christian" (26:28).[44] Thus while not actually rejecting Paul, Agrippa nevertheless remained noncommittal. Though faced with evidence that would lead him inescapably to the knowledge of the resurrection, he was unwilling to own up to it.

The reason for these rejections—to follow Luke's understanding—was not that the evidence for the resurrection was not persuasive in itself, but that these men were devoid of the grace of God that would have made them want to own up to the validity of the evidence. For Luke, revelation is to be found in history, but history itself is not sufficient to produce faith. Faith comes only when one is the recipient of special grace that turns one from the powers of darkness to light so that he will be willing to own up to the persuasiveness of the historical evidence.

C. Faith from Simply Hearing the Gospel

Not all men are capable of carrying out the historical reasoning that the argument of Acts would have one follow in order to know the resurrection. Therefore, if historical reasoning is the only way by which men can attain faith, then faith becomes the possibility for only the few who can think historically, and faith for the common man is possible only if he is willing to commit himself to the authority of a priesthood of historians.

Pannenberg, it will be remembered, wants to make faith the possibility for all men by having what is, virtually, a priesthood of historians. Theology's task, as he sees it, is to assert the credibility of the Christian proclamation, so that laymen can believe it because of the authority that the theologian,

[44] The author's translation. Paul's reply in verse 29, "Whether short or long, I would to God that not only you but also all who hear me this day might become such as I am—except for these chains," does not fit well with that interpretation of verse 28 (H.A.W. Meyer, Lake, and Cadbury) that regards Agrippa's statement as irony. Haenchen (*op. cit.*, p. 615) argues that Paul's reply is more suited to a sincere statement on the part of Agrippa than an ironical one.

with special historical skills, can provide. It does not seem, however, that Luke, who also finds the basis for revelational knowledge in history, makes historical reasoning the exclusive way to such knowledge. Acts 11:24 is a passage of particular interest in this connection because it tells how a number of people came to believe on the basis of the moral impact of the minister, rather than by accepting his authority or by employing historical reasoning to get back to the truth of the resurrection. "[Barnabas] was a good man, full of the Holy Spirit and of faith. And [as a result] a large company was added to the Lord."

Is Luke then saying in such a passage that, whereas faith for the apostles and for a Theophilus is based on incontrovertible evidence, it is possible for the ordinary multitudes to believe without evidence, so that faith for them is simply a "leap"? In answering this question it should first be observed that the argument for the resurrection from Paul's leadership of the Gentile mission is based ultimately on a change in Paul's conduct. There was a time when Paul's whole purpose in life was to persecute the Christians. The Jewish opposition to the Christians arose from the fact that their message, rather than complimenting the Jews for their good works, condemned them for having killed their Messiah. To receive the salvation set forth in the Christian message meant that a Jew could no longer pride himself on his distinctives of circumcision, Sabbath-keeping, and dietary regulations, for how could Jews find these a basis for approval if they as a nation had been guilty of rejecting and killing their Messiah? Some such thinking was the reason for Paul's persecution of the church, for in Philippians 3:4-6 Paul recalled how before his conversion his basis for pride had been such Jewish distinctives as his circumcision and his flawless keeping of the Pharisaic interpretation of the law. In Galatians 1:13-14 Paul explicitly links up his having persecuted the church with his zeal to keep the Jewish distinctives. But without relinquishing his regard for Judaism, Paul had ceased to have pride in the Jewish distinctives as the mainspring of all his actions. He came to consider Jews and Gentiles as equally in need of the grace of God, which was to be obtained purely through faith in what God could do. Paul was no longer a man who tenaciously clung to the Jewish ways for having a sense of superiority, as though to lose them would be to lose all meaning in life. No longer did he elevate himself and the Jews at the expense of the Gentiles. On the contrary, he had the confidence of a man who is filled with hope because his salvation has been assured by God himself. Having no need, therefore, to strive to maintain his own security, he did not subjugate others as means to his ends but rather made himself the means to the ends of others. He sought to bring to the Gentiles as well as to the Jews the blessings of the salvation God had promised originally to the Jews. The change that occurred in Paul could not be explained by Paul or by the Judaism by which he lived, for both were wholly opposed to such a change. His testimony of his encounter with the risen Jesus is the only plausible explanation.

But according to Luke, the darkness of the Jews that led Paul to behave as he did before his conversion is the plight of all men. All men are seeking to use what bases they may have to gain a sense of superiority over their fellow men. In their efforts to maintain these bases, they evince an anxiety and a fear lest these should somehow slip from their grasp. But in contrast to the darkness of the Jews and Greeks who lived at Antioch, there was the life of Barnabas. As he preached the Gospel the people of that city could sense that he was seeking to fulfill their ends, for he was a good man. Furthermore, he evinced a confidence that excluded an anxious grasping to hold on to the security of this world, for he was filled with the Holy Spirit and faith. Barnabas did not follow the analogy of men who were under darkness and the power of Satan. In addition, he declared that the only way such power could be broken and such darkness dispelled was through the risen and living Lord Jesus Christ. Barnabas was a living example of the truth of such a claim, and his example was a verification of its truth in the same way that Paul's change was a verification of his claim that he had encountered the risen Christ, for in neither case could the change be accounted for from men as they are. Since men cannot by themselves be good and have faith and hope, the cause for goodness, faith, and hope must lie apart from their capabilities and in the living Christ whom such men proclaim as Saviour.

Thus it is understandable how Luke could have stressed that the faith of the apostles and of a Theophilus must come through a reasoning based on infallible proofs, and yet declare that many believed as Barnabas preached, for Barnabas was himself an infallible proof of his message. Therefore the people at Antioch came to faith in a manner not essentially different from that of the apostles and Theophilus. It required simply a reasoning (not carried out necessarily in a deliberate, conscious way) that would acknowledge that Barnabas had moral qualities men could not produce and which must therefore result from the Christ whom Barnabas preached.

To be sure, not all men would be convinced by such an example, for men in their darkness (e.g., the Jews who persecuted Paul) have no desire to give up their bases for feeling superior and humbly to acknowledge that their salvation depends upon the grace of God. Instead, they will fight to the death to preserve their bases for pride. According to Luke, men must have grace to own up to the infallible evidences that would lead them to accept the grace of God.

If this analysis of Luke's thinking is correct, then faith is possible for every man who is confronted with a Barnabas, for everyone who is rational is capable of seeing the infallible proof represented by such a man. Such a system of thought does keep Christianity as an historical religion, rather than one whose knowledge is immediately accessible to all. Men cannot believe unless they encounter a Barnabas.[45] But such a system does not make all men dependent upon a priesthood

[45] The Bible functions as a Barnabas because its message of God's grace produces an atmosphere of love and hope.

of theologians who can follow historical reasoning to know that Jesus rose from the dead. Therefore it would seem that Luke has bridged Lessing's ugly ditch without involving himself in the difficulties of Pannenberg.

Chapter Eight

An Evaluation of Luke's Approach

The foregoing understanding of the purpose of Acts can only be of service in solving the problem of faith and history to the extent that the inadequacies of certain objections against the thinking of Luke can be made evident.

One of the most penetrating criticisms of Luke comes from Hans Conzelmann, professor at Göttingen.[1] Conzelmann has sensed how important it was for Luke to regard the events of his Gospel as distinct from those of Acts and yet consider both the Gospel and Acts as parts of one redemptive history. Luke, declares Conzelmann, was the first one in the early church to make a distinction between the time of Jesus and the time of the church. "It is not until Luke that . . . the period of Jesus and the period of the church are presented as different epochs in the broad course of saving history" (13). Prior to Luke, the church had come into being and derived its life simply from the proclamation of the message of Jesus. In the years immediately following the departure of Jesus, the church had lived from the *kerygma* as though Jesus himself were with them and preaching it to them. This sense of being contemporaneous with Jesus and his message was bolstered by the conviction shared by the church in those early years that Jesus would return very soon to set up his kingdom. But as the years passed by and Jesus did not return,

[1] H. Conzelmann, *The Theology of Saint Luke.*

it became more difficult for the church to maintain this sense of contemporaneity. It was Luke who came to the rescue with his concept of the differences between then and now, between the events of the Gospel and the events as set forth in Acts. According to Conzelmann, Luke was saying to the church that it should not feel any embarrassment or increasing tension in the fact that there was no present appearance of Jesus to compensate for the fact that the time of his first appearance was receding farther into the background, for God was with his people and working during the present period of the church as much as during the past ministry of Jesus or when he would return in the future. "Luke is confronted by the situation in which the church finds herself by the delay of the Parousia and her existence in secular history, and he tries to come to terms with the situation by his account of historical events" (14).

According to Conzelmann, the distinction Luke drew between the time of Jesus and the time of the church by no means involved a complete separation between them. On the contrary, Luke stressed the continuity between the past, when Jesus walked the earth, and the present age of the church. There was continuity because Jesus had risen, and thus it was possible for his heavenly ministry to be the continuation of his earthly ministry. And it is the risen Lord who gives promise of the future resurrection as the destiny toward which the church is moving (205f.).

The fidelity with which Conzelmann reproduces Luke's concept of a history of redemption whose center is the resurrection of Jesus is commendable. The only question to be raised with him is that of the ultimate origins of this concept. Conzelmann understands it to arise from the delayed Parousia, which became increasingly apparent to the church as the years passed. Luke, on the other hand, wants his readers to understand that God's continued working in behalf of the church became possible because Jesus rose from the dead, ascended into heaven, and continued his working through the outpoured Holy Spirit.

Oscar Cullmann is convinced that Luke's own explanation for the origin of the idea of redemptive history is the correct one.[2] Cullmann argues that the idea of God working contemporaneously with the early church finds a better explanation in the fact that the early Christians were experiencing the working of God through the outpouring of the Holy Spirit than that they created this idea in order to fill a void that was becoming increasingly painful each year the promised Parousia did not materialize. "And behind God's intervention in the daily life of the early church," declares Cullmann, "was the joy of Easter that Christ is risen" (12).

Hence Cullmann believes that Luke was stating the truth in his insistence that the subsequent redemptive history of the church was the outworking and the fulfillment of the resurrection and ascension of Christ, but Conzelmann believes that Luke was wrong, for although he may not have realized it, it was really the delay of the Parousia that led him to think of the resurrection as opening the door to God's present working. Which view is correct?

In answering this, it should be observed, first of all, that Luke was not the only New Testament writer who set forth his thinking in terms of continuing redemptive history. As Cullmann never tires to point out (and he is not alone in this[3]), all the writers of the New Testament understand the church as existing in a redemptive history that finds completion in the future, because Jesus Christ has already wrought full redemption in his death and resurrection and is causing the benefits of this to be partially enjoyed by the church at the present time. The New Testament writers think of themselves as existing between an "already fulfilled" and a "not yet completed." It is easier to account for this common understanding as deriving from a tradition and experience shared in common by each writer instead of from a theological concept which each of the New Testament writers would arrive

[2] O. Cullmann, "Parusieverzögerung und Urchristentum," *Theologische Literaturzeitung*, 83 (1958), cols. 1-12.

[3] See, e.g., U. Wilckens, "Die Offenbarungsverständnis in der Geschichte des Urchristentums," *Offenbarung als Geschichte*, pp. 42-90.

at independently in order to relieve a growing tension in the church.

It should also be noted that Luke's argument that God's present working in the Gentile mission is the fulfillment of the resurrection depends for its validity upon what actually occurred in the inauguration of this mission. If Paul's leadership of it really could not be explained either by his loyalty to Judaism or by his revolt against Judaism, but only by recourse to the fact that Jesus appeared to him, then indeed there was a continued working of God in connection with the church. Such a working would be entirely adequate to account for the New Testament concept of God's continued activity in redemptive history. Such a concept could easily embrace the fact of a delayed Parousia, for the time of the church would be when God was pleased to carry on redemptive history through the Holy Spirit and the church, rather than through the return of his Son to earth.

But are the facts valid that are essential to Luke's argument that the Gentile mission can only be explained by the resurrection? The essentials for Paul's argument are (1) his continued loyalty to orthodox Judaism after his conversion, (2) the Jews' hatred of the Gentile mission, and (3) Paul's testimony that he carried out this mission because of a commission received from the risen Jesus. These three essentials are not only set forth in Acts but also in the Pauline epistles. Paul forthrightly asserted his loyalty to Judaism. In his epistle to the Romans, with its classical emphasis on justification by faith alone, apart from the deeds of the law, he nevertheless declared that Judaism had a great advantage and that there was much profit in circumcision (Rom. 3:1). In Romans 9:1-5 he revealed his love for his own kinsmen, the Jews, and listed the many advantages and prerogatives they had. This loyalty to Judaism was not, of course, that which demanded that the Gentiles be circumcised, for this would have taken the heart out of the Gospel and marked the end of the Gentile mission (Gal. 2:3-5). However, Paul was perfectly willing to demand circumcision of Timothy in order to keep peace with the

245

Jews, for he himself declared (I Cor. 9:20), "To the Jews I became as a Jew, that I might gain Jews; to them that are under the law, as under the law, not being myself under the law. . . ." Paul also attested the Jewish hatred of Christianity and its Gentile mission. In I Thessalonians 2:14ff. he said,

> You, brethren, became imitators of the churches of God in Christ Jesus that are in Judea: for you suffered the same things from your own countrymen, as they did from the Jews, who both killed the Lord Jesus and the prophets, and drove us out and displease God, and oppose all men, by hindering us from speaking to the Gentiles. . . .

Finally, Paul made it clear that it was the appearance of the risen Jesus that led to the Gentile mission: "When . . . he was pleased to reveal his Son to me, in order that I might preach him among the Gentiles, I did not confer with flesh and blood . . ." (Gal. 1:15-16). Before this time, Paul was consumed with those things in his life whereby he felt he could earn favor with God: being circumcised, being a Pharisee, and zealously adhering to all the law (Phil. 3:4-6). But after his conversion his only concern was to glory in Christ (Phil. 3:7-16). According to I Corinthians 9:1, he was an apostle by virtue of having seen the risen Lord. In I Corinthians 15:8-10 Paul asserted that it was simply through God's grace that he, a persecutor of the church, had come to see Jesus and thus through the grace of God to labor more abundantly than the rest. This ministry was directed primarily to the Gentiles, according to Romans 15:14-29, Ephesians 3:1-13, and Colossians 1:24-29, and thus the language of I Timothy 2:7, "I was appointed a preacher and apostle . . . a teacher of the Gentiles . . ." is a summary of Paul's understanding of his life and work.

Thus Luke's argument can be formed from the data of the Pauline epistles: since the Gentile mission stemmed from a man who was and who remained a loyal Jew, and since this mission was opposed by the Jews who thought and felt as Paul did before his conversion, therefore Paul's testimony that it was the gracious appearance of the risen Christ to him that changed him and led to the Gentile mission must be true.

The fact that there are *two* sources for the data essential to this argument would have little weight if it were evident that the material in Acts was derived simply from the Pauline epistles. However, there is almost unanimous agreement that Acts does not have a literary dependence on the Pauline epistles. Acts' source of knowledge regarding Paul, therefore, is the general milieu surrounding him in which Luke moved, and not merely the Pauline epistles. Hence, there is a real sense in which Acts and the Pauline epistles are independent sources for our knowledge of Paul, and consequently we have an historical control which validates the three essentials for the argument.

But it might be suggested that Paul was simply an impostor, who fabricated these statements in his epistles and misled the author of Acts. It would be difficult to support such an hypothesis, however, because the same objection would rise against such a reconstruction as arose against Reimarus' hypothesis that the disciples stole the body of Jesus so that the empty tomb could argue for their claim that Jesus had risen. How could Paul be willing to suffer deprivation and the threat of death for an idea he knew was only a fabrication? A more promising way to escape the power of Luke's argument is to grant that Paul was sincere in his conviction that Jesus rose from the dead and then attempt to explain his conviction in some immanental way.

Perhaps the most sophisticated attempt to do this is that of the famous French New Testament scholar Maurice Goguel.[4] He was not impressed with the ordinary method of explaining the conversion of Paul as resulting from a troubled conscience whose nagging became more and more insistent as he recalled the sublime attitude of Stephen as he died and the superior ethical teaching of the Christian church. According to such a theory, Paul's troubled conscience became

[4] M. Goguel, *The Birth of Christianity*, pp. 75-86.

247

so unbearable that it was only relieved by an hallucination in which he supposed he saw Jesus and thus became convinced that it was the will of God to give up his Pharisaism and embrace Christianity. Goguel rejected such a reconstruction because Paul himself, in speaking of his activity as a persecutor, does not indicate that he had any remorse while carrying on this work but was acting fully in accord with his convictions. Therefore Goguel asserts that before Paul's conversion he had a clear conscience and was convinced that he was "blameless" in his keeping of the law (Phil. 3:6). The moral struggle depicted in Romans 7 must have occurred *after* his conversion, when he realized that it was impossible to fulfill the condition for justification through the law, for this would mean, as Jesus taught (Matt. 5:18), having a righteousness that was greater than that of the scribes and Pharisees.

Goguel understands Paul's conversion to have taken place not because of a conscious moral struggle but because of an unconscious one in his subliminal self. In his conscious thinking Paul regarded Christianity as blasphemous, because it worshiped a man who had been crucified and who, therefore, on the basis of the law, was accursed (cf. Deut. 21:23). This conviction dominated Paul's conscious thinking so that he carried out his activity as a persecutor with the single-minded devotion he speaks of in various passages in his epistles. But in Paul's subliminal self,

> the affirmations of Christians concerning their master's resurrection and their expectation of his return on the one hand and on the other the new ethical ideal preached by Jesus had been secretly working upwards, gathering strength, while on the level of consciousness they were repressed by the statement of the law concerning a curse belonging to the cross and by loyalty to the traditional forms of Judaism. [But] . . . a moment came when the activity in the unconscious gained such strength that it . . . burst forth in the field of consciousness and became objectified in a vision which the apostle judged to be the direct presence of Christ himself. Trying to account for what happened to him, he considered that Christ had personally intervened in his life and had caused his conversion (85).

It is significant that Goguel must postulate an immanental cause for Paul's conversion of which even Paul was not aware and for which there is not a shred of evidence. This is an acknowledgment that the data regarding Paul's conversion provides no hint that would open the way for an immanental explanation of it. But to advance such an explanation Goguel must have some control, that is, some case in human experience that is analogous to his understanding of how Paul was converted. Goguel attempts to find this in the way the Sikh, Sundar Singh, was converted to Protestantism and in the way the Jew, Ratisbone, was converted to Roman Catholicism. Goguel claims that both of these men were so committed to their original religions that so far as their conscious life was concerned, they were not aware of any tug toward Christianity. Yet, strangely, in recounting the stories of their conversions, Goguel includes incidents concerning which it would be difficult to say that they did not involve conscious tugs toward the religions finally espoused. Ratisbone had experienced some strange emotions upon visiting a Roman Catholic church some time before his conversion, and Sundar Singh was so attracted to the Bible before his conversion that "he could not stop himself from reading it secretly" (77). It seems, therefore, that these men did experience conscious tugs before conversion and that therefore they were in a different category from Paul, for whom Goguel himself confesses that all the evidence leads to the conclusion that "Paul's conversion was not preceded by any crisis of which he was aware" (85).

But to place Paul in a different category from that of Sundar Singh and Ratisbone is to say that his conversion came from a source other than the powers and possibilities latent in himself or in his environment. If Paul was not conscious of any tug in himself toward Christianity, and if the Judaism by which he lived could not have produced a Gentile mission, then Paul's conversion constitutes what Marc Bloch called "an overly-pronounced deviation."[5] It is overly-pronounced because it is an effect for which there is no cause in Paul

[5] See Chapter 1, p. 23.

or his environment that can account for it. In Paul's conversion, therefore, the cause-effect sequence that accounts for ordinary human behavior is broken.

Marc Bloch and other historians have refused to allow the possibility of such a deviation because of the conviction that it would mean that all historical knowledge would henceforth be impossible. Since it is absurd to deny the possibility of gaining historical knowledge, then Luke must be wrong to report that Paul was converted by a supernatural intervention, if Bloch's understanding of reality is the only possible alternative.

According to Bloch, one can distinguish between false and true reports of what happened only by holding to the principle that things do not happen in this world without adequate immanental causes. A report that involves an occurrence that coheres with preceding causes is true, while one that is contradictory to them must be false. Thus, to use Bloch's illustration, when the braggart Marbot came up for promotion, he could not have failed to cite how he freed the French soldiers by crossing the Danube river at flood stage, for under such circumstances one was supposed to cite his record, and Marbot had never been loath to do that. To insist that he nevertheless did perform this brave deed, even though he failed to report it, is to say that history can be spontaneous and that things can happen in contempt of antecedent causes. If this be so, then there is no reason to deny what Marbot wrote in his Memoirs. Hence one has lost all control for distinguishing between false and true reports, and historiography is no longer possible. Thus James Robinson joins Marc Bloch in excluding the possibility of miracles:

> The historian must always weigh the probabilities of contradictory reports. But this procedure of the historian becomes an impossibility whenever one believes that the interconnectedness of history is constantly disturbed by miracles. The possibility of miracles must be excluded from positivistic historiography, not because of certain dogmatic presuppositions, but because of the demands of the historical method itself.[6]

[6] J. Robinson, *Kerygma und historischer Jesus*, p. 14, note.

But Pannenberg denies that the admission of the possibility of unanalogous events makes historiography impossible.[7] Pannenberg argues that when the *report* of the unanalogous cannot be explained as the work of the imagination of the reporter, then it must have occurred. What this means is simply that the historical method remains intact despite overly-pronounced deviations, so long as it can be assumed that the reporter is reacting in a way that is commensurate with reality and not in contempt of it. Thus, while the resurrection of Jesus was in contempt of antecedent causes in this world, yet the apostles' report of it was not. Their report could not have been the result of their imagination, for their morale had been so shattered by the crucifixion that their inclination was only to disbelieve. Therefore, in denying the possibility that the apostles' report was the result of their imagination, Pannenberg is saying that it must be assumed that men imagine things only when they are so predisposed. In other words, when it comes to the activity of reporting what happened, effects do not occur that are in contempt of antecedent causes. The report was therefore the result of actually having seen the risen Jesus, for his appearances and not the apostles' imagination was the only way such a report could have been given.

Thus, according to Pannenberg, overly-pronounced deviations can occur without destroying the possibility for historical knowledge, as long as it can be assumed that these deviations take place in a milieu that behaves according to analogy. The one who reports an overly-pronounced deviation is a part of this deviation's milieu, and in order for his report to be controlled and credited it must be assumed that the reporter himself is not an overly-pronounced deviation like the event he is reporting. To extend the possibility for an overly-pronounced deviation into the milieu in which it occurs is indeed to make historical knowledge impossible, for then every report of every incident could be spontaneous and need not be related to the reality in which it is given.

[7] See Chapter 6, pp. 179-82.

It is just at this point, however, that a difficulty in Pannenberg appears, for history for Pannenberg (and also for Richard Niebuhr) is a complete intermingling in events of both connectedness and contingency. For them every event in history is a testimony both to cause-effect connectedness and to spontaneous contingency, with the emphasis on spontaneity. But if spontaneity is the primary characteristic of all existence, then it is impossible to control the reports of historical events on the basis of cause-effect and analogy. Consequently, all historical knowledge would become impossible. Even knowledge through immediate sense perception would become impossible, for then one's senses would be reporting data to the brain with a spontaneity that had little regard for what was in the outside world.

But it is possible to maintain the validity of historical knowledge in general and even reports of overly-pronounced deviations so long as the milieu in which these deviations take place continues to behave in accordance with antecedent causes and not in contempt of them. Such a concept of reality, however, implies a continuum of cause-effect sequence in the world as we know it and yet implies that causes can be introduced into this continuum that do not originate from it but from somewhere above it. In other words, despite Pannenberg's and Niebuhr's rejection of a two-story world (the first story natural, the second story supernatural), it is this sort of a system that would enable them to assert the possibility of overly-pronounced deviations without destroying the possibility of historical knowledge.

Luke regarded reality as a two-story affair. There is the first story, in which events occur as effects of antecedent, immanental causes. There is also the second story, from which causes come and introduce effects on the first story that would never come to pass from first-story causes. But first-story effects are so tuned to act in accordance with antecedent causes and not in contempt of them that when a second-story cause comes downstairs, a commensurate effect is produced on the first story. Thus Paul, so long as he was left untouched by the supernatural in the form of the resurrection appearance of Jesus, continued to act as the epitome of the Jewish culture of which he was a part. But when Jesus appeared to Paul on the Damascus road, he confronted him with the grace and love of God that was not analogous to anything in Judaism. In response to the antecedent cause of the appearance of Jesus, Paul reacted in a way that was completely commensurate with it, for he headed up the Gentile mission, which was the perfect expression of the grace of God that became manifest to him on the Damascus road. Paul reacted not with spontaneity but with correspondence to the antecedent cause, for in Luke's understanding of reality, second-story causes do come down without causing first-story phenomena to cease to be tuned to react in a way that corresponds to antecedent causes. In other words, according to Luke, the milieu of an overly-pronounced deviation does not, because of the deviation, become loosed from the necessity to obey antecedent causes so that henceforth it behaves with pure spontaneity. Instead, it continues to behave with a regularity that is always commensurate with antecedent causes, whether these be first-story or second-story. Thus Luke does not, like Pannenberg and Niebuhr, run the danger of destroying the possibility of all knowledge of the world.

Hence, according to Luke, the resurrection of Christ as the basis for faith can be known through historical reasoning as having taken place in history. The objection might then be raised that faith becomes a matter of knowledge and ceases to be a matter of commitment. Furthermore, if faith is based on knowledge, it would then seem that the Biblical antithesis between faith and sight ("We walk by faith and not by sight" —II Cor. 5:7) is broken down. However, as Pannenberg points out, our faith (or knowledge) that Christ is risen also embraces the promise that the people of God shall rise from the dead in the future. This future resurrection is not seen but only promised on the basis of the resurrection of Jesus. His resurrection has come from the second story into our world and carries with it the promise that believers too shall rise from the dead. This promise contradicts the cause-effect continuum on the first story, for by itself this continuum leads only to death and deterioration. So far as this world is concerned, there is no hope. All its paths of glory lead but to the grave, and the best course of action for a man shut up to the possibilities of the first story of this world is to "eat, drink, and be merry, for tomorrow we die" (I Cor. 15:32). However, the Christian does not walk by sight in the sense of living his life in accordance with the things that are seen in this world; rather, he is to live according to the things that are not seen, according to the resurrection from the dead, whose promise he knows in the resurrection of Christ but does not as yet see in the reality around him. By walking according to the knowledge of this promise and not by the world around him, he walks by faith and not by sight. Though this faith consists in owning up to knowledge and is anything but a "leap," yet it involves not only intellectual assent but also a wholehearted commitment to the promise of the resurrection from the dead, and thus to the living Christ who made the promise. Because faith is thus a commitment based upon knowledge, it therefore involves the Christian in a life which is based on hope rather than on the despair that arises from a consideration of the visible world.

To be thus committed to Christ means to enjoy that which (to use the words of Kierkegaard) satisfies "an infinite personal interest in an eternal happiness." According to Luke, this commitment is based wholly upon an historical fact. But it was Kierkegaard who said that an historical truth could never provide such a basis because historical truths can never go beyond being mere approximations and probabilities.[8] In saying this, Kierkegaard was following the inspiration he received from Lessing, who had said that "the accidental truths of history can never become the necessary truths of reason."[9] It was only the ultimate knowledge of what *is*, rather than

[8] S. Kierkegaard, *Concluding Unscientific Postscript*, pp. 25f. Cf. Chapter 1, pp. 24f.
[9] H. Chadwick (ed.), *Lessing's Theological Writings*, p. 53.

mere historical fact, that could provide for both Lessing and Kierkegaard a basis upon which they could rest their souls. Thus while Lessing (though with tongue in cheek) declared that he believed in the resurrection of Jesus, yet he added that he could not "jump with that historical truth to a quite different class of truths . . . and alter all my fundamental ideas of the nature of the Godhead because I cannot set any credible testimony against the resurrection of Christ."[10]

It should be noted that in making these statements both Lessing and Kierkegaard were voicing the age-old philosophical problem of how to find "being" beyond mere "becoming," or how to find what *is*, and thus what is ultimate, in the midst of a fluctuating and possibly ambiguous sense experience. Hence both men thought that to find ultimate truth they must turn away from history and the empirical world. Lessing found ultimate reason in his own soul,[11] and Kierkegaard declared that he had found the knowledge of God not in what existed inherently in his own soul, but in a miracle God had performed in his soul whereby he was able to know that the Jesus who had lived about two thousand years ago was indeed the Son of God who came to save sinners.[12]

For both of these men, therefore, faith did not rest upon history but upon a knowledge found immediately in the soul. But for Luke the certainty, and thus the knowledge of the things in which Theophilus had been instructed, was to be found in history, so that faith rested upon an historical knowledge.

In trying to decide whether to follow Lessing and Kierkegaard, or Luke, one should note that it is difficult to see how either Lessing or Kierkegaard was able to prove that he had found in his own soul a knowledge that was ultimate and free from the possible ambiguities of feeling. How, for example, was Kierkegaard able to claim with such certainty that his knowledge of Jesus as deity truly stemmed from God and was

[10] *Ibid.*, p. 54. Cf. Chapter 2, pp. 34f.
[11] See Chapter 2, p. 32.
[12] See Chapter 4, p. 81.

not a deception that originated from some other source? How was he sure that this knowledge was not the work of Descartes' malevolent demon or the fruit of some pathological state of mind? True assurance can only be found through the use of criteria by which the true can be distinguished from the false. But in applying such criteria Kierkegaard would be evaluating the claim to truth advanced by his own soul in exactly the same way that an historian evaluates an ancient document. How then could Kierkegaard assume that the claim to knowledge advanced by his own soul was free from the threat of approximation and probability that, in his view, inevitably accompanied every claim to empirical knowledge?

It would seem, therefore, that before we affirm something that confronts us—whether it be the assertion of an historical document or some impulse that arises from our souls—we must use criteria to determine whether it should be affirmed or not. One would be as foolish to commit himself to every inclination and impulse of his heart as he would be to credit every statement found in historical documents without first checking their credibility. No claim to truth should ever be accepted until its validity is checked by relevant criteria.

At this point at least two alternatives are open in the quest for an adequate basis for faith. One can say that faith in Jesus' resurrection can never be based on objective evidences and that therefore one can only have faith in the resurrection of Jesus because one *wants* to believe in it, and particularly in its concomitant promise that those believing it will rise from the dead. Such faith is nothing more than a leap into the void, for it is plain wishful thinking. Of course, it may be argued that believing in the resurrection deters one from evil deeds, since the resurrection asserts that death is not the last word and that God will bring men to judgment. But it is fallacious to assume that since it is *useful* to believe in the Biblical claim to the resurrection, therefore we *should* believe in it. If the resurrection of Jesus be not objectively and historically true, and there be no future resurrection from the dead, then Nietzsche might very well have been right that the best thing for one to do is to exercise as much power as he can to gain happiness in this world, even though this sometimes involves one in the injustice of using others as a means to his ends. If there be no resurrection, then why not be as happy as possible while one can? Furthermore, really to order one's life to the Biblical concept of the resurrection involves one in a clash with this world and consequent suffering. Because Christians suffer on account of their faith, Paul declared that if in this life only they have hope in Christ, they "are of all men most to be pitied" (I Cor. 15:19). Thus Paul affirmed that if there be no resurrection, he would live simply to extract as much happiness as possible from life: "If the dead be not raised, let us eat, drink, and be merry, for tomorrow we die" (I Cor. 15:32).

The second alternative is to say that faith only has a right to exist when it can be based on evidences that people can credit as trustworthy according to the verdict of suitable criteria. But this alternative must come to terms with the charge that perhaps, after all, our world of experience is really only a delusion produced by a malevolent demon. According to this charge it is impossible to demonstrate with absolute certainty that our experience is not a delusion. The only things a person can know with certainty are that he exists, and the truths of formal logic and mathematics. One can verify his own existence with Descartes' argument, "I doubt; therefore I exist." Thus the validity of truth remains certain despite the threat of a malevolent demon.

But the mere knowledge of one's existence and the validity of a syllogism falls far short of satisfying the soul's longing after an infinite personal happiness. However, this lack is of no consequence, for no one limits himself to such a small circle of data. We all take in dead earnest the world around us, and nobody seriously entertains the hypothesis of a malevolent demon. Suppose a speeding automobile bears down upon me while I am crossing a street. Rather than pausing to consider whether I and the automobile really exist, I leap out of the way. When the calendar shows that one day remains to pay the income tax, I do not question the reality of time. Rather, I proceed to fill out my income-tax forms. When a loved one dies, there are facts within the sensible world that produce the profoundest emotions within my heart. If the sensible world can produce such wholehearted responses, then it is not impossible for an empirical fact to satisfy the longing of my soul after an infinite personal happiness. Sophistry might try to deny this, but sophistry is irrelevant, for I realize that my life is already irretrievably governed by the sensible world around me.

Luke argues the certainty of an historical event whose meaning satisfies the deepest longings of the heart, for it brings the knowledge of God and the certainty of a triumph over death. It may be objected, however, that Luke bases his argument on historical knowledge, and that historical knowledge is so problematical that it can never provide sufficient certainty to support something of ultimate concern.

To be sure, there are many pieces of historical knowledge that are asserted only on the basis of the barest probability, and all historians are humbled by the consideration that, in comparison with all that has occurred, only a few crumbs of knowledge of what took place are available from the extant evidences. But neither the fact that much historical knowledge is missing nor the fact that much historical knowledge wavers in the twilight zone of conjecture and minimal probability means that *all* historical knowledge is problematical and must be less certain than knowledge gained by immediate sense perception. There are some things in history, like the existence of Julius Caesar, that are as certain as the ground we are standing on. It is not possible to explain either the existence of the extant sources that tell of a Julius Caesar or Roman history without asserting that a Julius Caesar existed.

A consideration of Luke's argument for the resurrection of Jesus shows that it is just as impossible to deny his resurrection as it is to deny the existence of Julius Caesar. How can the historical fact of Christianity's mission to the Gentiles and its origin in Judaism be explained unless we include the resurrection of Christ? Apart from Christ's resurrection, these two historical facts remain an insoluble riddle, for how could the Jews of that day admit Gentiles to a place of equal standing apart from supernatural intervention? To try to explain this without reference to the resurrection is as hopeless as trying to explain Roman history without reference to Julius Caesar.

Luke's argument contains, along with the establishment of the resurrection of Jesus, the establishment of the fact that the apostles were endowed with a teaching office, whereby through supernatural inspiration they were enabled to impart the God-given *meaning* to the fact of the resurrection of Christ.[13] One of the most salient features of the apostolic meaning of the resurrection is that it carries with it the promise that believers will rise from the dead to a life of unending bliss with God. Such a meaning is the answer to the soul's infinite interest in and quest for an eternal happiness, for the soul can ask nothing more than to know God forever.

Although Luke's method for coming to such knowledge focuses attention upon an ancient historical fact, it does not do so in such an exclusive way that it makes faith a possibility only for those who are capable of following out historical reasoning. For Luke faith is also a possibility for those confronted with a Barnabas who is "full of the Holy Spirit and of faith" (Acts 11:24). Since the atmosphere of love and hope that surrounds such a man cannot be reproduced by one who is confined to the possibilities of this world, which is characterized by sin and death, men sense intuitively that such love, faith, and hope originate from outside the possibilities of this world. As Barnabas preaches the Gospel that Christ died for men's sins and rose again the third day, and as he testifies to the change that came about in his own life as he believed this message, the hearers, sensing the supernaturalness of the Barnabas, are confronted with sufficient evidence to credit his message regarding the risen Christ.

Of all those who have come to embrace faith in Christ, no

[13] See Chapter 7, pp. 223-29.

doubt by far the great majority have done so through confrontation with a Barnabas, rather than by reasoning historically regarding the origins of Christianity. But it should be noted that the method of knowing, whether it be via Christianity's historical origins or via a contemporary Barnabas, depends on a life that has been changed and whose change cannot be explained by recourse to causes existing within this world. When one views a Barnabas, a life is seen that is out of keeping with this world characterized by the struggle for survival and by death; likewise, when one views the apostles, lives are seen that produce a Gentile mission entirely out of keeping with the Judaism of that day. But in both cases there is an empirical fact that can only be explained by reference to the risen Christ.

Since faith can always come into existence through a Barnabas, it might be supposed that a knowledge of the resurrection by recourse to Christianity's historical origins is quite unnecessary. There are times, however, when it is needful to check the historical foundation of the message of a Barnabas in a more direct way than by the argument that his message regarding Christ must be true since his life cannot be explained by causes within the world. The following are occasions when this can be highly desirable: (1) when certain people claim to be Barnabases but teach something other than the grace of God, that is, when it is necessary to reassert Christianity's foundation in overcoming heresy; (2) when the church is reproached with the charge that it is inconsistent to claim an historical faith and yet not be able to verify its center, the resurrection of Jesus, through the historical method; and (3) when those who have believed through a Barnabas become aware of the historical method and might therefore be troubled if their faith, which depends on the assertion that God has effected redemption in history, could not be verified in the same way that all other historical knowledge is verified.

Luke, writing for the second generation of Christians, has provided the church with a way of obtaining historical knowledge concerning the resurrection, the center of all its instruction. By providing this argument from the Gentile mission, Luke was far from saying that the church should confine its attention to the past, for he himself spoke of the present work of Christ, mediated through the filling of the Holy Spirit, as much as any New Testament writer. The church should therefore live through the Holy Spirit unto Christ in the present, while always remembering and considering the redemptive history of the past, which makes present knowledge of Christ possible. Through this method that Luke has provided, the church can also verify the central fact of its past whenever the need arises. Thus the Easter history continues to be vital for the faith of the church as it lives for Christ in the present.

A Bibliography of Works Cited in This Book

Althaus, Paul. "Offenbarung als Geschichte und Glaube," *Theologische Literaturzeitung*, 87 (1962), cols. 321-30.

————. *Das sogenannte Kerygma und der historische Jesus* (Beiträge zur Förderung christlicher Theologie, 48). Gütersloh: Carl Bertelsmann Verlag, 1958. Cf. *The So-Called Kerygma and the Historical Jesus*. Trans. by David Cairns. Edinburgh: Oliver & Boyd, 1959.

Baldensperger, Guillaume. *Le tombeau vide*. Paris: Liberairie Felix Alcan, 1935.

Barrett, C. K. *Luke the Historian in Recent Study*. London: Epworth Press, 1961.

Barth, Karl. *Church Dogmatics*. 4 vols.; Edinburgh: T. & T. Clark, 1936-1962. Trans. from *Die kirchliche Dogmatik* (I/1, Munich: Chr. Kaiser Verlag, 1932; I/2–IV/3, Zollikon/Zurich: Evang. Verlag, 1938-1959) by G. T. Thomson (I/1); G. T. Thomson, Harold Knight (I/2); T. H. Parker *et al* (II/1); G. W. Bromiley *et al* (II/2); J. W. Edwards *et al* (III/1); Harold Knight *et al* (III/4); G. W. Bromiley (IV/1); G. W. Bromiley (IV/2); G. W. Bromiley (IV/3).

————. "Ein Briefwechsel mit Adolf von Harnack," *Theologische Fragen und Antworten*. Zollikon/Zürich: Evang. Verlag, 1957. Pp. 7-31.

————. *The Epistle to the Romans*. London: Oxford University Press, 1933. Trans. by Edwyn C. Hoskyns from *Der Römerbrief*. 6th ed.; Munich: Chr. Kaiser Verlag, 1928.

————. "Evangelical Theology in the 19th Century," *Scottish Journal of Theology Occasional Papers*, 8. Edinburgh: Oliver & Boyd, 1959. Pp. 55-74. Trans. by J. S. McNab from *Evangelische Theologie im 19. Jahrhundert* (Theologische Studien, 49). Zollikon/Zürich: Evang. Verlag, 1957.

————. *From Rousseau to Ritschl*. London: SCM Press, 1959. Trans. by Brian Cozens from 11 of the 29 chapters of *Die protestantische Theologie im 19. Jahrhundert*. Zollikon/Zürich: Evang. Verlag, 1952.

————. *Die Lehre vom Worte Gottes*. Prolegomena zur christlichen Dogmatik. Munich: Chr. Kaiser Verlag, 1927.

————. "How My Mind Has Changed," *Christian Century*, 77 (1960), 72-76.

A Bibliography of Works Cited in This Book

————. *The Resurrection of the Dead.* New York: Fleming Revell, 1933. Trans. by H. J. Stenning from *Die Auferstehung der Toten.* Munich: Chr. Kaiser Verlag, 1924.

————. "Rudolf Bultmann — An Attempt to Understand Him," *Kerygma and Myth,* 2 vols.; H. W. Bartsch (ed). London: S. P. C. K., 1953, 1962. II, 83-132. Trans. by R. H. Fuller from *Rudolf Bultmann: Ein Versuch, ihn zu verstehen* (Theologische Studien, 34). 2nd ed.; Zollikon/Zürich: Evang. Verlag, 1953.

Berkouwer, G. C. *The Triumph of Grace in the Theology of Karl Barth.* Grand Rapids: Wm. B. Eerdmans Publishing Co., 1956. Trans. from the Dutch by Harry R. Boer.

Bloch, Marc. *The Historian's Craft.* Manchester: Manchester University Press, 1954. Trans. by Peter Putnam from *Apologie pour l'histoire ou, Métier d'historien.* Paris: Librairie Armand Colin, 1949.

Bornkamm, Günther. *Jesus from Nazareth.* New York: Harper & Row, 1960. Trans. by Irene and Fraser McLuskey with James M. Robinson from the 3rd edition of *Jesus von Nazareth.* Stuttgart: W. Kohlhammer Verlag, 1959.

Bruce, F. F. *The Acts of the Apostles.* Grand Rapids: Wm. B. Eerdmans Publishing Co., 1952.

Brunner, Emil. *The Christian Doctrine of Creation and Redemption,* vol. II. *Dogmatics,* 3 vols. Philadelphia: Westminster Press, 1950-1962. Trans. by Olive Wyon from *Die christliche Lehre von Schöpfung und Erlösung,* vol. II. *Dogmatik,* 3 vols. Zurich: Zwingli Verlag, 1946-1960.

Bultmann, Rudolf. "Autobiographical Reflections," *Existence and Faith. Shorter Writings of Rudolf Bultmann.* Schubert M. Ogden (ed.). London: Hodder and Stoughton, 1961. Pp. 283-88. Trans. by Schubert M. Ogden from "Lebenslauf," an autobiographical statement prepared by R. Bultmann in 1956 at Ogden's request.

————. "Bultman Replies to His Critics," *Kerygma and Myth,* 2 vols. H. W. Bartsch (ed.). London: S. P. C. K., 1953, 1962. I, 191-211. Trans. by R. H. Fuller from a part of "Zum Problem der Entmythologisierung." *Kerygma und Mythos* II. H. W. Bartsch (ed.). Hamburg/Bergstedt: Herbert Reich Evang. Verlag, 1952. Pp. 179-208. Pp. 191-95 are omitted from the English translation.

————. *Die Geschichte der synoptischen Tradition.* Göttingen: Vandenhoeck & Ruprecht, 1921. Cf. *The History of the Synoptic Tradition.* Trans. by John Marsh. New York: Harper & Row, 1963.

————. *Jesus and the Word.* Students' edition; New York: Charles Scribner's Sons, 1958. Trans. by L. P. Smith and E. H. Lantero from *Jesus.* Berlin: Deutsche Bibliothek, 1926.

————. "Karl Barths 'Römerbrief in zweiter Auflage," *Die Christliche Welt,* 36 (1922), cols. 320-23; 330-34; 358-61; 369-73.

————. "Karl Barth, 'Die Auferstehung der Toten'," *Glauben und Verstehen* I. 4th. ed.; Tübingen: J. C. B. Mohr (Paul Siebeck), 1961. Pp. 38-64.

————. *History and Eschatology.* Harper Torchbook edition; New York: Harper & Row, 1962. Published by Harper & Row in 1957 as

The Presence of Eternity, the title of Bultmann's 1953 Gifford Lectures, which were the first presentation of this work.

————. "Die liberale Theologie und die jüngste theologische Bewegung," *Glauben und Verstehen* I. 4th ed.; Tübingen: J. C. B. Mohr (Paul Siebeck), 1961. Pp. 1-25. This article was first published in 1924.

————. "New Testament and Mythology," *Kerygma and Myth.* 2 vols.; H. W. Bartsch (ed.). London: S. P. C. K., 1953, 1962. I, 1-44. Trans. by R. H. Fuller from "Neues Testament und Mythologie," *Kerygma und Mythos,* I, H. W. Bartsch (ed.). Hamburg/ Bergstedt: Herbert Reich Evang. Verlag, 1948. Pp. 15-53. This famous essay first appeared under the title *Offenbarung und Heilsgeschehen.* Munich: A. Lempp, 1941.

————. "The Problem of Hermeneutics," *Essays.* New York: Macmillan, 1955. Pp. 234-61. Trans. by C. G. Greig from *Glauben und Verstehen* II. Tübingen: J. C. B. Mohr (Paul Siebeck), 1952. Pp. 211-35. This essay first appeared in *Zeitschrift für Theologie und Kirche,* 47 (1950), 47-69.

————. *Theology of the New Testament.* 2 vols.; New York: Charles Scribner's Sons, 1951, 1955. Trans. by Kendrick Grobel from *Theologie des Neuen Testaments.* Tübingen: J. C. B. Mohr (Paul Siebeck), 1948-1953.

————. *Das Verhältnis der urchristlichen Christusbotschaft zum historischen Jesus.* (Sitzungsberichte der Heidelberger Akademie der Wissenschaften, philosophisch-historische Klasse, Jahrgang, 1960; 3. Abhandlung). 2nd ed.; Heidelberg: Carl Winter, Universitätsverlag, 1961.

————. "Zum Problem der Entmythologisierung," *Kerygma und Mythos II.* H. W. Bartsch (ed.). Hamburg/Bergstedt: Herbert Reich Evang. Verlag, 1952. Pp. 180-90.

————. "Zu J. Schniewinds Thesen," *Kerygma und Mythos I.* H. W. Bartsch (ed.). 4th ed.; Hamburg/Bergstedt: Herbert Reich Evang. Verlag, 1961. Py. 122-38.

Cadbury, H. J. "Commentary on the Preface of Luke," *The Beginnings of Christianity.* 5 vols.; F. Foakes-Jackson and K. Lake (eds.). London: Macmillan, 1920-33. II, 489-510.

————. "Roman Law and the Trial of Paul," *The Beginnings of Christianity.* 5 vols.; F. Foakes-Jackson and K. Lake (eds.). London: Macmillan, 1920-23. V, 297-338.

Collingwood, R. G. *The Idea of History.* T. M. Knox (ed.). Oxford: Clarendon Press, 1946.

Conzelmann, D. Hans. *Die Apostelgeschichte* (Handbuch zum Neuen Testament, 7). Tübingen: J. C. B. Mohr (Paul Siebeck), 1963.

————. *The Theology of St. Luke.* New York: Harper & Row, 1960. Trans. by G. Buswell from *Die Mitte der Zeit.* (Beiträge zur historischen Theologie, 17). Tübingen: J. C. B. Mohr (Paul Siebeck), 1953.

Cullmann, Oscar. *Christ and Time.* Philadelphia: Westminster Press, 1950. Trans. by Floyd Filson from *Christus und die Zeit.* Zollikon/ Zürich: Evang. Verlag, 1946.

A Bibliography of Works Cited in This Book

—————. *The Christology of the New Testament*. Philadelphia: Westminster Press, 1959. Trans. by Shirley C. Guthrie and Charles A. M. Hall from *Die Christologie des Neuen Testaments*. Tübingen: J. C. B. Mohr (Paul Siebeck), 1957.

—————. *The Earliest Christian Confessions*. London: Lutterworth Press, 1949. Trans. by J. K. S. Reid from *Les premières confessions de foi Chrétiennes*. Presses Universitaires de France, 1943.

—————. "Parusieverzögerung und Urchristentum," *Theologische Literaturzeitung*, 83 (1958), cols. 1-12.

Dibelius, Martin. *Jesus*. Philadelphia: Westminster Press, 1949. Trans. by C. B. Hedrick and F. C. Grant from *Jesus*. Berlin: W. de Gruyter, 1939.

—————. *Studies in the Acts of the Apostles*. London: SCM Press, 1956. Trans. by M. Ling and P. Schubert from *Aufsätze zur Apostelgeschichte*. H. Greeven (ed.). Göttingen: Vandenhoeck & Ruprecht, 1951.

Diem, Hermann. *Dogmatics*. Edinburgh: Oliver & Boyd, 1959. Trans. by Harold Knight from *Dogmatik: Ihr Weg zwischen Historismus und Existenzialismus*. Munich: Chr. Kaiser Verlag, 1955. This latter volume appeared as vol. II of *Theologie als kirchliche Wissenschaft: Handreichung zur Einübung ihrer Probleme*.

—————. "The Earthly Jesus and the Christ of Faith," *Kerygma and History*. C. Braaten and R. Harrisville (eds.). New York: Abingdon Press, 1962. Pp. 197-211. Trans. by C. Braaten and R. Harrisville from "Der irdische Jesus und der Christus des Glaubens," *Der historische Jesus und der kerygmatische Christus*. H. Ristow and K. Matthiae (eds.). Berlin: Evangelische Verlaganstalt, 1960. Pp. 219-32. This is a somewhat revised version of Diem's inaugural address as he became Professor of Theology at Tübingen in 1957.

—————. *Grundfragen der biblischen Hermeneutik*. (Theologische Existenz heute, N. F., Vol. 24.) Chr. Kaiser Verlag, 1950.

Dodd, C. H. "The Appearances of the Risen Christ: An Essay in Form-Criticism of the Gospel," *Studies in the Gospels*. D. E. Nineham (ed.). Oxford: Basil Blackwell, 1957.

Easton, Burton Scott. *Early Christianity. The Purpose of Acts and Other Papers.* F. C. Grant (ed.). London: S. P. C. K., 1955.

Ebeling, Gerhard. "The Significance of the Critical Historical Method for Church and Theology in Protestantism," *Word and Faith*. London: SCM Press, 1963. Pp. 18-61. Trans. by J. W. Leitch from *Wort und Glaube*. Tübingen: J. C. B. Mohr (Paul Siebeck), 1960. This article first appeared as "Die Bedeutung der historisch-kritischen Methode für die protestantische theologie und Kirche," *Zeitschrift für Theologie und Kirche*, 47 (1950), 1-46.

Filson, Floyd. *Jesus Christ the Risen Lord*. New York: Abingdon Press, 1956.

—————. *Three Crucial Decades*. Richmond: John Knox Press, 1963.

Foakes-Jackson, F. J., and Lake, Kirsopp. "Christology," *The Beginnings of Christianity*. 5 vols.; F. Foakes-Jackson and K. Lake (eds.). London: Macmillan, 1920-33. I, 344-418.

Frankfurter Zeitung, October 4, 1914.

Fuchs, Ernst. "Die Frage nach dem historischen Jesus," *Zur Frage nach dem historischen Jesus.* Tübingen: J. C. B. Mohr (Paul Siebeck), 1960. Pp. 143-67. First published in *Zeitschrift für Theologie und Kirche,* 53 (1956), 210-19. Cf. "The Quest of the Historical Jesus," *Studies of the Historical Jesus.* (Studies in Biblical Theology, 42). Trans. by A. Scobie. London: SCM Press, 1964. Pp. 11-31.

Goguel, Maurice. *The Birth of Christianity.* London: George Allen & Unwin, 1953. Trans. by H. C. Snape from *La naissance du Christianisme,* vol. 2. *Jésus et les origines du Christianisme.* 3 vols.: Paris: Payot, 1932-1947.

Grass, Hans. *Ostergeschehen und Osterberichte.* 2nd ed.; Göttingen: Vandenhoeck & Ruprecht, 1962.

Haenchen, Ernst. *Die Apostelgeschichte.* (Kritisch-exegetischer Kommentar über das Neue Testament, begr. von H. A. W. Meyer, 3. Abt. 12th ed.) Göttingen: Vandenhoeck & Ruprecht, 1959.

—————. "Das 'wir' in der Apostelgeschichte und das Itinerar," *Zeitschrift für Theologie und Kirche,* 58 (1961), 329-66.

Harnack, Adolf. *The Acts of the Aposles.* New York: G. P. Putnam's Sons, 1909. Trans. by J. R. Wilkinson from *Die Apostelgeschichte.* (Beiträge zur Einleitung in das Neue Testament, 3). Leipzig: J. C. Heinrichs'sche Buchhandlung, 1908.

—————. *The Date of the Acts and of the Synoptic Gospels.* New York: G. P. Putnam's Sons, 1911. Trans. by J. R. Wilkinson from *Neue Untersuchungen zur Apostelgeschichte.* (Beiträge zur Einleitung in das Neue Testament, 4). Leipzig: J. C. Hinrichs'sche Buchhandlung, 1911.

—————. *Luke the Physician.* New York: G. P. Putnam's Sons, 1907. Trans. by J. R. Wilkinson from *Lukas der Artz, der Verfasser des dritten Evangeliums und der Apostelgeschichte.* (Beiträge zur Einleitung in das Neue Testament, 1). Leipzig: J. C. Hinrichs'sche Buchhandlung, 1906.

—————. "Rede zur deutsch-amerikanischen Sympathiekundgebung," *Aus der Friedensund Kriegsarbeit.* Giessen: Alfred Topelmann, 1916. Pp. 283-290.

Hegel, G. W. F. *On Christianity: Early Theological Writings.* Harper Torchbook edition; New York: Harper & Row, 1961. Trans. by T. M. Knox from *Hegels theologische Jugendschriften.* Herman Noel (ed.). Tübingen: J. C. B. Mohr (Paul Siebeck), 1907.

—————. *The Philosophy of History.* Trans. by J. Sibree. *Great Books of the Western World.* 54 vols.; R. M. Hutchins (ed.). Chicago: Encyclopedia Britannica, Inc., 1952. Vol. 46, pp. 151-369.

Herrmann, Wilhelm. *The Communion of the Christian with God.* 2nd ed.; New York: G. P. Putnam's Sons, 1906. Trans. by J. Sandys Stanyon and enlarged and altered in accordance with the 4th edition of *Der Verkehr des Christen mit Gott.* Stuttgart, 1903.

Hobart, William K. *The Medical Language of St. Luke.* Reprint. Grand Rapids: Baker Book House, 1954.

Holtzmann, Heinrich Julius. *Lehrbuch der neutestamentlichen Theologie.* 2 vols.; 2nd ed.; Tübingen: J. C. B. Mohr (Paul Siebeck), 1911.

A Bibliography of Works Cited in This Book

————. *Die synoptischen Evangelien.* Leipzig: Wilhelm Engelmann, 1863.

Kähler, Martin. *Der sogenannte historische Jesus und der geschichtliche, biblische Christus.* (Theologische Bucherei, 2). E. Wolf (ed.). Munich: Chr. Kaiser Verlag, 1956. A reprint of pp. 1-95 of the 2nd edition of 1896. Cf. *The So-called Historical Jesus and the Historic, Biblical Christ.* Trans. and ed. by Carl E. Braaten. Philadelphia: Fortress Press, 1964.

————. *Der sogenannte historische Jesus und der geschichtliche, biblische Christus.* 2. Aufl. Leipzig: A. Deichert, 1896.

Käsemann, Ernst. "Das Problem des historischen Jesus," *Zeitschrift für Theologie und Kirche,* 51 (1954), 125-53. Cf. "The Problem of the Historical Jesus," *Essays on New Testament Themes.* (Studies in Biblical Theology, 41). Trans. by W. Montague. London: SCM Press, 1964. Pp. 15-47.

Kant, Immanuel. *Religion within the Limits of Reason Alone.* Ed. and trans. by T. M. Greene and H. Hudson. Chicago: Open Court Publishing Co., 1934.

Kepler, Thomas S. *The Mystery of the Resurrection.* New York: Association Press, 1963.

Kierkegaard, Søren. *Concluding Unscientific Postscript.* Trans. by D. F. Swanson. Princeton: Princeton University Press, 1944.

————. *Philosophical Fragments.* Trans. by D. F. Swanson. Princeton: Princeton University Press, 1936.

Klostermann, Erich. *Das Lukas Evangelium.* (Handbuch zum Neuen Testament, 5). Tübingen: J. C. B. Mohr (Paul Siebeck), 1929.

Knox, John. *The Church and the Reality of Christ.* New York: Harper & Row, 1962.

Koch, Gerhard. *Die Auferstehung Jesu Christi.* (Beiträge zur historischen Theologie, 27). Tübingen: J. C. B. Mohr (Paul Siebeck), 1959.

Kümmel, Werner Georg. *Das Neue Testament.* (Orbis Academicus, III/3). Freiburg: Verlag Karl Alber, 1958.

————. "Das Urchristentum," *Theologische Rundschau,* N.F. 22 (1954), 138-70; 191-211.

Künneth, Walter. *Theologie der Auferstehung.* 4th ed.; Munich: Claudius Verlag, 1951.

Lachmann, Karl. "De ordine narrationum in evangeliis synopticiis," *Theologische Studien und Kritiken,* 8 (1835), 570-90.

Lake, Kirsopp, and Cadbury, H. J. *The Acts of the Apostles,* vol. 4. *The Beginnings of Christianity.* 5 vols.; F. Foakes-Jackson and K. Lake (eds.). London: Macmillan, 1920-1933.

Masson, Charles. *L'épitre de Saint Paul aux Ephésiens.* (Commentaire du Nouveau Testament, 9). Neuchatel: Delachaux & Niestlé, 1953.

McNeile, Alan Hugh. *The Gospel According to St. Matthew.* London: Macmillan, 1949.

Menoud, Philippe H. "Remarques sur les textes de l'ascension dans Luc-Actes," *Neutestamentliche Studien für Rudolf Bultmann zu seinem siebzigsten Geburtstag.* Walter Eltester (ed.). (Beihefte zur Zeitschrift fur die neutestamentliche Wissenschaft, 21). Berlin: Alfred Topelmann, 1954. Pp. 148-56.

Meyer, Eduard. *Ursprung und Anfänge des Christentums,* 3 vols. Stuttgart: J. G. Cotta, 1921-1923.
Meyer, H. A. W. *Critical and Exegetical Handbook to the Acts of the Apostles.* (Critical and Exegetical Commentary. W. Dickson and F. Crombie, eds.). Edinburgh: T. & T. Clark, 1877. Trans. from the 4th edition of the German by P. Gloag.
Moulton, James Hope, and Milligan, George. *The Vocabulary of the Greek New Testament.* Grand Rapids: Wm. B. Eerdmans Publishing Co., 1952.
Niebuhr, Richard R. *Resurrection and Historical Reason.* New York: Charles Scribner's Sons, 1957.
O'Neill, J. C. *The Theology of Acts.* London: S. P. C. K., 1961.
Ott, Heinrich. *Geschichte und Heilsgeschichte in der Theologie Rudolf Bultmanns.* (Beiträge zur historischen Theologie, 19). Tübingen: J. C. B. Mohr (Paul Siebeck), 1955.
————. "Objectification and Existentialism," *Kerygma and Myth,* 2 vols. H. W. Bartsch (ed.). London: S. P. C. K., 1953, 1962. II, 306-335. Trans. by R. H. Fuller.
Pannenberg, Wolfhart. "Einsicht und Glaube," *Theologische Literaturzeitung,* 88 (1963), cols. 81-98.
————. "Heilsgeschehen und Geschichte," *Kerygma und Dogma,* 5 (1959), 218-37; 259-88. Part of this article has been translated by Shirley Guthrie as "Redemptive Event and History," *Old Testament Hermeneutics.* Claus Westermann and J. L. Mays (eds.). Richmond: John Knox Press, 1963. Pp. 314-35. Editors James Robinson and John Cobb plan to reproduce this article in its entirety in the third volume of their *New Frontiers in Theology,* which will be entitled *Theology as History* and will be devoted to a discussion of Pannenberg's system.
————. "Did *Jesus* Really Rise from the Dead?" Lecture delivered at Fuller Theological Seminary, May 8, 1963. Cf. "Ist Jesus wirklich auferstanden?" *Geistliche Woche für Südwestdeutschland der Evang. Akademie Mannheim vom 16 bis 23. Februar 1964.* Karlsruhe/Durland: Gebr. Tron KG, 1964. Pp. 23-33.
Pannenberg, Wolfhart (ed.). *Offenbarung als Geschichte.* (Kerygma und Dogma, Beiheft 1). 2nd ed.; Göttingen: Vandenhoeck & Ruprecht, 1963. In this joint effort, the articles by Pannenberg are of particular interest: "Dogmatische Thesen zur Lehre von der Offenbarung," pp. 91-114, and "Nachwort zur zweiten Auflage," pp. 132-48.
Ramsey, Michael. *The Resurrection of Christ.* Philadelphia: Westminster Press, 1946.
Reicke, Bo. *Glaube und Leben der Urgemeinde. Bemerkungen zu Apg. 1-7.* (Abhandlungen zur Theologie des Alten und Neuen Testaments, 32). Zürich: Zwingli Verlag, 1957.
————. "The Risen Lord and His Church," *Interpretation,* 13 (1959), 157-69.
————. "Zum sprachlichen Verständnis von Kol. 2:23," *Theologica Studia,* 6 (1953), 39-53.
Rengstorf, D. Karl Heinrich. *Die Auferstehung Jesu.* 4th ed.; Witten/Ruhr: Luther-Verlag, 1960.

Richardson, Alan. *The Bible in the Age of Science.* London: SCM Press, 1961.

Ritschl, Albrecht. *The Christian Doctrine of Justification and Reconciliation.* 2nd ed.; H. R. Mackintosh and A. B. Macaulay (eds.). Edinburgh: T. & T. Clark, 1902. Translated by R. H. Mackintosh and A. B. Macaulay from the 3rd edition (1888) of *Die christliche Lehre von der Rechtfertigung und Versöhnung,* the third of three volumes on the subject of justification and reconciliation which originally appeared between 1872 and 1874.

Robinson, James. "The German Discussion of the Later Heidegger," *The Later Heidegger and Theology.* J. Robinson and J. Cobb, Jr. (eds.). 2 vols.; New York: Harper & Row, 1963-. I, 3-76.

—————. *Kerygma und historischer Jesus.* Zürich: Zwingli Verlag, 1960. More than a translation of *The New Quest of the Historical Jesus,* this is a second and revised edition of that book.

—————. *A New Quest of the Historical Jesus.* (Studies in Biblical Theology, 25). London: SCM Press, 1959.

—————. "The Recent Debate on the 'New Quest'," *The Journal of Bible and Religion,* 30 (1962), 198-208.

Sahlin, Harald. *Der Messias und das Gottesvolk.* A. Fridrichsen (ed.). (Acts Seminarii Neotestamentici Upsaliensis, 12). Upsala: Almqvist & Wiksells boktyrckeri, 1945.

Schleiermacher, Friedrich. *The Christian Faith.* H. R. Mackintosh and J. S. Stewart (eds.). Edinburgh: T. & T. Clark, 1928. Trans. by D. M. Baillie *et al.,* from the 2nd edition of *Der christliche Glaube* published in 1830.

—————. *On Religion: Speeches to Its Cultured Despisers.* New York: Harper & Row, 1958. Trans. by John Oman from the 3rd edition of *Ueber die Religion. Reden an die Gebildeten unter ihren Verächtern.*

Schlier, Henrich. *Der Brief an die Galater.* (Kritisch-exegetischer Kommentar über das Neue Testament, begr. von H. A. W. Meyer, 7. 12th ed.). Göttingen: Vandenhoeck & Ruprecht, 1962.

Schmidt, K. L. "Jesus Christus." *Die Religion in der Geschichte und Gegenwart,* 6 vols. 2nd ed.; Hermann Gunkel and Leopold Zscharnack (eds.). Tübingen: J. C. B. Mohr (Paul Siebeck), 1927-1932. III, cols. 110-151.

Schweitzer, Albert. *The Mystery of the Kingdom of God.* London: A & C. Black, 1914. Trans. by Walter Lowrie from the second part of *Das Abendmahl im Zusammenhang mit dem Leben Jesu und der Geschichte des Urchristentums,* Leipzig, 1901, entitled *Das Messianitats-und Leidensgeheimnis. Eine Skizze des Lebens Jesu.*

—————. *The Quest of the Historical Jesus.* 2nd ed.; London: A. & C. Black, 1931. Trans. by W. Montgomery from *Von Reimarus zu Wrede. Eine Geschichte der Leben Jesu Forschung.* Tübingen: 1906.

Stauffer, Ethelbert. *New Testament Theology.* New York: Macmillan, 1955. Trans. by John Marsh from the 5th edition of *Die Theologie des Neuen Testaments.* Stuttgart: W. Kohlhammer Verlag, 1948[4].

Strauss, David F. *The Life of Jesus.* 2nd ed.; New York: Macmillan,

1892. Trans. by George Eliot from the 4th edition (1840) of *Das Leben Jesu.*

Table Talk of Martin Luther. Trans. by William Hazlitt. 2nd ed.; Philadelphia: Lutheran Board of Publication, 1868.

Taylor, Vincent. *The Names of Jesus.* New York: Macmillan, 1954.

Tenney, Merrill C. *The Reality of the Resurrection.* New York: Harper & Row, 1963.

Tillich, Paul. *Systematic Theology,* 3 vols. Chicago: University of Chicago Press, 1951-1963.

Tödt, Heinz E. *Der Menschensohn in der synoptischen Ueberlieferung.* Gütersloh: Gerd Mohn, 1959.

Trocmé Étienne. *Le "Livre des Actes" et l'histoire.* (Études d'histoire et de philosophie relgieuses, publiées sous les auspices de la faculté de théologie protestante de l'université de Strasbourg, 45). Paris: Presses Universitaires de France, 1957.

Troeltsch, Ernst. *Die Bedeutung der Geschichtlichkeit Jesu für den Glauben.* Tübingen: J. C. B. Mohr (Paul Siebeck), 1911.

————. "Ueber die historische und dogmatische Methode in der Theologie." *Zur religiösen Lage. Religionphilosophie und Ethik,* Vol. II, 729-53, Gesammelte Schriften, 4 vols. Tübingen: J. C. B. Mohr (Paul Siebeck), 1912-1925.

van Stempvoort, P. "The Interpretation of the Ascension in Luke and Acts," *New Testament Studies,* 5 (1958), 30-42.

von Campenhausen, Hans F. *Der Ablauf der Ostereignisse und das leere Grab.* (Sitzungberichte der Heidelberger Akademie der Wissenschaften, philosophisch-historische Klasse, Jahrgang 1958; 2nd Abhandlung.) 2nd ed.; Heidelberg: Carl Winter Universitätsverlag, 1958.

Voysey, Charles (ed.). *Fragments from Reimarus.* Lexington, Kentucky: American Theological Library Association Committee on Reprinting, 1962. A reprint of the 1879 edition. Trans. anonymously.

Wallbank, T. Walter, and Taylor, Alastair M. *Civilization Past and Present.* 2 vols., 4th ed.; Chicago: Scott, Foresman, 1961.

Weber, Otto. *Karl Barths kirchliche Dogmatik.* 4th ed.; Neukirchen/ Moers: Verlag des Erziehungsvereins, 1958. This edition summarizes I/1 to IV/2 of *Die kirchliche Dogmatik. Cf. Karl Barth's Church Dogmatics.* Trans. by A. C. Cochrane (Philadelphia: Westminster Press, 1953), which covers I/1-III/4.

Weiss, Johannes. *Die Predigt Jesu vom Reiche Gottes.* 2nd ed.; Göttingen: Vanderhoeck & Ruprecht, 1900.

Weisse, Christian Hermann. *Die evangelische Geschichte kritisch und philosophisch bearbeitet,* 2 vols. Leipzig: Breitkopf & Härtel, 1838.

Westcott, Brooke Foss. *The Gospel of the Resurrection.* 4th ed.; London: Macmillan, 1879.

Wilckens, Ulrich. "Die Offenbarungsverständnis in der Geschichte des Urchristentums," *Offenbarung als Geschichte.* W. Pannenberg (ed.). Gottingen: Vandenhoeck & Ruprecht, 1963, Pp. 42-90.

Wilke, Christian Gottlob. *Der Urevangelist.* Dresden: G. Fleischer, 1838.

Williams, H. A. *Jesus and the Resurrection.* 2nd ed.; London: A. R. Mowbray, 1960.

Wingren, Gustav. *Theology in Conflict.* London: Oliver & Boyd, 1958. Trans. by E. H. Wahlstrom.

Wrede, Wilhelm. *Das Messiasgeheimnis in den Evangelien.* 3rd ed.; Gottingen: Vandenhoeck & Ruprecht, 1963.

Yarnold, G. D. *Risen Indeed.* New York: Oxford University Press, 1959.

Zahn, Theodor. *Introduction to the New Testament,* 3 vols. Grand Rapids: Kregel Publications, 1953. Trans. by M. W. Jacobus *et al.,* from the 3rd edition of *Einleitung in das Neue Testament.* Leipzig: Deichert, 1924.

Aristotle. *Prior Analytics*. Organon I, 181-531. Trans. by H. Tredennick. Loeb Classical Library. Cambridge, Mass.: Harvard University Press, 1955.

————. *The Art of Rhetoric*. Trans. by John H. Freese. Loeb Classical Library. Cambridge, Mass.: Harvard University Press, 1947.

Digest of Justinian, Part II. The Civil Law, 4 parts, 17 vols. Trans. by S. P. Scott. Cincinnati: The Central Trust Company, 1932.

Dio's Roman History, 9 vols. Trans. by Earnest Cary. Loeb Classical Library. Cambridge, Mass.: Harvard University Press, 1954.

Josephus. 8 vols. Trans. by H. St. J. Thackeray. Loeb Classical Library. Cambridge, Mass.: Harvard University Press, 1956- . Includes all of Josephus' works except the last three books of the *Antiquities of the Jews*.
Against Apion, I, 161-411.
The Jewish War, vols. II, III.
The Life, I, 1-159.

————. *The Antiquities of the Jews*. The Works of Josephus. Trans. by William Whiston. Illustrated ed.; New York: Thomas Nelson & Sons, 1886. Pp. 27-550.

Pliny. *Letters*, 2 vols. Trans. by W. Melmoth and W. Hutchins. Loeb Classical Library. Cambridge, Mass.: Harvard University Press, 1953.

Suetonius. 2 vols. Trans. by J. C. Rolfe. Loeb Classical Library. Cambridge, Mass.: Harvard Univ. Press, 1950.
The Deified Claudius, II, 1-84.
The Deified Julius, I, 1-120.

Tertullian. *The Apology*. Vol. III, 17-55. Trans. by S. Thelwall. Ante-Nicene Fathers, 9 vols. Alexander Roberts and James Donaldson (eds.). Grand Rapids: Wm. B. Eerdmans Publishing Co., 1951.

Index of Subjects

Apostles: teaching office, 226ff.; witness to resurrection, 149f., 153, 156, 166, 174f., 176, 177, 224-27

Demythologizing: authentic vs. unauthentic living, 96f., 130f., 136; basic problem encountered, 100, 136; Bultmann's reasons for demythologizing, 93f., 99f.; *Dass* vs. *Was*, 98f., 110, 116f., 131, 142, 167, 170; definition of "myth," 94, 169; examples of, 97f., 168f.; "prior understanding," 108, 130, 135, 138

Dialectical theology: background in Kierkegaard, 80ff.; rapid rise of, 85f.; why "dialectical"? 85, 138

Enlightenment: beginnings, 27f., confidence in man its basic theme, 76f., 78f., 80, 81; Deism as its thology, 28f., difficulties encountered by, 29f.

Faith: distinct from sight, 183, 253f.; Holy Spirit's role in. 185f., 187, 230, 232-37, 239ff.; why only some believe, 186f.

Form criticism: 86, 113ff., 126f., 132, 141

Gentile mission: demonstrated God's grace, 208f., 216f.; possible only because of resurrection, 219f., 221ff., 245, 258

Hermeneutics: of Karl Barth, 84f., 87-93, 102, 107ff.; of Rudolf Bultmann, 88ff., 93-100, 107ff.; of Hermann Diem, 112, 136f.; of Martin Luther, 25; of Origen, 24f.

History: existential understanding of, 114f., 126-29; happenings always analogous? 173f., 179f.; *Historie* vs. *Geschichte*, 69f., 71, 84, 105f., 119, 148; knowledge of dependent upon analogy? 23, 180ff., 187, 250-54; problems posed for faith, 25f.; provides a basis for faith? 34, 37, 72f., 76f., 81, 87, 89f., 134f., 150f., 178, 182f., 254-59

Historical method: capable of ascertaining meaning of an event? 172, 182f., 223-29; outline of, 20-24; problems posed for faith, 24f., 61, 71, 183f., 230, 237; provides relevant knowledge of Jesus? 117f., 120, 123f., 132f., 137f.; supernatural events known thereby? 25, 186f.

Inspiration of the Bible, 228f.

Jesus Christ: ascension, 39, 152, 169, 196-99; basic purpose, 53f., 56,

273

Index of Names

Index of Scripture